Integ
Arts t
in

Spillman, Carolyn V.

LB
1576
S744
1996

Integrating language arts through literature in elementary classrooms

DATE DUE		

AUDREY COHEN COLLEGE LIBRARY
75 Varick St. 12th Floor
New York, NY 10013

Integrating Language Arts through Literature in Elementary Classrooms

by Carolyn V. Spillman

Oryx
1996

The rare Arabian Oryx is believed to have inspired the myth of the unicorn. This desert antelope became virtually extinct in the early 1960s. At that time several groups of international conservationists arranged to have 9 animals sent to the Phoenix Zoo to be the nucleus of a captive breeding herd. Today the Oryx population is over 800 and nearly 400 have been returned to reserves in the Middle East.

© 1996 by The Oryx Press
4041 North Central at Indian School Road
Phoenix, Arizona 85012-3397

All rights reserved. No part of this publication may be reproduced or transmitted in any form or by any means, electronic or mechanical, including photocopying, recording, or by any information storage and retrieval system, without permission in writing from The Oryx Press.

Published simultaneously in Canada
Printed and Bound in the United States of America

∞ The paper used in this publication meets the minimum requirements of American National Standard for Information Science—Permanence of Paper for Printed Library Materials, ANSI Z39.48, 1984.

Library of Congress Cataloging-in-Publication Data

Spillman, Carolyn V.
  Integrating language arts through literature in elementary classrooms / by Carolyn V. Spillman.
    p. cm.
  Includes bibliographical references (p.) and index.
  ISBN 0-89774-897-2 (pbk.)
  1. Language arts (Elementary) 2. Children's literature—Study and teaching (Elementary) 3. Interdisciplinary approach in education. I. Title.
LB1576.S744 1995   95-35683
372.6044—dc20   CIP

CONTENTS

• • • • • • • •

Preface .... *vii*
    How to Use This Book   viii
    One Final Note   x

1. Integrating Literature with Language Arts 1
    The Integrated Language Arts   1
    The Literature Base   2
    Using Literature in the Classroom   3
    Other Sources for Reading about Literature-Based Language Arts   7
    Notes   8

2. Genres 10
    Fiction   10
    Poetry   11
    Nonfiction   11
    Primary Resources   13
    Intermediate Resources   32

3. Structures 52
    Narrative Forms   53
    Expository Forms   54
    Poetic Forms   54
    Primary Resources   54
    Intermediate Resources   76

4. *Themes* 102
   Primary Resources   103
   Intermediate Resources   133

5. *Evaluating a Literature-Based Language Arts Program* 168
   Program Goals   169
   Continuous Assessment and Evaluation   171
   Looking at the Total Program   176

Appendix: Selected Book Titles for Author Studies 181

Index 189

PREFACE

• • • • • • • •

The young teachers gathered before their university course meeting began, discussing what had happened in their classrooms during the previous week. They talked of books they had read, of strategies they had tried, of problems they had faced.

"I wish I had summaries of all the books we've talked about over the last few weeks," said one teacher.

"We have our lit. logs," chimed another, "but mine is not organized well enough to find books for a unit."

"I have mine on a database that has cross references that will help me match books by genre and subject," said a recent graduate who was comfortable with technology.

"What I would really like is a reference that gives examples of books by genre and grade level," replied the first teacher.

"That would be great but we need more than that. I'd like examples of books in different text structures and maybe some suggestions for theme studies. And while I'm wishing, I'd also like some help in using literature as a base for all of my language arts," requested another.

One who had been quiet throughout the conversation offered, "I always like to choose the books that I use, but I would love to have suggestions for books that could be used for certain language activities."

All of these teachers acknowledged that such a collection of information would be helpful to them. As teachers who were early in their careers, they had been concentrating on management, the prescribed curriculum, and the overwhelming task of recordkeeping. Until taking this graduate course, they had not read much current children's literature. A few of them had tried integrating language arts around literature, but they lacked confidence that they could provide enough structure for the achievement of the language processes with this approach. Up to this point they had depended on teachers' manuals to ensure their accountability to required curriculum. The task of planning, implementing the plan, securing appropriate materials, and assessing the process was formidable. They felt they needed a guide.

This book is for teachers who, like these, need additional guidance in using language arts and literature in the classroom. It was written in part for beginning teachers, although I hope teachers at all stages of their careers will find it a useful resource.

I wrote the book for teachers who believe that language arts should be united for communication purposes, not separated into its various components. These teachers know that children deserve opportunities to use language in meaningful combinations and that experiencing fine literature is an authentic and purposeful way to use the language arts. These teachers also know, however, they cannot possibly read every children's book that is published.

The majority of the selections in this book were published within the last four years; it is a deliberate objective to present summaries of fresh books that teachers may not have read. Scattered among the bright new stars, however, are a few choices nearing the classic status.

I also wrote this book for media specialists and librarians who share their knowledge and excitement about books with children. I hope they, too, will find some new titles or activities to suggest to teachers or to use as they conduct literary focus studies from the media center.

This book is intended as a classroom guide to recommended books for genre studies, text structure studies, and theme studies. It is designed to provide a framework for integrating language arts experiences. Activities for using literature for literature's sake as well as for instructional purposes are also included.

HOW TO USE THIS BOOK

The first chapter, "Integrating Literature with Language Arts," gives a succinct overview of the rationale and theoretical background for integration of language arts and for using literature as a curricular base. The reasons for integrating the language arts are indicated, and three ways to experience literature are specified: personal responses to literature, learning about literature and literary conventions, and using literature for developing literacy processes. A list of other sources for continued reading on a specific topic is also included.

Chapters 2 through 4 share the same structure: Book summaries are provided, usually clustered by groups of three books and are designated for primary (kindergarten to second grade) or intermediate (third through sixth grade) age levels. Activities follow each cluster and are denoted as "Integrated Language Experiences," "Literature Approaches," and "Story Branches." Any of the language arts or literature activities may be used with one or more of the books in the cluster, so teachers may select activities or take ideas for further development. The *integrated language arts experiences* are combined activities that promote the use of reading, writing, listening, and speaking as well as mechanical support skills when appropriate. The activities reflecting *literature approaches* fall under the three approaches to using literature in the classroom: personal experiences, literary conventions, and literacy processes. If students are particularly interested in one of the books, or if the teacher would like to plan for extensions, suggestions are given in *story branches* for story-specific experiences.

Chapter 2, "Genres," presents books and activities that can be used when teachers concentrate for a period of time on a particular literary genre. Students may examine the characteristics of the genre and read and compare examples. In Chapter 2 there are 36 book summaries and more than 200 language arts and literature activities.

The six genre clusters consist of three books each (per age level) for folk literature, fantasy, contemporary realistic fiction, historical realistic fiction, poetry, and nonfiction. Book summaries and activities for primary levels are at the beginning of the chapter, followed by those for intermediate age levels.

The third chapter, "Structures," examines topics such as narratives, expository text, and poetry, revealing substructures within each that are recognizable by children. Once children recognize the text structures, they can use them in their own writing. This chapter presents 57 text summaries and more than 260 language and literature activities for both primary and intermediate age levels. There are 24 examples of narratives, 18 examples of expository texts, and 15 examples of poetry.

The fourth chapter, "Themes," features nine themes related to interpersonal interactions. With six books for each theme (three are primary and three are intermediate), topics include: Kaleidoscope, Changes, Beginnings and Endings, Surprises, Perspectives, Courage, Considering Others, Families and Friends, and Comparisons. The 54 book summaries and more than 300 activities related to these themes can be used as stand-alone studies or can be incorporated into large units.

The fifth chapter, "Evaluating a Literature-Based Language Arts Program," discusses the assessment and evaluation of students who are learning language arts and literature through this focus as well as programmatic evaluation. Student involvement through self-assessment is supported with specific strategies. Questions a teacher may ask in determining the effectiveness of the entire program complete the chapter.

Throughout the book, teachers are encouraged to make decisions on what is appropriate for their students. Although grade level recommendations are made, teachers may find activities at both levels that meet their needs. It is my intent that teachers will look at the books recommended in a genre, text structure, or theme cluster and determine which ones are available and how many of the three are appropriate for the time and purposes of the study. The activities are varied and may be used selectively. To integrate completely all of the language arts and the mechanical support skills, however, most of the "Integrated Language Arts Experiences" should be ventured by the students. The decision to use all or part of the suggested experiences is the teacher's.

The appendix lists titles by various authors, some of whom are featured in this book. The appendix should be helpful in building a classroom library to accommodate the literature studies suggested here.

ONE FINAL NOTE

Over the past year, I have read most of these books for the first time, as many of them are newly published. Although many of the books have been reviewed, others were without recommendations, and I have made my own decisions about their worthiness in a classroom. Reading the books and savoring each word and illustration in them has been a great joy, and I recommend that practice to all teachers. The very best way to know the literature that will "touch" your students, that will model the use of language for them, and that will capture them as life-long readers is to let it snare you! I strongly urge teachers to use a computerized database to record bibliographic information, genre, theme, text structure, and any other information needed to guarantee current and appropriate literature selections for the students.

Thanks to all of the teachers over the years who have influenced me in the writing of this book.

Integrating Language Arts through Literature in Elementary Classrooms

CHAPTER 1

Integrating Literature with Language Arts

When children acquire the foundation for reading and writing through high quality stories and poems, they make associations with literature and literary processes that last a lifetime. Learning to read and write, listening to the words of others who read and write well, and patterning their own language after quality literature are experiences that children deserve. These experiences are more likely when teachers recognize the resources available in various literary genres, structures, and themes and when they can provide ways for children to enjoy literature while developing language and reading abilities and interests. To do that, teachers must be aware of the relationships and interdependencies among reading, language arts, and literature.

THE INTEGRATED LANGUAGE ARTS

The language arts include speaking, listening, writing, reading, literature, and the mechanical support for these processes, such as spelling, handwriting, language usage, grammar, phonics, and vocabulary. Traditionally, each area of language arts was a separate course of study that was taught and practiced independently. In the schools of early America, students commonly spent a block of time practicing speaking, or elocution, then moving to reading from texts or copying for penmanship. All of these studies may have had completely different and isolated content. Contrast that practice to today's classrooms where curriculum is integrated: students read, write, speak, and listen with purposeful and connected content. They may read from literature, write a letter to the author of the story, talk to peers about why the story may have been written, listen to others' opinions, and further practice their communications skills by creating additional dialogue for one of the characters.

As today's classroom educators know, language subjects and the processes involved in their use are not segmented but are parts of a whole. How can one speak without also listening? How can one write without also reading? The language arts are inherently integrated, and the isolation of any part is artificial. Even the support system, composed of mechanical functions such as spelling, is meaningless outside the purposes of communication. There is little reason for spelling unless one is writing. The purpose for handwriting is to provide the courtesy of legibility to promote communication. When language arts are viewed as a process of communication, the need for integration is clear.

In a classroom where interdependence of language arts is the prevailing philosophy, children experience the integration naturally. The processes come together in meaningful ways for authentic purposes. Students read from published authors, from authors among their peers, and from their own authorship. They are aware of why an author writes, and they, too, search for communication. They write because they have something to say, and they know that someone will read it. They listen and speak for the same communication purposes; oral and written language are part of their lives. It comes as no surprise to children for whom language arts have been integrated that authors draft, revise, edit, and use mechanical conventions to communicate more effectively. They see a reason for learning where to place commas or how to spell words they frequently use.

Children who have learned to communicate by exploring texts in this way are also acutely aware of the differences among types of text. They know that some texts tell stories and that others give information. They can hear the difference between poetry and prose. When all of the processes are used in combination for real purposes, language learning is truly integrated.

THE LITERATURE BASE

Literature can easily become the foundation for literacy and the focus for subsequent oral and written experiences. Students learn to listen to their language through the projected sounds, rhymes, and modulations of literary selections. They expand their vocabularies and their knowledge base by hearing the thoughts and expressions of literary characters in words, phrases, and sentences. They learn that punctuation on the page is a courtesy to the listener and that comprehension declines without it. They begin to realize that the written text is intricately related to the spoken word and to meaning expressed by an author or speaker. They begin to discern that written texts have different meanings to different people and that new insights can be gained by talking to others about a story or a piece of text. As students enter the communication process, they recognize that practitioners of language arts not only speak and listen, but they read and write; so students find models for all language arts as they experience literature and communicate their experiences with others.

Literature is a major medium through which language arts processes can take on meaning. For some children, being able to read stories, poems, essays, letters, and all forms of literature becomes the driving motivation for proficiency with these processes. Readers want to know what happens to a character, the description of a curious event, or they may simply want to read more for the sheer enjoyment of the words. They may want to learn about something that occurred before they were born, or they may like to imagine living in a fantasy world that is yet to be. If there is motivation for reading, if there is a reason to write, if there are interesting things to talk about, and interesting things to listen to, there is a real basis for using language to communicate. It would be hard to find an equal to the power of literature for involving students in literacy development.

When literature is used as the base for learning content in the school curriculum—in language arts, social studies, or science—the term literature-based curriculum is often used. Frequently, basal texts in these subject areas are difficult for many students to read. Text books usually are written in an expository style—sequence, cause and effect, or problem-solving—that does not draw readers in as well as stories or narratives, and interest frequently is lost. Reading and writing with expository text is a goal of the elementary curriculum, but when the objective is to understand science or social studies concepts, a narrative style may capture student interest and promote greater perception.

Although many language process objectives are met incidentally every time a student uses a trade book on a social studies theme, the literature-based, integrated language arts program focuses on additional language experiences. When the language arts processes are woven into a literature program, with or without a broader curricular theme study, literature-based, integrated language arts become the foundation for literacy development. Skillful teachers become aware that literature may be used as a scaffold to support novice level language-users in their efforts to become proficient communicators. Teachers know that literature provides models of various genres that may be enjoyed, examined for their literary qualities, and used as patterns for individual development. They know that literature has connections to real life issues and emotions and that personal constructions of meaning and individual responses to literature linger long after the initial reading of a text. Teachers also acknowledge that through literature intertextuality is fostered as students build on what they learn in one text and apply it to another. Once a student has read a folktale with the typical story grammar of the "once upon a time" beginning and the "happily ever after" ending, other tales with such features will be familiar and will provide a measure of security for the child.

Narrative stories with connections to curricular content are often used as springboards for a theme study promoting the content objectives. Within the theme study, stories in narrative form as well as trade books with expository text may be used to extend experiences and understandings. Through these stories, students will meet objectives for integrated content.

Teachers are the avenue through which students gain access to the world of literature. Most teachers have not been trained in using literature as a base for the integration of language arts, but they are finding ways to integrate language arts, and they are constantly seeking literature that will provide meaningful experiences for their students. Many teachers are joining what is being called "the literature-based reading revolution."[1]

USING LITERATURE IN THE CLASSROOM

Approaches

Over the past few years, awareness of the value of literature-based, language arts integrated curriculum has heightened along with research indicating that many teachers use literature either for pleasure reading to children or for teaching specific skills. Those who use literature in the classroom do so for two basic reasons: (1) as an approach to reading instruction; and (2) as an avenue for teaching the appreciation of children's literature.[2] Another influence on teacher practices has been the recognition that literature is a way to construct personal meaning with texts that leads to aesthetic appreciation and the insightful gain of knowledge and information.[3]

Teachers approach the use of literature in several different ways.[4] One way to use literature is to encourage personal transactions with texts. The seminal work of Rosenblatt[5] underscored the uniqueness of individuals, whose backgrounds, belief systems, experiences, and education merge with the text to produce original interpretations, reactions, and responses to a story or poem. A reader's response to a text is personal, and therefore, if teachers value students' meaningful involvement with literature, various responses must be accepted. In the classroom, personal transactions occur as children write in journals, sometimes called literature logs, or as they converse with other children in literary circles. Sometimes teachers guide children's responses with questions that cause them to look at the story in a different way. For example: "If you could be any character in the story, whom would you be? Why or Why not?"; "Do you share any of the feelings of the characters in the story? Explain;" and so on.[6] Having *personal experiences* with literature is the focus of this approach.

Another way that literature can be used in the classroom focuses on the structure of literature and the conventions that define its rules and elements. When these elements take a central role in the use of literature, we have literary criticism at an elementary level.[7] Through the discovery of *literary conventions* such as the elements of characters, setting, theme, plot, and point of view, children develop a common vocabulary for comparing one book with another or one genre with another.

Another approach is to use literature as a source for directly or indirectly teaching content, concepts, or processes. Using *literacy process,* teachers approach reading as an interactive process.[8] Reading is emphasized as a strategic mechanism in which meaning is constructed by the reader in a deliberate, although sometimes facilitated, manner. The other literary processes are integrated around the reading text with the goal of literacy development clearly in mind.

Although some teachers may prefer one or more of these approaches to using literature over the others, it is likely that if given opportunities and suggestions for resources, many would advocate a balance of all three.

Strategies

As teachers search for ways to ensure meaningfulness and real purpose in the ways their students experience and respond to literature, strategies are surfacing that have been tried and that meet the standards. Selected processes and experiences are discussed in general terms. More specific uses for these and other techniques are suggested in the chapters that follow.

Literary Circles
In small groups, students respond to a literary selection, expressing feelings and emotions evoked by the text. They analyze literary elements such as plot, setting, characters, theme, and point of view as developed by various authors.[10]

Literature Logs
Response journals take many forms; some are teacher directed in which discussion prompts are presented for children's consideration and written response; others are personal response journals where students write spontaneous entries about stories they have read or heard. Sometimes they take the form of dialogue journals in which teachers or other students participate.

Cooperative Book Sharing
From cooperative learning, numerous strategies are appropriate for reading, writing, and sharing literature. One type that has had good results is coopera-

tive book sharing (CBS), in which students cooperatively read sections of a book and then tell their part in sequence during a large group sharing session. Sometimes teachers literally tear a book apart and give sections of it to small groups of two to three students who collaboratively read the section. They may take turns reading aloud, reading together in pairs, or selecting one reader from among the group to read the story. As the total group sharing begins, the teacher will ask which group has a section that seems to be a beginning. From that point on, students offer sections that may follow and they develop consensus on which sections "make sense" next. Sometimes with chapter books, the chapters are numbered and the focus on sequence is not as important as sharing the plot, so groups tell their chapter as they know they follow numerically. For those who read the beginning of the book, the revelation of the plot is often startling; for those who read only the end of the book, there are many "ahas" as they hear the story unfold. Intense discussion usually follows this type of activity as students have sincere and spontaneous responses. Sometimes, students return to their base group after the presentation of the whole story for literary discussions.

Sharing Groups

In some reading programs, such as readers' workshop, students self-select their reading texts from the library or a pre-selected group of books.[11] In such cases, sharing groups become a socialization outlet for students to share the books they have read. Because other children may or may not have read the same books, these sharing groups are sources for students to present information to an audience who may not know a book. In some cases, the student may operate as an "expert" or the only one who has read a book. In this case, the sharing session may serve a purpose as old fashioned book reports once did: to entice other children to read a book. These sessions hold students accountable for what they are reading.

Literary Publications

Because writing is an integral part of the literary process, students need opportunities to write about what they are reading, as in book reviews, to "copycat" or pattern after a given author or illustrator, or to create from the various genres and forms and to have an audience for their creations. Some classes publish newsletters that include original writings as well as book reviews; others produce magazines and have a full-fledged literary review process. These experiences show children that reading, writing, literature, and the support processes are real-life experiences.

OTHER SOURCES FOR READING ABOUT LITERATURE-BASED LANGUAGE ARTS

The following references are suggested as resources for guiding classroom experiences that will lead to the meaningful, integrated use of the language arts with a literature base.

Books

Barchers, S. 1994. *Teaching language arts: An integrated approach.* Minneapolis-St. Paul: West.

Hancock, J., and S. Hill, eds. 1988. *Literature-based reading programs at work.* Portsmouth, NH: Heinemann.

Johnson, T. D., and D. R. Louis. 1987. *Literacy through literature.* Portsmouth, NH: Heinemann.

Laughlin, M. K., and L. S. Watt. 1986. *Developing learning skills through children's literature: An idea book for K-5 classrooms and libraries.* Phoenix: Oryx Press.

Savage, J. F. 1994. *Teaching reading using literature.* Dubuque: Wm. C. Brown.

Tchudi, S. 1994. *Integrated language arts in the elementary school.* Belmont, CA: Wadsworth.

Thompson, G. 1991. *Teaching through themes.* New York: Scholastic.

Tompkins, G. E., and L. M. McGee. 1993. *Teaching reading with literature: Case studies to action plans.* New York: Macmillan.

Yellin, D., and M. Blake. 1994. *Integrating language arts: A holistic approach.* New York: HarperCollins.

Journal Articles

Aiex, N. K. 1988. Literature based reading instruction. *The Reading Teacher* 41:458–61.

Bergeron, B. S. 1990. What does the term whole language mean? Constructing a definition from the literature. *Journal of Reading Behavior* 22:301–29.

Cheek, E. H., Jr. 1989. Skills-based vs. holistic philosophies: The debate among teacher educators in reading. *Teacher Education Quarterly* 16:15–20.

Crook, P. R., and B. A. Lehman. 1991. Themes for two voices: Children's fiction and nonfiction as whole literature. *Language Arts* 68:34–41.

Culinan. B. E. 1989. Latching onto literature: Reading initiatives to take hold. *School Library Journal* 35:27–31.

DeFord, D., and J. Harste. 1982. Child language research and curriculum. *Language Arts* 59:590–99.

DeGroff, L. J. 1989. Developing writing processes with children's literature. *The New Advocate* 2:115–23.

Freppon, P. A., and K. C. Dahl. 1991. Learning about phonics in a whole language classroom. *Language Arts* 68:190–97.

Fuhler, C. J. 1990. Let's move toward literature-based reading instruction. *The Reading Teacher* 44:312–15.

Galda, L. 1988. Readers, texts, and contexts: A response-based view of literature in the classroom. *The New Advocate* 1:92–102.

Hade, D. 1994. Aiding and abetting the basalization of children's literature. *The New Advocate* 7:29–44.

Hiebert, E. H., and J. Colk. 1989. Patterns of literature-based reading instruction. *The Reading Teacher* 43:14–20.

Langer, J. 1994. Focus on research: A response-based approach to reading literature. *Language Arts* 71:203–11.

Paradis, E., B. Chatton, A. Boswell, M. Smith, and S. Yovich. 1991. Accountability: Assessing comprehension during literature discussion. *The Reading Teacher* 45:8–17.

Roser, N. L., J. V. Hoffman, and C. Farest. 1990. Language, literature, and at-risk children. *The Reading Teacher* 43:554–59.

Savage, J. F. 1992. Literature-based reading instruction: It works! *The New England Reading Association Journal* 28:28–31.

Silva, C., and E. Delgado-Larocco. 1993. Facilitating learning through interconnections: A concept approach to core literature units. *Language Arts* 70:469–74.

Stahl, S., and P. D. Miller. 1989. Whole language and language experience approaches for beginning reading: A quantitative research synthesis. *Review of Educational Research* 59:87–116.

Trachtenburg, P. 1990. Using children's literature to enhance phonics instruction. *The Reading Teacher* 43:648–52.

Tunnell, M. O., and J. S. Jacobs. 1989. Using "real" books: Research findings on literature based reading instruction. *The Reading Teacher* 42:470–77.

Villaume, S. K., and T. Worden. 1993. Developing literate voices: The challenge of whole language. *Language Arts* 70:462–68.

Zarrillo, J. 1989. Teachers' interpretations of literature-based reading. *The Reading Teacher* 43:22–28.

NOTES

1. McGee, L. M. 1992. Focus on research: Exploring the literature-based reading revolution, *Language Arts* 69:529–37.

2. Walmsley, S. A. 1992. Reflections on the state of elementary literature instruction, *Language Arts* 69:508–15; Pearson, P. D., ed. 1984, *Handbook of reading research,* New York: Longman; Huck, C. Hepler, and J. Hickman 1987. *Children's literature in the elementary school,* 4th ed., New York: Holt.

3. Rosenblatt, L. 1978. *The reader, the text, the poem: The transactional theory of the literary work*, Carbondale: Southern Illinois Press.

4. Tompkins, G. E., and L. M. McGee 1993. *Teaching reading with literature. Case studies to action plans*, New York: Merrill.

5. Rosenblatt, L. 1938. *Literature as exploration*, New York: Progressive Education Association.

6. Kelly, P. R., and N. Farnan 1991. Promoting critical thinking through response logs: A reader-response approach with fourth graders, in J. Zutell and S. McCormick, eds., *Learner factors/teacher factors: Issues in literacy research and instruction*, 277–84, Chicago: The National Reading Conference.

7. Tompkins and McGee, *Teaching reading*, 210–49.

8. *Ibid.*, 142–52.

9. Mauro, L. H. 1983. Personal constructs and response to literature: Case studies of adolescents reading about death. *Dissertation Abstracts International* 4407A.

10. Edelsky, C. 1988. Living in the authors' world: Analyzing the authors' craft, *California Reader*, 21:14–17; Urzua, C. 1992. Faith in learners through literature studies. *Language Arts*, 69:492–501.

11. Tompkins, G., and L. McGee 1993, *Teaching reading with literature: Case studies to action plans*, New York: Merrill.

CHAPTER 2

Genres

When students have opportunities to experience a variety of literary genres while learning the language arts processes, they begin to recognize the characteristics of these genres and notice how writing differs depending on the purpose of the communication. Children quickly notice differences in texts used for entertainment as opposed to texts that give directions for building a bird house. Through experience, children learn the differences among narrative texts that tell stories, nonfiction texts that give information, and texts written in poetic form. The term "genre," meaning "kind," "style," or "sort," is used frequently in writing, as well as in reading programs, and has become a commonplace term, even for children to use as they designate different types of texts.

FICTION

Folk literature consists of tales originally told in oral or written form but for which the first telling has been lost in history. The original authors generally are not known because most of the tales and verses have been passed down through oral storytelling and have many variants, as they have crossed cultures and time for hundreds of years.

For most folktales, the plot begins quickly and unfolds without much detail. The characters are usually one-sided and exhibit only one or two traits. The reader never really gets to know folk characters. Plots are often simple and predictable, ending quickly with satisfying resolutions.

Subgenres of folk literature include folktales, fairy tales, myths, legends, fables, explanatory animal tales, trickster tales, tall tales, nursery rhymes, ballads, and epics. The last three subgenres may also be classified as poetry, while the rest were told or written in prose form. Certain characteristics are found frequently in the subgenres. For example, fables usually have a moral at the end, and phrases such as "once upon a time" are found in folk and fairy tales.

As a fiction genre, *fantasy* displays distinct characteristics. Plots concern a world not like our own. There are elements of reality with which readers identify and that make the stories believable, but there are also impossibilities for the world in which we live. Fantasy stories can be simple tales with animals acting as humans, complex science fiction, or compelling stories of utopian existence. The characters in high level fantasy, often dealing with good versus evil, are usually fully developed, giving readers insights and understandings of their motivations as well as their actions.

Realistic fiction, in historical and contemporary settings, reminds readers of some of their own experiences. These narratives are set in time periods that readers either know personally or may easily identify. Current sociological issues often become the focus of the plot, which may be a simple sequence of events or may have subplots, flashbacks, and suspenseful, sometimes cliff-hanging conclusions. Characters are fully developed in most cases, with all of their strengths and weaknesses evident. It is through these stories that readers may unintentionally or incidentally establish values, receive motivation, confidence, or direction regarding their own lives.

POETRY

Poetry comes in many forms, from the simplest nursery rhymes sung to infants to the complex epics of Homer. In between, there lies a wonderful world of rhythm, rhyme, alliteration, pleasing sounds, visualized images, and lyrical and narrative tales. Children enjoy listening, reading, and replicating the patterns found in many of the forms.

NONFICTION

Biographies and autobiographies may tell a complete life story or may focus on some segment of a person's life. In titles of high quality, the characters are given honest portrayals that reflect their lives—the positive and the negative events.

Information books include factual data on subjects known to readers. Travel books, how-to books, and subject-specific books such as weather, machines, and life in medieval ages are some of the types that children frequently select. Accuracy in presenting facts clearly, with reputable documentation and current terminology, is important.

Types and Traits of Various Genres and Subgenres

Genre	Text Type	Setting	Plot	Characters
Folk Literature folk and fairy tales "how" stories trickster tales legends tall tales nursery rhymes folk songs	Narrative text in prose; poetic text in nursery rhymes and folk songs.	Unknown lands, far-away places, long-ago times.	Predictable, fast beginning, problem unfolds quickly, series of attempts and results easily identified; ends with a satisfaction.	One or two traits are evident; reader knows very little of thoughts or feelings.
Fantasy low fantasy high fantasy science fiction	Narrative text.	Past, present, or future; realistic or totally fantastic.	Low fantasies are simple: one or more fantastic elements such as talking animals, animate objects. High fantasies are complex: other worlds, quests, and struggles.	High fantasy characters are well-developed with multifaceted traits; readers get to know the characters well and identify with them.
Realistic fiction historical contemporary	Narrative text.	Realistic and authentic for the period.	Often complex, dealing with issues of the period. Readers identify with situations and possible solutions. Often parallel plots, sub-plots, or flashbacks. Endings are not always happy; sometimes open-ended.	Characters are well-rounded; readers understand them and their plights. Many stories are written from the point of view of one or more character with clearly evident thoughts and motives.
Poetry	Poetic, narrative poetic.	Varies.	Varies; may have none.	Varies.
Nonfiction biographies, travel, how-to information	Expository or narrative text.	Varies.	Varies; may have none.	Varies.

PRIMARY RESOURCES

Folk Literature

Ehlert, L. 1992. *Moon Rope—Un lazo a la luna.* San Diego: Harcourt.

Summary. This Peruvian folktale with text in English and Spanish is about a fox who wants to go to the moon and decides to make a rope of grass to get there. He asks birds to carry the rope and hitch it over one corner of the crescent moon. They return and tell him that his rope is ready for climbing. Fox, along with Mole, climb paw over paw up the rope toward the moon until Mole slips and falls. He lands on a bird's back and is carried to earth. The creatures watching chide Mole, so he digs a deep hole and crawls into it. To this day, he prefers that deep hole and comes out only at night. What happened to Fox? It appears that he may have made it to the moon as his face is seen there occasionally.

Hong, L. T. 1991. *How the Ox Star Fell from Heaven.* Morton Grove, IL: Albert Whitman.

Summary. This Chinese tale tells of the oxen that live in the heavens among the stars. They have easy lives, are dressed in silk, and have no labor to perform. But down on earth, the farmers have a very hard life because they have no animals to help with the planting or harvesting of their crops; they are so poor they go days without food. The Emperor of all the Heavens looks down on the poor farmers and feels sorry for them. So he sends the Ox Star as a messenger to tell the people that they must eat at least every three days. When the Ox Star arrives, he misreads the message and tells the people they should eat three times a day! The people are thrilled, but the Emperor is furious. When Ox Star returns to the heavens, the door is locked and he is hurled back to earth. He has remained on earth since then. Along with other oxen, he helps the farmers tend their crops and produce food so people can eat three times a day.

Dixon, A. 1992. *How Raven Brought Light to People.* Illustrated by James Watts. New York: Margaret McElderry Books.

Summary. This tale told by the Tlingit of Alaska is one of many stories about Raven. In this narrative, Raven is unhappy because a great chief keeps the sun, moon, and stars hidden in boxes, making the world very dark. When Raven sees the chief's daughter by the river, he turns himself into a spruce needle and drops into the water, where he is scooped up by the woman's hands as she drinks. She swallows the needle, and inside her body Raven turns into a baby and is born a boy.

He is the chief's grandson and is loved dearly. When he cries to play with the boxes that hold the stars and the moon, they are given to him. Even after being told not to open them, he does, letting the stars pepper the sky and the moon shine at night. The people are pleased. The chief has lost two of his treasures, but does so as a doting grandfather. After a while, the boy wants to play with the box that holds the sun. He cries and will not eat, so finally the chief gives in and lets him have that box too. He turns himself back into Raven and tries to carry the box through the smoke-hole in the top of the lodge. The chief realizes what has happened and, by magic, makes the hole smaller. Raven struggles and pushes himself and the box through the hole, but the soot from the smoke hole clings to his feathers. He releases the sun from the box, so now the people of the world have light during the day from the sun and at night from the stars and moon. Raven is still black from the sooty smoke hole.

Integrated Language Arts Experiences
- Children will listen to the story read aloud.
- They will fold a paper with three horizontal creases; draw a scene from the sky, from the earth, and from the area between them. They will turn the paper into a horizontal accordion story and write words to go with the pictures. Then they may share the story with a friend.
- Retell the story as a group. Teacher will write the retelling on chart paper.
- Children take home copies of the retelling of the story and read it to their family.
- Children listen to the story again and listen for questions the story answers: (Why does Mole live underground? Why do the oxen work so hard? Why is Raven black?)
- Write a question; use a question mark.

Literature Approaches
- Before hearing the story, children will talk about the way things look from far off or way up high; the teacher may ask them to remember a time when they looked down to see something (from a plane or building). (personal experiences)
- Children predict what will happen in the story. (literary conventions)
- Children realize that they can guess what the story is about through its title. (literary conventions)
- Children recognize the "how" or "why" form of story—an explanatory tale—by hearing more than one of them and comparing. They see how

these stories are alike by using Venn diagrams of two of the stories. (literary conventions)
- Children turn statements or titles into questions: How did the moon rope help Fox? How did Raven bring light to the people? How did the Ox Star fall from heaven? (literary processes)
- By generating, reading, writing, and answering questions, children learn a convention of the writing process. (literary processes)

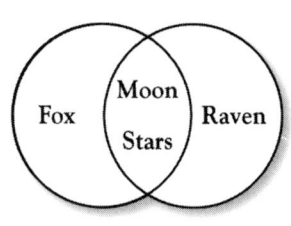

Story Branches

Moon Rope
- Children will group write a climbing chant to help Fox climb to the moon. They can sing the chant at the appropriate place while the story is read again.
- They may cut geometric shapes from silver, gold, and brightly colored paper to make characters from the book. Then they can place the characters on a bulletin board attached to a rope that goes from the earth to the moon.
- Children can listen to the sound of the /oo/ in moon and find other words with the same sound. A collection of /oo/ words might be placed on display: moon, loon, soon, raccoon, noon.

How the Ox Star Fell From Heaven
- Children dress dolls and toy animals in silk fabrics as the oxen were in heaven.
- As a class, cook rice and steamed vegetables and eat as the people did three times a day.
- After reading and experiencing the story, some time might be spent on the irregular verb "fell," so children might realize that all past tense verbs do not end in "ed." Other examples are ran, did, went, thought, and drew.

How Raven Brought Light to People
- Listen to the story in the dark; each child will have a flashlight and be assigned to be a star, moon, or sun. Children will turn on individual flashlights when the appropriate box is opened in the story.
- They can draw pictures of Raven as he looked before and after going through the sooty smoke-hole.

- In this story, children may also experience an irregular verb in the past tense. Although teachers will decide whether or not to use the term "irregular verb," children may profit from emphasis on how to express this word in the past tense (saw, spoke, flew).

Fantasy

McDermott, G. 1992. *Papagayo, The Mischief Maker.* Orlando: Harcourt, Brace, Jovanovich.

Summary. From the Amazon rain forest, Papagayo is a parrot that makes a raucous sound every morning as he greets the new day, much to the dismay of his night creature friends. He not only makes noise, but he is also mischievous, scaring butterflies and dropping nuts on the shell of the armadillo. The struggle between Papagayo and the night creatures continue until something happens that none of them expect: An ancient monster dog's ghost awakens from a deep sleep and soars to the sky to taste the moon. He does this every night, and the night creatures are afraid. So worried are they that they begin losing sleep and remaining awake during the day when Papagayo is also awake. He decides to help them, so he stays awake the next night and orchestrates loud chanting, which scares the moon-dog back into his hiding place. After helping the night creatures, Papagayo is no longer their enemy.

Auch, M. J. 1993. *Peeping Beauty.* New York: Holiday House.

Summary. This fantasy is the story of Poulette, a chicken, whose greatest dream is to dance. The chickens live in the farmyard and all but Poulette are leery of the fox and his promises. He beguiles Poulette into believing that she will star in his production, Peeping Beauty. As Poulette's friends, Philomena and Gertrude, predict, Poulette is in danger when the production plans to be more of a dinner than a show. Poulette outwits the fox by doing ballet moves—a tour jeté and a tour grandé—to knock the fox out and get the better hand. She finally lets the fox go after her friends scare him into thinking he is going to be a fox burger.

Yorinks, A. 1986. *Hey, Al.* Illustrated by R. Egielski. New York: Farrar, Straus and Giroux.

Summary. Al, a nice, quiet janitor, and his dog, Eddie, become disenchanted with the hum-drum of daily life in a one-room apartment in a big city. They long for more in life than working and coming home to the same apartment each day. One day a big bird sticks his head in Al's bathroom window and offers him and Eddie an opportunity for change. The next morning, Al and Eddie are waiting for the bird and are delighted to be ferried toward an island in the sky. It is a beautiful tropical island full of lush trees and colorful birds. For a few days, they have a wonderful time, eating, drinking, sunbathing with the birds—until they discover they are turning into birds, too! With the wings they have sprouted, they flap into the sky and fly toward home. Enroute, Eddie drops into the ocean, so Al arrives alone and heartbroken that he has lost his dog. Eddie is a good swimmer, however, and he swims to shore and arrives home shortly after Al. They are so happy to be back in the one room apartment.

Integrated Language Arts Experiences
- As a group, cluster concepts about birds through webbing terms known to students before reading the story.
- In pairs, students will create their most "fantastic" bird story by planning where it takes place (setting) and what the bird characters look like. They may draw pictures or write the words for their story. Older students may also plan the bird's problem and how it is solved in the story. Sharing these bird stories with small or large groups may be a part of the prereading session.
- The teacher may read the story to the students telling them this is another "fantastic" bird story. For a second reading, show part of the text on an overhead transparency and allow for choral reading.
- Individual students may write or draw a comparison of a bird character in the story to the bird character previously created with a partner.
- Children may tell their neighbor (students talk to a partner for a given number of minutes about a given topic) what they think was the best part of the story that the teacher read and why.

Literature Approaches
- On a timeline prepared by the teacher that specifies beginning, middle, and end, children will suggest events that may be written there that are part of each of the segments of the story. (literary conventions) Once the sequence has been negotiated by the class and students are in agreement on what constitutes the beginning, middle, and end of the story, the class may be divided into three groups for dramatizing the parts of the story. All children should participate, so some extra parts may be needed or two or more children might play the same role in the same segment of the story.
- Students quickwrite on index cards (draft, without any intention of carrying the piece through the writing process) and share thoughts with a small group or later with the teacher. (literary processes) Topics for quickwrite might be one of the following:

My favorite fantasy is . . .
I knew this story was make-believe when . . . (personal experiences)
- Students may select a bird and look it up in the encyclopedia. (literacy processes) Use a CD-ROM multimedia encyclopedia if available. Complete the following chart with the information obtained:

Name of Bird	Where It Lives	What It Eats	What It Sounds Like	What It Uses for a Nest

Story Branches

Papagayo
- Children may sing the crooning songs and the chant that the night creatures sang. Record both the quiet night croons and the loud, raucous scary chants. Finger paint to the sounds as they are replayed.
- Children may make masks of the animals in the forest and perform a dance.
- The rhythm of the title of the book is created to a great degree by the use of vowels. Because young children are learning about vowel sounds, they will want to examine the word carefully, perhaps substitute some other vowels (or consonants) to see the sounds that might be represented. They will also see both short (a) and long (o) vowels in this word (Papagayo).

Peeping Beauty
- Children may dress dolls in tutus like Poulette wore. Practice the tour jeté and the grand jeté as Poulette must have done. (Children taking ballet lessons will be able to teach the rest.)
- Children may plan what they would have said to the fox if they had been Poulette.
- Children can find words that rhyme with "peep," paying attention to the long e sound. As they are exploring this word, they may find other words that have similar meanings: call, squeal, cheep, chirp, titter, squeak, tweet.

Hey, Al!
- Children will plan a bird chant to break the spell for Al.
- They may use a map and find out where Al might have gone to get to a tropical island.

- They may build a shoe box diorama with one side being the small apartment and the other side his tropical island.
- Students may expand on the cliches in the story ("ripe fruit spoils soon" or "paradise lost is sometimes heaven found"), and make a chart of other such sayings that could apply to this story.

Realistic Fiction

Johnson, A. 1992. *The Leaving Morning.* Illustrated by David Soman. New York: Orchard.

Summary. A mama, daddy, and two children are moving from an urban apartment to a different one. They say goodbye to their friends, cousins, and the people in the building; they have hot cocoa and find strength among themselves to look forward to their new place.

Bunting, E. 1988. *How Many Days to America?* Illustrated by Beth Peck. New York: Clarion.

Summary. After many hardships crossing a body of water in a small, cramped boat with little food, two nameless children and their parents, along with a boat full of people, land in America on Thanksgiving Day, and they, too, give thanks. The lingering fear of oppression from their former country (the Caribbean is implied), danger from soldiers who might catch them, and uneasiness about the ride across the waters in the small boat are shown clearly.

Altman, L. J. 1993. *Amelia's Road.* Illustrated by Enrique O. Sanchez. New York: Lee & Low Books.

Summary. The migrant farm family of which Amelia Luisa Martinez is a part moves frequently, and Amelia does not feel like she has a home. At one of their seasonal stops, she finds a road and calls it the "accidental road" because it is more like a path that accidentally happens than a real road. On this road, she finds a favorite place to sit after school: a wonderful tree. Everyday, she walks past it and sits for a while. As the picking season for the farm workers pass, it becomes time to leave again. She finds an old metal box and fills it with things that she possesses, such as a hair ribbon. She draws a map of the accidental road, writes "Amelia's road" on the map, and puts it in the box. She buries her box with treasures in it under the tree and vowes to come back. For the first time, she feels as if she belongs.

Integrated Language Arts Experiences
- Before reading the story, children will dramatize moving. Many will have moved before, so a discussion to highlight what the conversations and feelings might be like at moving time will be appropriate.
- Children will listen while the teacher reads the story aloud.
- They may draw or write how it feels to move.
- Children will read or show their pictures or stories to a friend.
- The class may group write (or individually, if possible) a script for saying goodbye, then chorally read as a group if written as a group.
- They will experience a mini-lesson on quotation marks.

Literature Approaches
- Children will identify cause and effect in the story. With teacher guidance, they may look for events that made characters happy or sad. For example, leaving made one sad; having hot chocolate made one happy; saying goodbye made one sad; thinking about a new house made one happy. (personal experiences)
- Children may select an event and write a cause and effect sentence to go with it. They may then draw a happy or sad face to show the effect. These cause and effect signs may be shared and displayed. (literacy processes)
- Students may use puppets to pretend about moving or leaving days. They may play act these roles during center or activity time. (personal experiences)

Story Branches

The Leaving Morning
- Children will "tell their neighbor" how they think the child in the story felt at the end. They should tell how they know and how they felt.

- Children will think or write about pretending to be the new neighbor. They will decide what to do to make the child feel better about a new neighborhood.
- Children will examine the title and think of other words that would convey the same message. Let the class vote on another title for the book.

How Many Days to America?
- The teacher may bring in newspaper accounts of refugees so children may talk about what immigrants experience today.
- As a group, talk about feelings of homelessness and immigration; web feelings on chart.
- Children will construct a timeline to recount the story of the crossing to the United States in the story.
- They can research and draw a map of the Caribbean, find newspaper clippings of immigrants coming from South or Central America, and make a bulletin board of the clippings.

Amelia's Road
- Children will draw a map of favorite places.
- They may look at maps of where Amelia traveled; they might discover foods grown in each area, describe them, and share the description with someone.
- Children will determine something they might call their own as Amelia called her road. Give them time to practice writing it as in Amelia's road. For example: Emma's building, Kelly's orchard, or Katrina's church.
- Children will each prepare a keepsake box like Amelia's and decide where it could be hidden. They may write about the "hiding place."

Historical Fiction

Cooney, B. 1982. *Miss Rumphius*. New York: Trumpet.

Summary. In this story, the Lupine Lady, who grows flowers at her house by the sea, remembers her life as a child named Alice. Alice could see wharves, and she lived at the top of the shop where her father made carvings and art work. He often told her to do something to make the world more beautiful. When Alice grows up, she works in a library and they call her Miss Rumphius. She travels to a tropical island; she meets Bapa Raja, king of a fishing village; she climbs mountains, and travels to the land of Lotus-Eaters. She decides to find her own place by the sea and makes the world more beautiful. She does it by planting lupines.

Houston, G. 1988. *The Year of the Perfect Christmas Tree.* Illustrated by Barbara Cooney. New York: Dial.

Summary. Ruthie and her papa find a perfect Christmas tree early in the spring of 1918 and mark it to be cut for the church later in the year. It is a good thing they mark it early because Ruthie's papa has to go to fight in the big war across the sea. Papa sends Mama silk stockings and promises to be home in time for Christmas. They wait and wait and finally Ruthie and her mama find and bring the marked tree to the church in the middle of the night. At the service on Christmas night, Ruthie is the heavenly angel, but her papa is missed. When gifts are given from the tree, Ruthie is sad until Santa pulls the tiniest angel doll from the top of the tree and gives it to Ruthie. It looks just like her and has a face that looks just like the silk stockings Papa has sent Mama. There is another surprise waiting as they leave the church: There in the snow stands Ruthie's papa.

Yolen, J. 1992. *Letting Swift River Go.* Illustrated by Barbara Cooney. Boston: Little, Brown.

Summary. Narrated in first person by a young girl, Sally Jane, this story tells of her friends, the places in the Swift River Valley, and how they walk to school, play in the cemetery, sleep under the huge maples, catch fireflies in jars and let them go, and catch maple syrup in the late winter. Eventually the valley is flooded to provide a reservoir so people in Boston can have water. They dig up the cemetery and move the bones, cut all the timber, move or tear down the houses, build dikes and dams, and flood the area. Sally Jane later comes back and rows with her father over the reservoir. He knows where everything used to be. She remembers what her mother said: "You have to let them go, Sally Jane." And she does. The setting is the Quabbin Reservoir, New England, from 1927 to 1946.

Integrated Language Arts Experiences
- Before reading one of the stories, children should spend time looking at the illustrations by Barbara Cooney. Quaint drawings with incredible detail give an authentic view of life in another time, another place. The teacher should provide books illustrated by Cooney so that children in pairs or groups may examine the books and talk about the pictures. All three books in this cluster are illustrated by Cooney and a list is included in the appendix.
- Children may draw a picture or write in a literature response log about how the life of one of the characters is different from their lives. Responses may be shared and drawings may be placed on a bulletin board entitled: The Way It Was Back Then.

- Because it is important for people to have their names spelled correctly, make name labels for each character in the book and place them on a chart. Then have each child print his or her first name on the chart for display in the classroom. Each child will be given three names of other children in the class and will select two of those names to include on a personal spelling list. Each child may be expected to use those names over the next week in writing notes to the children with those names. This activity not only focuses on the importance of spelling people's names correctly but also encourages children within the classroom to get to know classmates better.
- The teacher will read one of the books to the children. Then as a group project children will retell the story for a group write. The teacher may copy their story on chart paper and allow many opportunities for rereading; duplicate and let each child take home a copy of the retold story to read to parents.

Literature Approaches
- Review each story with discussions on point of view. Children may think or talk in groups about:
    the minister's point of view regarding having a Christmas tree in the church;
    the people of Boston's point of view regarding having drinking water from the river;
    the point of view of Miss Rumphius' neighbors when she began planting flowers. (literary conventions)
- Children write in their logs on one of these topics:
    I know how Ruthie felt because . . .
    I know how Miss Rumphius felt because . . .
    I know how Sally Jane felt because . . . (personal experiences)
- Children write a newspaper report on one of the stories giving the factual information and leaving out the emotions of the story:
    the return of Ruthie's father from the war;
    the flooding of the valley to provide water for Boston;
    a travelogue on Miss Rumphius' travels. (literacy processes)
- Children may have an option of drawing a picture to represent the factual information.

Story Branches

Miss Rumphius
- Copycat illustrations will be exciting for some students who have examined Cooney's art and would like to try to imitate this great illustrator. The teacher will provide acrylic paints or thick tempera for their art projects.

- As a class, plant a flower garden and grow lupines.
- Children may write or draw additional stories of Miss Rumphius' adventures through her world travels.
- Have children practice writing titles for people at school, such as Miss, Mr., Mrs., or Ms.

The Year of the Perfect Christmas Tree
- Make "perfect" Christmas trees by folding two sheets of construction paper together to create a long fold with both sheets together. Turn the paper so the fold is facing the child who writes his or her name in very large letters with the lower edges of the letters on the fold. Being careful not to cut completely through the fold, cut around the letters with scissors. Unfold, turn one page inside out, and staple the two pages together. The capital letter forming the first letter of the name is taller than the rest of the name, so the cutout, when held up, will resemble a Christmas tree that may be decorated and hung from the ceiling.
- Children will draw a picture or write a story to express how Ruthie must have felt when her wishes came true at Christmas time.
- Children will describe a perfect Christmas tree using as many descriptive words as possible. They may dictate or write their descriptions.

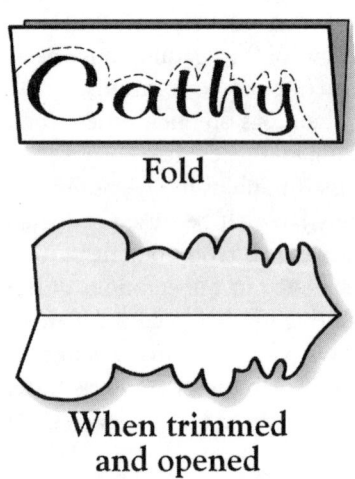

Fold

When trimmed
and opened

Letting Swift River Go
- As a group, make a list of names of rivers known by the children in the class.
- Children may look up pictures of rivers and find out where they run.

- Each child may plan what he or she would take along if forced to leave home because it was going to be covered with water.
- Children may draw a map of the inside of their bedroom, showing where the treasures are that they would want rescued if their house were going to be flooded.

Poetry

Nightingale, S. 1991. *A Giraffe on the Moon.* San Diego: Harcourt, Brace, Jovanovich.

Summary. This is a very simple book of couplets (two-line rhymes) beginning with "I didn't expect to see . . ." Following are rhyming fantasies including a cat, a snowman, a scarecrow, fishes, and other assorted creatures, each in a strange place. The little child decides that anything can be in his dreams—even a giraffe on the moon.

Hopkins, L. B. 1992. *To the Zoo.* Illustrated by John Wallner. Boston: Little, Brown.

Summary. This collection of animal poetry is written with a variety of poetic styles. From poets such as Myra Cohn Livingston to his own creations, Hopkins covers the span of zoo animals from giraffes to snakes to raccoons.

Yolen, J. 1993. *Raining Cats and Dogs.* San Diego: Harcourt, Brace, Jovanovich.

Summary. This book is a delight for young children because when reading it from one direction it is full of poems and pictures of cats and when flipped and read from the other direction, its subject is dogs. Of course, from either starting direction there comes a point in the middle of the book when it has to be turned up-side down! On one page in one direction is "Raining Dogs," and on the other page from the opposite direction is "Raining Cats." Several poems have opposites, such as "I Am Dog" and "I am Cat," both written with descriptions full of imagery, and "House Dog Speaks" and "Alley Cat Speaks," written in comparable patterns. Large type and large illustrations make this an easy book to share with a group of children.

Integrated Language Arts Experiences
- The teacher selects animal poetry to read to the children. The teacher or the children write the poem on chart paper following the initial reading and post in the classroom. Ask children for suggestions on which poems they want to hear again. When children can read charts, they should be encouraged to read along with the teacher.

- As children listen to some of the poetry, they close their eyes and imagine what they are hearing. They think, share in a pair, and then share their images with the whole group.
- Poems should be typed or printed and copied for children to have personal copies. Some children will be able to copy their own from the chart; others will need a close up copy and some may not be able to copy. In that case, a copy should be provided. They may be encouraged to read the poems at home to their parents.
- After much exposure to poetry through listening and reading, they should be able to try to write their own animal poems. Brainstorming rhyming animal words and other words that will be useful in the poems will be helpful. These words may be written as pairs on the chalkboard or on a chart.
- After drafting poems, children are encouraged to revise and edit their poems for standard spelling and punctuation as required by the grade level curriculum.

Literature Approaches
- Children will find favorite animal poems, copy them correctly, and place them on a bulletin board with an illustration or a note about why they are favorites. (personal experiences)
- Children will have opportunities to see and hear couplets (two-line rhyming poetry), triplets (three-line rhyming poetry), and quatrains (four-line rhyming poetry). They will identify poetry by its form (two, three, or four lines) or by its name (couplet, triplet, or quatrain). As they write their own poetry, they will be able to identify its form. (literary conventions)
- Children will participate in the classroom preparation of an anthology of favorite poems. Children will locate, copy, and submit poems to be selected for the anthology. Each child will have an opportunity to participate in the selection process. The teacher will lead the class in determining criteria for the selection of a poem. For example, perhaps the anthology will have a certain theme; if so, the poem should relate to the theme. There may be size limits on the length of the poem, or other criteria, such as whether or not most of the children like the poem. After the poems are selected for the anthology, children in pairs will write to the poet or the book publisher and request permission to use the poem in the class anthology. Return letters from publishers and poets should be motivating to the children. (literacy processes)

Story Branches

A Giraffe on the Moon
- Children will close their eyes as the book is read, and they will imagine the sights (giraffe on the moon, for example).
- They may create other unusual sights and write a couplet about the sight.
- They may draw a picture to accompany the couplet and make a border on the picture as is in the book.
- They may tell a partner about an unusual dream they have had.

Raining Cats and Dogs
- As a class, group write a two directional poem book about birds and mice, horses and cows, lions and elephants, goats and ponies, or any other combination of animals.
- Children plan and sing a rain dance to make it rain cats and dogs.
- Children may make an animal poetry book and collect poetry to copy in it.

To the Zoo
- Children may visit the *San Diego Zoo Animals* on CD Rom. (Address: Software Toolworks, Inc., 60 Leveroni Ct., Navato, CA 94949). They will keep a list of animals they have read about as it will take some time to read about all of them.
- Take them to a local zoo with their animal checklist from the CD ROM and check off the animals they see there.
- They may write animal poetry.
- They may sit on blankets with animal designs and read animal books and poetry.

Nonfiction: Biographies and Autobiographies

Aardema, V. 1993. *A Bookworm Who Hatched.* Katona, NY: Richard C. Owens.

Summary. In this autobiography written in first person, Verna Aardema states in the first sentence that she is a reteller of folktales. Her reputation as a reteller of more than 25 tales is wide, so most children who read or hear this story will have already met Verna in one of her many books: *Why Mosquitoes Buzz in People's Ears; Oh, Kojo! How Could You!; Anansi Finds a Fool;* and

Borrequita and the Coyote. Verna tells of her childhood and the inspirations to her imagination; she tells of the secret thinking and writing place and of her mother's prediction that she would become a writer. The book is full of photographs as well as simply stated text to allow children to know this author personally through this book and to gain insight into the process that authors maneuver as a book is conceived, written, illustrated, and published. Children who read or hear this book will be inspired to find the folktales she has masterfully retold. (A complete list of her books is in the appendix.)

Towle, W. 1993. *The Real McCoy*. Illustrated by Wil Clay. New York: Scholastic.

Summary. Elijah McCoy was born in Canada on May 2, 1844, to escaped slaves from Kentucky. His father fought in the 1837 Rebel War in Canada and was given 160 acres of land. On this land, Elijah and his brothers and sisters are raised as free Canadian citizens. Elijah goes to school and is interested in mechanical things. When he is 16 his parents send him to school in Edinburgh, Scotland, to study engineering. Elijah goes to the United States at the end of the Civil War and can only find a job with the Michigan Central Railroad as a fireman-oilman. He wants to find a better way to oil the train. He works for two years to perfect an oil cup and applies for a patent in 1872. Others try to invent an oil cup also, but his is always better, so people ask for the "real McCoy." He leaves Ypsilanti, Michigan, and goes to Detroit where he is a respected consultant to Detroit Lubricating and other companies. He also invents a lawn sprinkler, a better rubber heel for shoes, and makes designs for tires and tire treads. In 1916, he invents the graphite lubricator. He sets up his own company to sell his lubricator, but unfortunately has bad luck and does not get to develop it. After his wife dies he enters an infirmary for poor elderly people and dies in 1929.

Accorsi, W. 1992. *My Name is Pocahontas*. New York: Holiday House.

Summary. In this story the author-illustrator allows Pocahontas to tell her story of life in the Algonquin tribe with her brothers, sisters, pets, friends, and her powerful father, Chief Powhatan. Through the expressionistic illustrations and Pocahontas' story, the reader is carried through daily life to the day when she hides in the thick grass and watches a confrontation between the white settlers and warriors of her tribe. She is confused with the events as she believes that peoples of many colors can live harmoniously, but her father is suspicious of the settlers. When John Smith is captured, she takes advantage of a tribe member's right to save someone, making that someone a member of the tribe. She becomes John Smith's sister, and he spends much time with her family and friends. After he leaves the village, more trouble erupts, and

Genres

Pocahontas is captured and taken to live at the Jamestown settlement. There she marries John Rolfe and they have a son named Thomas. Pocahontas later goes to England and is presented to the court as the daughter of the Great Powhatan. She meets John Smith again in England, but never returned to her native land.

Integrated Language Arts Experiences
- The teacher will read one of the books to the children following this preparation experience:
- Show the children a biography block that you have completed. It will contain information on yourself as the teacher or on a personality well-

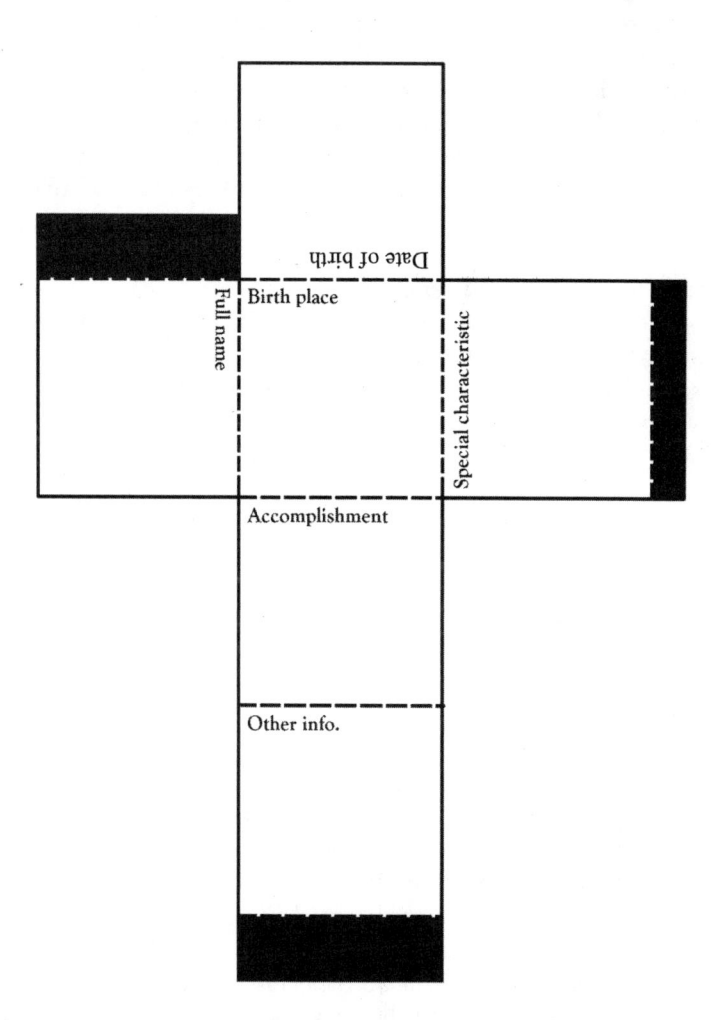

known to the children. Read from all six sides and include the following information:
Month and day of birth
Full name
Birth Place
A special characteristic of the person
An accomplishment of the person
One more piece of information
- Place the areas of information on a chart so children may listen for information on the person about whom the story is written while hearing the biography.
- After the reading, solicit the information from the children and list it on chart paper.
- Divide the class into six groups, one group for each of the six areas of information. Each group will take a sheet of posterboard already cut to a square measurement and will record the information from the chart as assigned. Some children may illustrate while others will write the information in large letters. When the writing has been completed, place the posterboard pieces on the floor in a large open area and tape them together to form the cube (biography block).
- Allow each child to select a person, read about that person, and make a biography block. Information is available through encyclopedias, trade books, and a list of biographies for kindergarten through grade three in the appendix.

Literature Approaches
- Children will recognize the differences between biographies and autobiographies by looking at the authors of the collection of books in the classroom. A table should be prepared near the bookshelf with a dividing line of masking tape. A sign on one side will read "Biographies" and on the other side, "Autobiographies." Groups of children may have several opportunities daily to sort the books into the two categories. (literary conventions)
- Following the reading aloud of one or more of the stories, children may be asked to think and talk about what the person in the biography or autobiography accomplished and what challenges were overcome to make these achievements possible. They may be given paper for drawing a picture or writing about the person and his or her challenges. Children may also be asked to think of their own challenges and draw a picture of their efforts toward a goal also. (personal experiences)
- After each child has read or heard a biography of choice, there will be time for reading, talking about the book, looking up additional informa-

tion, and trying to involve the home in the project. When possible, parents may assist in making simple costumes for a mix-and-meet bio party, where each child will dress like his or her character. Each child will have a paragraph written about the character, and it will be taped to the back of the character, (the child) so as they mix and meet each other, they can also read the cards and learn more about the characters. Each child will be responsible for the information on the card.
- Following the mix-and-meet bio party, a brown paper timeline will be taped around the classroom wall at child height. It will begin with the birthdate of the first character and continue until the current date. Children may place their cards (that were on their backs) on the timeline at the appropriate place in history. The finished timeline may be lowered for hanging under the chalkboard or raised above the chalk board for longer visibility. (literary processes)

Story Branches

A Bookworm Who Hatched
- Children may draw or write about their special places for thinking and writing. If they don't have one, they might decide on a place they could use for that purpose and draw or write about it.
- They may write to a book editor or a publisher and ask questions about the book publishing process (see publishers addresses on page 118).
- Children may make a folder for keeping a record of all the Verna Aardema books they have read. The record may look like this:

Title	Date I Read It	How I Liked It

The Real McCoy
- Children may draw pictures or describe some of his inventions.
- They may write him a letter telling him what they think of some of his inventions, such as the lawn sprinkler, rubber heels for shoes, or oil cups for oiling motors.
- Children will ask adults if they know where the phrase, "The Real McCoy" came from. If they don't, they will tell them the story.

My Name is Pocahontas
- Children will imitate the pictures in the book and draw others of what they think Pocahontas's world looked like.

- They may write a letter to Pocahontas and ask her why she thought the Indians and the "palefaces" could live together. Have them pretend that they can guess what she would have said and answer the letter.
- They may make a shoe box diorama of Pocahontas's world as an Algonquin woman and as the wife of an Englishman. Divide the shoe box in half and create half of the diorama for her Indian life and half for her English life.

INTERMEDIATE RESOURCES

Folk Literature

Aardema, V. 1992. *Anansi Finds a Fool.* New York: Dial Books for Young Readers.

Summary. In this West African folktale, Anansi is a man who is always trying to trick someone. He tells his wife that he is going to find someone to go into the fishing business with him—someone who will do all the work! Anansi's wife tells her friend about her husband's plan and her friend's husband, Bonsu, decides to teach Anansi a lesson, so he volunteers to go fishing with him. Being smarter than Anansi, Bonsu suggests that he do the work and let Anansi get tired, suffer, take the credit, or die if necessary. Well, Anansi thinks he is being tricked, so he insists on doing the work of building the fish trap and setting it while he lets Bonsu get tired, suffer, take the credit, or die if necessary. He even lets Bonsu take the large crayfish caught in the trap after Bonsu offers it to him first. When a python steals his fish and a crocodile damages his fish trap, Anansi realizes that he is not in a successful fishing business. He is still a trickster, but one who makes a fool of himself.

Hastings, S. 1988. *The Singing Ringing Tree.* Illustrated by Louise Brierley. New York: Henry Holt.

Summary. In this typical fairy tale, a prince falls in love with a selfish princess, brings her pearls, and asks her to marry him. She throws the pearls out and says the only thing she wants is the Singing Ringing Tree, which rings when the one who has it is in love. The prince goes to the place where it stands and meets an evil dwarf who gives him the tree but tells him that if the princess will not marry him, they will both be under evil power. The prince agrees, takes the tree, and the princess laughs at him. She takes the tree and it stops ringing. The prince does not know what to do, so he lies down beside the tree and goes to sleep. When he awakes, he has turned into a bear, and the princess is very ugly. The prince takes her to the dwelling of the evil dwarf, and there they live in a cave. She is willing to live there because she is so ugly she does not want anyone to see her. The prince provides food and she becomes uglier and meaner. She begins to realize, however, that the bear is taking care of her. She goes out by herself one day and finds a unicorn caught in a thicket. She rescues him—the first unselfish thing she has ever done in her life. The dwarf becomes very mad at her kindness and makes the river freeze over. The princess then sees a huge fish caught in the ice, so she uses her hands to dig out the ice and free the fish. Just then, the dwarf thaws the water and sends a giant wave crashing toward the princess. The fish takes her on his back and saves her. Then the dwarf sets the woods on fire, but the unicorn flies by and picks her up. She arrives safely back to the bear and puts her arms around him, telling him that she loves him. The spell of the dwarf is immediately broken, and they both turn back into a prince and princess. The dwarf is swallowed up in the ground, and the singing, ringing tree begins to ring again.

Zeman, L. 1992. *Gilgamesh the King.* **Montreal, Quebec: Tundra.**

Summary. This retold story from an ancient epic poem dating back 5,000 years is set in a kingdom of Uruk, in Mesopotamia, where Iraq and Syria are now located. Gilgamesh, part god and part man, is powerful but does not know how to relate to people. One day he decides to make his people build a towering wall around the city. They soon object to the long hours and senseless work, so they ask the sun god for help. The sun god creates a man, Enkidu, who is as powerful as Gilgamesh and sends him to live among the animals. The first man to see Enkidu, a hunter, takes word back to Gilgamesh that he has seen the strongest man in the world, because Enkidu rescues animals the hunter is chasing. Gilgamesh sends Shamhat, a beautiful singer, to lure Enkidu to Uruk. Shamhat falls in love with Enkidu. They return together, but Gilgamesh is angry, and he and Enkidu fight. Gilgamesh loses his footing and falls over the side of the towering wall, but Enkidu catches him and saves his life. They become friends, and Gilgamesh learns what it is like to have compassion for others.

Integrated Language Arts Experiences
- Before reading a story, the students may role play some of these character dichotomies: hateful vs. nice; deceitful vs. honest; vain vs. sincere; jealous vs. cooperative.
- They will read the story in individual settings with multiple copies, in pairs, or listen to the story read aloud.
- They can create character attribute charts, identifying characters and their traits. In such a chart, students place marks to identify traits that are present and question marks when unknown.

Character	Honest	Smart	Sense of Humor	Greedy	Lazy	Tricky
Anansi Aso Bonsu Laluah						

- Students write feelings regarding one or more characters in a response journal.
- Students draft an original tale from "folk literature" as told by a parent or friend. Many families have stories that are passed down about relatives. Others will have "baby" stories that parents may share orally for students to write. Continue the story with the option of carrying it through the writing process to publication.
- Students read independently several more examples of folk literature to determine literary conventions found in the genre that may be incorporated in the writing. Some examples are: beginning with "once upon a time...," having three incidents in the plot, heroes with extraordinary powers, and characters that we do not know very well.

Literature Approaches
- Students form groups to discuss the story with particular emphasis on the characters and their motivations. What caused them to act as they did? (literary conventions) Have students ever felt or acted as the characters did? (personal experiences)
- Students rewrite the story from the perspective of one character. (literary conventions) Instead of the objective perspective as found in most folk literature when the innermost thoughts and motives are never known, allow the character to think and plan while keeping the plot the same as the original.
- Students reread the story with readers' theater. The story may be read several times to give everyone an opportunity to read. Practice time will be important for everyone, so that an emphasis may be placed on fluidity and expression during the reading. (literary processes)

Story Branches
Anansi Finds a Fool
- Students write a note to tell Anansi that he is being made a fool. They take turns being Anansi and reading the notes aloud.
- Students read other African folk stories retold by Verna Aardema (see a list of books in print in the appendix). They make a list of the ideophones

used in these books (combinations of letters that represent sounds without real words).
- Using research skills of computerized title searches or card catalogues, students find as many spellings as possible of the character Anansi's name. They list all names on a chart and discuss the variants with the class.

The Singing Ringing Tree
- Students draw and label a plot diagram using a sequence stairstep chart. The first event will be listed and following events and results will be listed on lines drawn as stairs. The conclusion of the story will be written on the top step.
- Students compose and create the music played by the singing, ringing tree. They edit it for an audio-tape presentation to the class.
- Students determine other rhyming descriptions for everyday objects such as "singing ringing tree" or "snowing blowing wind" and use the descriptions as possible springboards for writing.

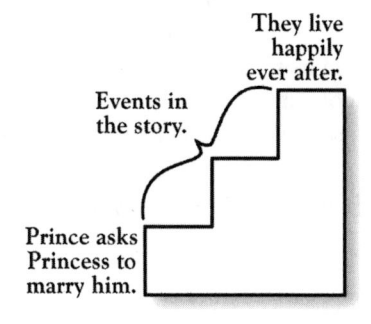

Gilgamesh the King
- Students may compare Gilgamesh to modern day heroes. Have them write a dialogue between the two characters.
- Have students listen to harp music as Shamhat might have played, then reenact an appropriate scene from the story with the music in the background.
- Examine the use of commas to set off a title, such as in Gilgamesh, the King. Other examples include: Mr. Jablonski, the teacher; Mrs. Voncannon, my neighbor; and Cinnamon Bun, my dog.

Fantasy

Steig, W. 1969. *Sylvester and the Magic Pebble.* New York: Simon & Schuster.

Summary. Sylvester Duncan is a donkey who lives with his parents and collects unusual stones and rocks. He finds an extraordinary rock and discovers that while holding it, he can make wishes that will come true. Upon confronting a lion on his way home, Sylvester wishes himself to be a rock, and he turns into one. Because the magic pebble is beside him, but not touching him, his wishes to be a donkey again are not answered. At home, his parents are worried and have neighbors and policemen looking for Sylvester. A month passes and his family is miserable in their loss. The seasons change and the leaves and the snow fall on the rock that is Sylvester. When spring comes, Sylvester's parents go on a picnic to the hill where Sylvester lies as a rock. His mother sits on the rock, and Sylvester tries so hard to call out to her, but to no avail. Mr. Duncan looks around and picks up the remarkable stone, saying that Sylvester would have liked it. He places it on the rock that is Sylvester, and as soon as he wishes himself to be himself again, he is! It is a wonderful moment for Sylvester to be back with his family. They put the pebble away in a safe place so accidents like that one cannot happen again.

Babbitt, N. 1975. *Tuck Everlasting.* **New York: Bantam.**

Summary. Winnie Foster dreams of running away from the house on the edge of the wood. Mae Tuck is going to meet her sons, whom she has not seen in ten years. Both of these events occur in the same area, near the mysterious wood. Another event is the appearance of a strange man in a yellow suit. The next morning, Winnie goes into the wood, just for a peek, and meets Jessie Tuck, one of Mae's sons who has looked 17 for 87 years. Winnie asks for a drink of water from the spring when she is seized and kidnapped to be taken away with Mae's family. Later they tell her their strange story of drinking the water from the spring and having eternal life; they are not able to die. Jessie is 17, and Miles, his brother, is 22 and married. When Miles' wife turned 40, she couldn't stand having a 22-two-year old husband, so she left.

Each year, the four members of the family meet near the spring for a reunion. This year, Winnie has gotten involved with them. They stay in a cottage deep in the wood where they had once lived. The man in the yellow suit offers to get Winnie back if the Fosters will give him their land. When he reaches the Tucks' cabin, he tells them of his plan to sell water from the spring. Mae is outraged and shoots him. When the constable comes, Winnie tells him that she is with the Tucks of her own free will, but Mae is taken to jail to stand trial for the shooting. Winnie is taken home and later hears that the man in the yellow suit has died. Mae is going to be tried for murder. Jessie visits Winnie at her house, giving her a bottle of water and advising her of the plan to free Mae. Jessie wishes that Winnie would wait until she is 17 and drink the water, so they would be the same age forever. Winnie watches from a distance as the Tucks break into the jail and carry Mae out and away in the wagon. Winnie thoughtfully pours the water from the vial onto a toad that has a hard time fighting off the dogs. The epilogue reveals that Winnie never drank from the spring, and long after she was gone, the Tucks visit her grave site.

Banks, L. R. 1992. *The Farthest Away Mountain.* New York: Avon Camelot.

Summary. Dakin, a small, dainty, 14-year-old girl, is called by a voice in the night to come to the farthest away mountain, where even her father has never gone. It is when the mountain top nods to her that she packs a knapsack and ventures toward the dark woods at the foothills of the mountain. She isn't sure why she picks up the tarnished brass troll that occupies a space on the mantelpiece, but when they are in the forest and she is scared, a teardrop on the brass troll brings him to life. He gives her some valuable advice, then retreats from the woods in fear. As she continues through her journey, she meets an old frog named Croak, three gargoyles named Og, Vog, and Zog, the Drackamag, a pitiful giant with his evil bird named Graw, and the most hideous of all creatures, the Wicked Witch, who paints the snow different colors by day and disappears into a mysterious form by night. Dakin is called by the mountain to free the creatures from the evil spell placed on them by the Wicked Witch and to return the Ring of Kings, which had been stolen 200 years ago. Through this adventure, Dakin learns her own strength and the intensity of her concern for others.

Integrated Language Arts Experiences
- Before reading the story, guide students to list actions, happenings, or objects that could make a story a fantasy. Some examples are: inanimate objects taking on animate characteristics; characters having traits that are not possible for humans; animals having human characteristics; worlds with principles of nature that are impossible in our world. Students may chart these characteristics of fantasy.
- Read the story in shared pairs with discussion time provided after each reading session. It will take several days to finish the reading of the books if read in pairs.
- Have the paired students keep a fantasy log of their reactions following each reading session. Ask them to collaborate on what they write in the log. It may also be illustrated with scenes from the story.
- Students examine the use of description in the story. Have students close their eyes while you reread a selection, leaving out all descriptors. Allow students to describe to a partner what they heard, then reread that selection and identify the descriptors in the text.
- Students add descriptors to a vocabulary bank kept in the classroom in the form of a card file, scrapbook, or picture dictionary.
- An alternative way of reading the book is to let pairs or small groups of students read various parts of the book simultaneously, sharing their parts of the story as it is told later in sequence. This technique, called cooperative book sharing (CBS), creates much interest. The groups only know their portion of the story until it unfolds as groups tell their part.

Paperback books literally are torn apart and pages are divided among the number of groups in the class. For a designated period of time, students read their sections aloud and in separate areas of the room. Following the reading, they are instructed to predict what may have happened prior to their section and what may happen later. Small group discussions occur until all have finished reading, then students in one group, believing to have the beginning of the story, retell in their own words their section. Whatever group has the next part of the story will continue and so on until the story has been told. Total group discussion will follow as students question each other about details regarding the story until everyone is satisfied.

Literature Approaches
- Students discuss why the elements of fantasy in the story were used and what might have happened if other elements had been present. Use the chart prepared earlier to consider how the story would have been different if the characters had not had the special traits or if the setting had been different. (literary conventions)
- Students remember a time when they were far from home and something scary happened to them. Find a way to share that experience with someone else: mobile, story, drawing, play, or other medium of choice. (personal experiences)
- Students draft a copycat story. Use the same characters and change the events in part of the story or keep the basic plot in the story and change the characters. (literacy processes)

Story Branches

Sylvester and the Magic Pebble
- On second and third readings of this story, have students find examples of the author providing clues to the meaning of specific words: extraordinary, ceased, panicked, confused, frantic, miserable. The meaning of each word is clearly found in the context of the story, with explanations closely following or preceding the word.
- From students' writing folders containing composition drafts, have them select a piece and edit it to provide vocabulary clues as Steig does in the examples uncovered by the students.
- Students complete character interactions between Sylvester and his parents, showing how they felt about each other.
    Mother and Father>>>>worried about him; missed him; babied him>>>>Sylvester
    Sylvester >>>>wanted to give them things; eager to show them his pebble; missed them >>>>Parents

Tuck Everlasting
- After discussion, students write epitaphs for the Tuck family in case they ever die.
- Discuss in small groups whether Winnie made a good decision in not drinking the water.
- Students write the continuing adventures of the frog that drank the water.
- They draw a relationship tree to show how the man in the yellow suit was related to the Tucks (which consequently allowed him to find out about the water, page 84).

The Farthest Away Mountain
- Teacher and students work together to make a collection of trolls for a display. Each student adopts a troll and keeps a diary for that troll, writing it from the troll's point of view and recalling events of the day. For example, "Today, I went to the playground and watched the children play a game. At lunch time, I sat in the middle of the table."
- Students paint a scene from the story showing how the Wicked Witch colored the snow on the mountain.
- Students compare this story to the *Frog Prince* with a Venn diagram. (Old Croak, the frog, is really a prince.)
- They may develop character webs for each of the characters in the story. Web information on how they look, what they can do, and what their hopes and fears are.
- Students research the use of the "est" in farthest. Exactly what does it mean? Are there other choices of words the author could have used to mean the same thing? Students should find ways to use the suffix in their own writing.

Realistic Fiction: Contemporary

Bunting, E. 1994. *Smoky Night.* **Illustrated by David Diaz. San Diego: Harcourt, Brace.**

Summary. Daniel, his mother, and his cat, Jasmine, look on in fear during the night of the Los Angeles riots. They are in their dark apartment watching from above as people below them are smashing and stealing. They see the grocery store across the street run by Mrs. Kim being robbed, while Mrs. Kim screams at them in an unknown language. Mrs. Kim is strange, and they have never shopped at her store. They are frightened, so they sleep with their clothes on, and all three (including the cat) sleep in the same bed. They awaken later to the smell of smoke and screams of others in the apartment that has caught on fire. In the excitement, Jasmine runs away. Daniel asks people if they have seen Jasmine. They go to a shelter in a church hall where a fireman later brings in two cats: Jasmine and one that belongs to Mrs. Kim. The cats make friends, and Daniel and his mother talk to Mrs Kim; they decide to shop at her store after it opens again.

Naylor, P. R. 1991. *Shiloh*. New York: Atheneum.

Summary. Marty Preston lives in the hills of West Virginia and is particularly close to the country and the wildlife. He faces some major issues when he finds a beagle (Shiloh) that has been abused. His problems include deciding if he can help the dog, and if he does, how his family will accept it. The problem is expanded with his interactions with the owner-abuser as Marty struggles under his own deceptions while trying to help the dog.

MacLachlan, P. 1993. *Baby*. New York: Delacorte.

Summary. Larkin is a 12-year-old girl who lives on a resort island off the New England coast with her parents and Byrd, an older family member. Larkin's mother is an artist, and she vents her feelings through art; her Papa dances on the coffee table when he gets home from work; and elderly Byrd observes the family and gives good advice. Larkin, however, can only talk to Lalo, a friend, about these family problems:

- Six months ago they buried an infant boy who lived one day. He was Larkin's brother, but she never saw him, they never named him, and no one will talk about him.
- A year-old child was left in their driveway at the end of the tourist season with a note that her name is Sophie; her mother loves her and will return for her.

Larkin learns to deal with her grief and lack of understanding through poetry, words, friendship, and Sophie's healing love. After the mother comes for Sophie a year later and explains that she left Sophie with the family deliberately because she thought they would take care of her while she nursed her sick husband back to health, Larkin is able to get her Mama and Papa to talk and to describe their baby. They name him William and have his name inscribed on his cemetery marker.

Integrated Language Arts Experiences
- Under the teacher's guidance, students explore types of families and how family members support and encourage each other. Students may list various family members and talk about how each plays an important role in the family (even the pets).

- *Smoky Night* is a picture book that the teacher may read aloud; the other books are chapter books that may be read aloud in installments or with multiple copies. Students may read in pairs or individually.
- If books are read over a period of days, each session should begin with small or large group talks to review what happened in the stories in previous sessions and to predict what might happen next. In literary circles of groups who have been working together for a few days, have students write predictions on cards and stack together for later discussion. Following the reading of the section of text, the prediction cards are a source for beginning the discussion.
- The teacher may select an entire book or a section of a text to read aloud. The students will each have an index card for making sketches while they listen to the story. (It is a good idea to read it once for their enjoyment and a second time for them to sketch their images.) Following the image sketching, groups of children show their cards and explain their images to others in the group.
- The sketch used in the image sketching may be used as a catalyst for writing a response to the story for a literature log or a writing entry.
- Drafts of written responses may later be edited for mechanics and completed as final pieces for publication.

Literature Approaches
- Following the reading of the story, divide students into pairs to write "dig deep probes." These are high level questions that begin with stems such as: What would have happened if . . . ? Why did . . . do . . . ? What did . . . really mean by this statement: . . . ? (literacy processes)
- Questions may be exchanged from one group to another for discussion. (personal experiences)
- The sequential plot of any of these stories may be the subject of a bulletin board. The outline may be placed on a background and students may identify the following parts by drawing pictures to represent the events. (literary conventions)
    1. The identification of the problem or goal
    2. The rising action toward the goal
    3. The climax or point of no return
    4. The falling action
    5. The resolution
- Students write letters to characters in the story as from one family member to another, trying to help them understand the feelings of another. For example, Daniel's mother (*Smoky Night*) might write to Daniel to explain how she could be so calm and nonjudgmental on the night of the riots. Marty might write to his father and tell him why he had

to keep Shiloh a secret for so long. Larkin might write to her parents and tell them how her heart was breaking that they had not even named the baby. The letters might be exchanged with different students responding as the character might have responded. (literary processes)

Story Branches

Smoky Night
- Students may research the newspaper files for more information on the Los Angeles riots. Look for human interest stories as well as factual reports. Compare the writing styles of the two types of stories.
- Using collage materials, they may replicate some of the art work in this book. It will require cereal, plastic laundry bags, paper bags, and other assorted fabrics. Heavy tempera paints will round out the supplies needed for making this project realistic.
- Students determine how words turn from nouns (smoke) into adjectives (smoky). Find other examples and use in writing.

Shiloh
- Have a classroom court to "try" Marty and Judd for what each did against the other or against the dog. Have a jury, judge, prosecutors, and defense lawyers who will play their roles based on the story.
- Have students write different endings to the story and spend a block of time allowing the endings to be read aloud to other students.

Baby
- Students explore the characters of Larkin and Lalo, the teacher and her boyfriend, Byrd, Larkin's parents, and Sophie's mother. Identify strengths and weaknesses in each character.
- Students select one paragraph or a short passage from the book and write a personal response to it in their literature log. Their response should help them remember something special about the book.
- Students compare the dancing daddy in this story to the grandfather in *Song and Dance Man*. Use a Venn diagram to compare the two dancers.

Realistic Fiction: Historical

Lowry, L. 1989. *Number the Stars.* **Boston: Houghton Mifflin.**

Summary. In Denmark in 1943, a family consisting of the parents and two daughters assist a neighboring family of Jews as they escape to Sweden. Anne

Marie Johansen and Ellen Rosen are friends who live in the same apartment building. It becomes more evident each day to Anne Marie and her parents that the Rosens are in danger from the German officers occupying Denmark. The boyfriend of the Johansen's oldest daughter, who had been killed the year before, visits often and passes information regarding the resistance. Mrs. Johansen, her two daughters, and Ellen, pretending to be their other daughter who had died, travel to the seashore on a "vacation." They are soon joined by the rest of the Rosen family as Uncle Henrik prepares to smuggle them out of Denmark and into Sweden where Jews can live freely. Clever planning for a family "funeral" and bravery on the part of Mrs. Johansen and Anne Marie aid in the Rosens' escape. The epilogue at the end of the story differentiates fact and fiction in the story.

Levitin, S. 1970, reissued 1993. *Journey to America*. Illustrated by Charles Robinson. New York: Atheneum.

Summary. The Platt family—father, mother, Lisa, who tells the story, Annie, the baby sister, and Ruth, the older sister—live in Berlin during the late 1930s. They escape to Switzerland and stay there while waiting to go to America to avoid the persecution of the Jews. The family has to leave everything they have except what they can carry with them without arousing suspicion that they are doing more than taking a vacation to Switzerland. Papa goes first to America and gets a job as a janitor; Mama and the three girls follow to Switzerland while he gets sponsors and makes enough money to send for them. When they get to Switzerland, they can not afford to stay together, so the older girls go to a refugee camp. It is unsatisfactory, so their mother takes them out of the camp and finds a good family to take care of the baby girl. After almost a year, they leave for America and are reunited with their father.

Rabin, S. 1994. *Casey Over There*. Illustrated by Greg Shed. San Diego: Harcourt, Bracc.

Summary. Aubrey is a seven-year-old boy when his older brother, Casey, joins the army and sails to France to fight in World War I. Aubrey writes letters from Brooklyn, while Casey fights in Europe. The family goes to the beach, and Casey waves across the Atlantic Ocean to his brother. When three months pass without a letter from Casey, Aubrey decides to write to Uncle Sam, who had recruited Casey. One day, a telegram arrives, and they are frightened, for telegrams often mean a soldier has been killed. It is a telegram from President Woodrow Wilson, telling Aubrey that Uncle Sam was not yet finished with Casey. Almost a year later, the war ends, and finally Casey comes home. Aubrey then writes another letter to thank Uncle Sam.

Integrated Language Arts Experiences
- The first two books are novel-length and will take several days to read whether the teacher reads aloud or the students have their own copies to read. The last book is a picture book with an intense story that probably should be read aloud and later placed on a table for students to examine the illustrations thoroughly.
- Prior to reading any of the books, a timeline and a world map or atlas may be shown with the setting of the story identified both in terms of when it happened and where.
- The teacher may show the cover of the book and invite students to speculate on the symbolism found on the illustrated cover. Perspectives will vary as there are a number of directions this discussion could take.
- If multiple copies of a novel are available, provide time for silent sustained reading (SSR), followed by group discussions.
- Use reciprocal questioning techniques so that students will question each other on items of interest in the story. Modeling by the teacher of appropriate questions will help students ask questions that will provide for higher level thinking.
- Suggest that students write acrostics for various characters in the story that will describe the strong traits found among them. For example:

    A friend to Ellen
    N ice
    N ot happy with the German occupation
    E llen's best friend
    M ore mature than her age
    A s brave as she needs to be
    R uns fast
    I s curious
    E scape plans are carried out

Literature Approaches
- As the story is read, students draw character webs to describe the Johansen and Rosen families or the Platt family or the Wheeler family. Add more insights into the descriptions, personalities, and motivations of the families with each day's reading. (literary conventions)
- Following the reading of the story, students revisit the predictions regarding symbols on the book jackets. Verify or negate the earlier predictions with small group discussions followed by share-back to the whole class. (literary conventions)
- Following the reading and the discussion of the entire story, students select a trait found in one of the characters and write of a time when someone they knew had demonstrated such a trait. Some possible traits: honesty, bravery, cleverness, and persistence. (personal experiences)

- Write a letter to the U.S. Naturalization and Immigration Department in Washington, D.C., explaining why the Rosen family or the Platt family deserves to come to America. Revise and edit for a grade on persuasive letter writing. (literacy processes)

Story Branches

Number the Stars
- Students list examples of bravery. Make a chart of brave characters in stories.
- Students write of a time when they needed to be brave.
- Students listen to Whitney Houston's *One Moment in Time* (©1987, Hammond Enterprises) on tape and quickwrite how the song applied to the story. After writing quickly on cards without using names, shuffle the cards, pass them out, and take turns reading them. Varying viewpoints will be expressed.

Journey to America
- Find stories in newspapers of families fleeing their countries. Have students try to imagine how they would feel if they were forced from their homes. Have them make a list of what they would take with them if they could only take one suitcase. Students may share thoughts after reading the story.
- Write in a personal literacy log how you think you would feel if your family was separated and some had to leave the country and others had to stay as the Platt family experienced.
- Continue interest in the Platt family with books: *Silver Days* and *Annie's Promise*, both published by Atheneum.
- The diary of Zlata Filipovic, referenced under nonfiction for intermediates, is a contemporary true account of a family under siege in Sarajevo. Have students write letters to Zlata and send them to her through her publisher.

Casey Over There
- Intermediate students should read this story aloud to a younger student and ask the younger one to explain the pictures. Good discussion and comprehension of the story will occur from both older and younger students.
- Students will research "The Great War," "Uncle Sam," "Woodrow Wilson," and what happened on November 11, 1918. Then they will make reports to display on bulletin boards or tri-fold boards.
- They may write a letter to a governmental official such as a governor or congressman. The letters should be addressed to him or her as "The

Honorable. . . ." Students should make sure their letters are written and addressed correctly before mailing them.

Poetry

Baylor, B. 1977. *Guess Who My Favorite Person Is*. Illustrated by Robert Parker. New York: Aladdin Books.

Summary. This book, written in free verse, tells a delightful story of a conversation between a man and a young girl about "favorites." They describe favorite lady bugs, favorite colors, favorite things to touch, favorite sounds, favorite places to live, favorite dreams, favorite things to see moving, favorite things to taste, favorite smells, and favorite time of day.

Osofsky, A. 1992. *Dreamcatcher*. Illustrated by Ed Young. New York: Orchard.

Summary. A lyrical, free verse poem written about the Ojibway method of freeing children of their bad dreams. The dreamcatcher is a woven circle with an eye hole designed to let the good dreams drift through and catch the bad ones and trap them until sunrise when they die. The story is of a day and a night in the life of a Native American family and their preparation and use of the dreamcatcher for their new infant in their family. Chalk illustrations reflect a gentle, soothing mood, projecting comfort in a culture of long ago.

Yolen, J. 1990. *Bird Watch: A Book of Poetry*. Illustrated by Ted Lewin. New York: Philomel.

Summary. Written in free verse, these poems celebrate the fowls of the air. Beginning with a statement of sorrow from a bird watcher whose loons are flying away, through analogies of the woodpecker to an oil drill or a dentist's probe, to a satisfying poem about Turkey Tom, these poems are language-fun with aesthetically charming illustrations. Reading them and enjoying them as a group will be delightful, but the real joy will come as each child has his or her own turn to savor this book.

Integrated Language Arts Experiences
- The teacher will read aloud to the class pages 10 to 15 from Lois Lowry's *Anastasia*. In this excerpt, Anastasia writes free verse poetry and is ridiculed by her teacher. Elicit students' reactions following the reading.
- Students will compare free verse to rhymed poetry using a Venn diagram. Highlight the likenesses and differences.

- As a group, list criteria for free verse. Some suggestions are:
  —may be any combination of words without regard for rhyming or syllabic patterns;
  —should evoke mental images for aesthetic appreciation;
  —may be long or short.
- Students may read a poem silently, then read it aloud to a partner.
- Students will listen to a partner read a poem aloud. They will imagine the picture created by their partner's words. They may ask questions to clarify the image received with the free verse poetry.
- They may work in teams to create a free verse poem on a topic of their choice. Then they can revise and edit for placement on a bulletin board.

Literature Approaches
- Teacher will say to students: Remember an experience you had when:
  you were thrilled to find that you could "play" with words;
  you made something for someone and knew that person would really like what you made;
  you were emotionally moved by something you saw in nature.
- Students will write about the experience using the free verse poetry style. (personal experiences)
- They may also make a puppet to read their poetry for them. The puppet will need to be an appropriate character and may be made from socks, paper plates, paper bags, or tongue depressors. (literary processes)
- Students may look for poetry in collections and anthologies with alliteration. ("Peter Piper picked a peck of pickled peppers.") They may try adding some alliteration to their free verse writing. (literary conventions)

Story Branches

Guess Who My Favorite Person Is
- Students make a list of favorite things; share with a friend. With that friend, find "different ways" to describe the things they like as was done in the text.
- Gather other Byrd Baylor books (see appendix) and read the free verse poetry aloud to a partner or within a group. Research Baylor's life and make a chart or video production of information on her career and books.
- They may try writing a poem that sounds like a Byrd Baylor poem.

Dreamcatcher
- Teacher should hang a dreamcatcher in the classroom. They are commercially available in many curio stores.

- Students make lists of bad dreams they would like to have the dreamcatcher catch; they also list the good dreams they would like to slip through to them.
- They may draw a dreamcatcher and write a story about how it is used.
- Students will use chalk as an art medium and draw a picture of the Ojibway using a dreamcatcher.

Bird Watch
- Students select various birds from the book for research reports and illustrate them in their habitat with watercolors.
- They may write a free verse poem about birds and bird watching.

Nonfiction: Diaries

Thaxter, C. 1992. *Celia's Island Journal.* Adapted and illustrated by Loretta Krupinski. Boston: Little, Brown.

Summary. This journal begins in 1839 when Celia is four years old and continues intermittently through 1846 as Celia grows up. The selections in this picture book are short and are framed with illustrations of wild life native to the Northeastern seacoast. Celia's father is a lighthouse keeper, and they live on White Island for many years. There is a baby brother and the parents, along with Celia. She tells of the seasonal changes, and how she watches them come and go, how she passes the time intricately involved with nature on the island. Celia grows up to be a published poet and writer, still living off the coast of New Hampshire, and later with her own family on the Isle of Shoals.

Whitely, O., and J. Boulton. 1994. *Only Opal, The Diary of a Young Girl.* Illustrated by Barbara Cooney. New York: Philomel.

Summary. The text in this book was selected from Jane Boulton's earlier publication of Opal Whitely's diary as a child in the lumbering camps in the Northwest. Opal's words are full of poetry, inspired perhaps by the memories of parents lost to her when she was very young; or inspired perhaps by the nature that surrounded her in the early 1900s in the West. Her diary tells of animal friends, of chores, of punishments, and of child like wonder and amazement. Whatever she endures, she always writes of the security of Angel Mother and Angel Father, her guardian angels, who are always with her.

Filipovic, Z. 1994. *Zlata's Diary.* New York: Viking.

Summary. Zlata Filipovic, an 11-year-old girl in 1991, living in Sarajevo, Bosnia-Herzegovina, formerly the country of Yugoslavia, keeps a diary of her daily life before the civil war there began and throughout the next two years. In this book, a typical pre-teenager begins the monologue; it turns to a diary when she begins writing to "Dear Mimmy" in imitation of Anne Frank's diary; and it continues with the philosophical wonderings of a too-soon-adult child trying to maintain sanity and life under the duress of war. The entries are child-like in that the excitements in her life are shown in capital letters, exclamation points, and onomatopoeia (SNIFFLE-SNIFFLE). The entries are far too mature for her age as she describes what has happened to her beautiful city, as she laments the death of friends due to the war, and as she contemplates suicide when the shelling, cold, hunger, and isolation are extreme. It is impossible for American children really to empathize with Zlata, but through the words of another child, some bare understandings of the horrors of war and the meaning of peace are possible.

Integrated Language Arts Experiences
- The diary as a genre of writing, with its unique characteristics, forms the basic structure for this language and literature experience. Students may brainstorm characteristics of "diary" and chart them. Some probable traits from the students are:
  first person point of view
  informal
  written to one's self as an audience
  omits details that the writer assumes are understood
  results in a chronological sequence of events since it is written over a period of time
  may be rhetorical as the writer tries to clarify issues or understand problems
  may show strong emotions as the "heart" of a person is often exposed in such writings
- If the two picture books are selected for this experience, the teacher will probably read them to the students following biographical introductions to the authors. Minimal information is available in the introductions and epilogues to the books. References are given in the books to other sources also. Both Celia and Opal have other published books for more in-depth study. If *Zlata's Diary* is the only book in this collection to be read, multiple copies may be obtained and students may read the book for several days to completion. Because of the powerfulness and currency of the content in this book, it is recommended that the teacher either read it to the students over a period of time or maintain whole class discussions before and after each independent reading session.
- Construct a timeline and assign different time periods to each student who will record the activities of the diary author on the timeline. For

example, with *Celia's Island* (1839 to 1846), seasons change during the span of time she lives on the island. Students may portray her activities during the various seasons. With *Only Opal* (around 1905), the timeline could be based on the different animals or people she met while at the lumbering camps. In *Zlata's Diary,* a two-year period (1991 to 1993) was covered. Because it is a time period known to the students, they might add other world happenings to the months and days referenced in her diary. The research could reveal much meaning to her story by knowing other episodes from the Serb-Croat-Muslim war.
- Students may research the time periods of the authors of the diaries and uncover other world events. Reports may be given to the class on the lifestyles and world history of their eras. Students may take on the role of another person living at the same time as the author and write a diary reflecting what the life of that person might have been like.
- Times and lives of those eras may also be dramatized, shown on bulletin boards, produced as video presentations, or visually displayed on tri-fold boards.

Literature Approaches
- Students need opportunities to reflect on their own emotions that were evoked from the diary. Provide silent, sustained writing (SSW) time for all to record personal thoughts and ideas from the diary. (personal experiences)
- Follow SSW with a simulated "news conference" when students volunteer to play roles from the diaries and have other student act as news reporters, asking questions during the "conference." Students may answer from implied meanings from the text if the question is not directly answered in the diary. (literacy processes)
- Students examine the conflicts in the plot in each diary. Compare and contrast the types of conflicts: person against nature (*Celia's Island*); person against society (*Only Opal*); person against person (*Zlata's Diary*). Students may participate in group discussions to support one of the types of conflict and show details from the story as evidence for that stance. Discussions may be lively as students perceive the character's actions and language differently. (literary conventions)

Story Branches
Celia's Island
- Students may locate other sources on seabirds and sea life on the Northeast coast of the United States. Compare the animal life with that of the local area.

- Students may make homemade toys and distribute either to children who are ill and cannot leave their homes or to children for winter days when they are snowbound and cannot get outside to play. As part of this project, students will imagine life for a child on an isolated island during winter storms.
- The teacher and students may locate books of poetry written by Celia Thaxter. As a group, students may read her poetry; individual students may write poetry back to her. As an example of responding with poetry to a poem, see Jane Yolen's "Note to Carl Sandburg" in response to Sandburg's "Fog" in *Weather Reports* by Jane Yolen.

Only Opal
- Students may research life in lumbering camps in the Northwestern states in the early 1900s. Reports may by made through various media. Multimedia video productions, such as Power Point by Microsoft, are challenging.
- They may investigate the namesake of each animal in the book—Felix Mendelssohn, Horatius, Lars Porsena, Michael Raphael, Elizabeth Barrett Browning, and Peter Paul Rubens— and make assumptions on how and why she selected each name. Displays presented to class showing biographical information on both the original namesake and Opal's animals will be appealing.
- Allow time for practice for oral reading of the text. The language is poetic and full of imagery. Oral interpretations may be practiced and performed to increase fluency.
- Students write using the first person perspective and first person pronouns.

Zlata's Diary
- Zlata Filipovic, who is now living in Paris, may be amenable to a personal contact through the mail or a telephone conference call. (She speaks English.) Students might directly ask her questions and respond to her diary. Contact her publisher (Viking) to investigate the possibilities.
- Students may compare the MTV favorites of Zlata as noted in the book to the favorites of students in the classroom. Survey and determine similarities and differences to her preferences.
- Examine the holiday and birthday celebrations in Zlata's family with those of students in the class. Comparison charts or Venn diagrams may be used to show similarities and differences of the two contemporary cultures. Students may make the comparisons individually as customs vary greatly in any classroom.
- Research the history of the former Yugoslavia and chart its recent upheaval.

CHAPTER 3

Structures

As children begin their paths to literacy and become more experienced with reading and writing, they discover that all stories are not written in the same style or for the same purpose. They notice that some books tell about people, about places, and about things in the world. They notice that other books tell stories in different ways; some tell stories with dialogue while others do not. Some stories are told in prose narrative while others are told in poetic verse. Of course, young children cannot explain how books are different, but they recognize the different forms and they like all of them.

This chapter is designed to give teachers some examples of various forms in narrative, expository, and poetic structures and some suggestions of ways to use them to heighten children's awareness of the differences. It is usually assumed that students read narrative and poetic structure for aesthetic purposes first and then may respond to the literary conventions, structure, or processes. The corollary assumption is that students read expository structure for the purpose of carrying away information—Rosenblatt's efferent purpose (see discussion in Chapter 1)—but expository text may also be used for aesthetic goals. Both aesthetic and efferent purposes are important in a balanced literature program; it is the responsiblity of the teacher to balance the group experiences and to guide students as they expand their independent literary encounters. Teachers will be able to use the materials in this chapter to plan such a balance and to increase their own awareness of how literature is used in their classrooms.

In this chapter, basic literary structures are clustered with text summaries, integrated language arts experiences, varied literature approaches, and specific story branches. As in the previous chapter, for each type of structure there will be a cluster of three stories for primary children and three stories for intermediate students. The teacher may select one or more of the stories to use with the suggested language arts and literature experiences.

As children begin listening to stories and reading them, they notice likenesses among the stories. They are able to predict what may happen, not only because of their increasing knowledge of the world but because they are developing intertextuality. They are becoming "text-wise," and they know that certain patterns are found in stories. They recognize beginnings, middles, and endings of stories. They know which stories lend themselves to exciting climaxes, because they have heard or read similar stories previously. As they acquire more experience with texts, they successfully discriminate among text types: narrative texts that tell a story, expository texts that provide information, and poetic texts. Because young readers can recognize the textual characteristics of different stories, they already have experience with literary structures.

Within text types—narrative, expository, poetic—there are other aspects of literary structure that children recognize as patterns and are able to emulate with their own writing. Selected patterns include narrative, expository, and poetic forms.

NARRATIVE FORMS

Repetitive patterns are especially enjoyable to children and make rereading easy. An example from a well-known story is: "Little Pig, Little Pig, let me come in." Related to the repetitive pattern is the *cumulative* form in which every part of the story builds onto the next part. In many cumulative stories, repetition is a key dimension, as well as the accumulation of events. *The House That Jack Built* is an example.

Cyclical patterns are easy to recognize and fun to create because with these stories, the beginnings and endings are the same. Remember *If You Give a Mouse a Cookie?*

I Have A Problem patterns are those forms with a character who asks various other characters to solve his problem. The classic example is *Are You My Mother?* A similar pattern for older students contains a plot with a clearly focused problem and its sequential efforts to find a solution.

Story grammar, or a predictable syntax of stories, includes noticeable indicators of the beginning, middle, and ending of stories with the systematic plot framework of setting a goal, attempting to reach the goal, evaluating the results of each attempt, and concluding the story after a climax. Folk literature has excellent examples, with the clearly stated tasks (attempts and results) found in many folktales.

EXPOSITORY FORMS

Sequence is used in expository text to show time, chronology, and progression of events. Found in both narrative and expository forms of writing, sequence is easily identified by young readers and writers.

Cause and effect is an identifiable pattern used in expository text to highlight problems and solutions. This structure may also be taught to young writers.

Problem-solution patterns are found at all levels of expository text. The efforts to delineate a problem and discuss a variety of possible solutions, along with the advantages and disadvantages of each are recognizable by both primary and intermediate age students.

POETIC FORMS

Rhyming poetry is a structure that is pleasing to the ear and easy to replicate. From couplets (two-line rhyming poems) to quatrains (four lines of rhyming poetry), children enjoy reading and writing this form of poetry.

Just for fun poetry is probably the favorite poetry of most children. This poetry may have humorous content, nonsensical language, or appealing alliteration. These are among the many ways poets invite children to read and experience this poetry.

Patterned poetry refers to selected poems used for form replication with different topics or word changes. It is similar to the popular "copycat" writing employed by many teachers. A poem with interesting and easily repeated meter is usually read and enjoyed by children, who then change the theme and insert their own language at various points.

PRIMARY RESOURCES: NARRATIVE TEXTS

The narrative structure tells a story with characters, settings, plots, point of view, style, and theme. The "story" is the prominent dimension of this literary form, and it may be told in prose or poetry.

Repetitive

Repetitive texts make use of duplication at various points in the story, so the audience will quickly learn to predict when the repeated text will appear again. When hearing these texts read aloud, children predict the duplications and read along with the reader.

Fox, M. 1994. *Tough Boris*. Illustrated by Kathryn Brown. San Diego: Harcourt Brace.

Summary. Boris von der Borch is a pirate to be feared. He is tough, massive, scruffy, greedy, fearless, and scary, but he has a soft spot for his parrot! Simple repetitive phrases allow children to read this book with the teacher on the first reading—and probably many, many more.

Wood, A. 1992. *Silly Sally.* **San Diego: Harcourt, Brace.**

Summary. Silly Sally is a little girl who "went to town, walking backwards, upside down." She meets a number of characters, such as a pig, a dog, a loon, and a sheep, and they all begin walking backwards, upside down also. Then "along came Neddy Buttercup, walking forwards, right side up." He turns all right side up until he tickles Sally and then she tickles him into walking backwards, upside down too.

Medearis, A. S. 1994. *Our People.* **Illustrated by Michael Bryant. New York: Atheneum.**

Summary. When a little girl tells what her daddy has said about the accomplishments of people of the black race, she repeats "Daddy says," and "I wish I could have been there. . . ." The repetition will be easy for children to follow along with reading aloud as a group.

Integrated Language Arts Experiences
- Teachers read one or more of these stories aloud to the students several times, encouraging their participation with the predictable phrases.
- Children group write a copycat story, changing the characters but keeping the repetitive phrases in the new story. Children may copy the story to take home to read to parents. They also need to copy the bibliographic information on the original story.
- Teacher or child may write story on large chart. As a group, examine the chart for the use of pronouns. Look for places where they are used or could be used.

Literature Approaches
- After listening to the story read aloud, have children buzz with a buddy for two minutes about what the story reminds them of in their own life. For two minutes, listen to their buddy's response, and then they will draw a picture of their thoughts. (personal experiences)
- As a group, children will retell the main story with five sentences. As children dictate, the teacher may write. The "story" found in each book forms the narrative structure. When all of the descriptions and side events are discarded, the "story" forms the concept that is important for children to recognize. (literary conventions)

- Children may write repetitive phrases on sentence strips and post so that with various stories using these phrases, children may join in and read chorally when a child reads a copycat story aloud. (literary processes)

Story Branches

Tough Boris
- Children will draw illustrations of pirates and parrots.
- They may write or tell a scary pirate story. Have them give their pirate a name that also begins with the /b/ sound.
- They may write in their journal about why they like or don't like Boris.

Silly Sally
- Have children draw a picture of Silly Sally walking upside down.
- They may write a sentence that the teacher might have said to Silly Sally if she had seen her. Have them practice making the letter "s" as they write the name of Silly Sally.
- Have them write or draw about Silly Sally and Neddy Buttercup the next day.

Our People
- As a class, find out about some of the people shown in the book. Examine the way the word "people" looks and find other words that also end with "le."
- Have children draw the little girl and her daddy as he told her about their people.
- Provide the words: "Daddy says . . ." and give time for children to dictate or write some things their daddy or mother has said.

Cyclical

Cyclical stories are those where the character begins at one place and goes through some experiences only to come back to the beginning.

Asch, F. 1994. *The Earth and I.* San Diego: Harcourt, Brace.

Summary. With simple geometric illustrations, the story is told of how the earth and a boy are friends. They go for walks, talk to each other, play together, grow together, and sing and dance together. When one is happy, the other is; when one is sad, so is the other. They are friends like all friends.

Carle, E. 1986. *The Grouchy Ladybug.* New York: HarperTrophy.

Summary. When a grouchy ladybug and a friendly ladybug have an early morning encounter over who will get some aphids on a leaf, the grouchy ladybug flies off to meet other creatures from the animal world. As she meets and challenges each succeeding opponent, the text repeats itself with, "'Oh, you're not big enough,' said the grouchy ladybug and flew off." Finally she meets and challenges the whale and is slapped by the whale's fin back to where she began. The friendly ladybug is still there and offers the grouchy ladybug some aphids.

Franklin, K. L. 1994. *The Shepherd Boy.* **Illustrated by Jill Kastner. New York: Atheneum.**

Summary. A Navajo boy named Ben takes his flock of sheep each day to a spring where they can get green grass. Each day they return to the fold. When a problem arises, Ben must rescue the missing lamb and get all 50 sheep back to the fold.

Integrated Language Arts Experiences
- The teacher will read aloud one or more of the cyclical stories to the children.
- Make a large circle on the floor with masking tape and place 6 to 12 children at equally divided points around the circle. Determine the number of events in the story to coincide with the number of children in the circle. As the story is retold, ask children along the circle to remember the event that happened in the progression of the story to correspond to where they are standing. Let them retell the story in order, showing the cyclical nature of the text. Have children trade places so everyone has a chance to participate as the story is retold many times.
- Write a place on the chalkboard, such as the bedroom, the kitchen, or the classroom, and ask children to write a story that begins and ends with that setting. They may use themselves or others as characters.
- Their final copies of the stories should use capital letters, periods, question marks, and exclamation points correctly.

Literature Approaches
- Make a circle on a bulletin board for students to post the titles of other stories they find that are cyclical. The title of the board may be "Circle Stories." (literary conventions)
- Children may write or draw pictures about the stories and connect their work to the titles of the stories with colored yarn. (literary processes)
- Children may write their own personal experience cyclical story beginning and ending in the same place. (personal experiences)

Story Branches

The Earth and I
- Children discuss or write in a journal the differences between the first and last pages of the book. (Both have same text and both feature the boy and a tree. It is day in the first picture and night in the second one.)
- Make flannel board symbols to represent the text (friends, walks, talks, listening, playing, etc.) and have them available for children to use them to retell the story with flannel board.
- Help children realize that we live on the earth and that we also live in a country, a state, and a city.

The Grouchy Ladybug
- The teacher will give children parts of storytext and they will prepare for a readers' theater. There will be a need for a narrator, lots of aphids, a friendly ladybug, a grouchy ladybug, a yellow jacket, a stag beetle, a praying mantis, a sparrow, a lobster, a skunk, a boa constrictor, a hyena, a gorilla, a rhinoceros, an elephant, a whale, and a leaf. After children have had time to read and practice their parts orally, they may read them. With readers' theater, props are unnecessary as the focus is on the oral reading of the text.
- Children may want to make a book that shows the time sequence as this one does.
- Have children make a wall of words that begin with the /gr/ blend.

The Shepherd Boy
- As a group, draw the path Ben takes each day to lead his sheep to the green grass. Individual children may draw the 50 sheep on the path.
- Give opportunities for children to pretend they are the lost sheep. Then have them write a sentence or a paragraph about how they are feeling.

I Have a Problem

The typical "I Have A Problem" story will feature a character with a problem who seeks advice from other characters and in the end finds a good solution to the problem. These stories are abundant for young children and are easy for the young writer to replicate.

Walsh, E. S. 1994. *Pip's Magic.* San Diego: Harcourt, Brace.

Summary. Pip is a salamander who is afraid of the dark. He asks other creatures to help, and they refer him to Old Abra, the wizard. As Pip asks various animals how to find Old Abra, they direct him over rocks, into the

Structures

woods, into a tunnel, over the hills, and into the night. As morning approaches, he finds Old Abra and asks for help to be brave in the dark. Old Abra tells him that he has already found it because he has been through the woods and over the hills, and into the dark without being afraid. And Old Abra is right.

Wormell, M. 1994. *Hilda Hen's Search.* **San Diego: Harcourt, Brace.**

Summary. Hilda, the hen, is looking for a place to lay her eggs. There is a problem with every place she looks. The henhouse is too full, the hay is too scratchy, the bicycle basket is too noisy, the clothes basket is too windy, and the horse trough is too risky. Then she finds a doll house, and it is just right. Her chicks hatch and have a wonderful place to play among the rest of the toys.

Binch, C. 1993. *Hue Boy.* **Illustrated by Carolina Binch. New York: Dial.**

Summary. Hue Boy, a little boy in a Caribbean village, is small in size, and he wants to grow taller. He asks for everyone's help. Here are the characters from whom he seeks advice and what each told him:
    Mama: Eat fruits and vegetables (tropical fruits listed).
    Gran: Get new clothes.
    Carlos: Exercise and stretch.
    Friends at school: Get high heel shoes (they are teasing him).
    Wise man: Where help is not needed, it cannot be given.
    Dr. Gamas: Some people are bigger than others; there is no problem.
    Miss Frangipani: Bathe in herbs.
Then he sees his father coming home, and he walks so tall through the village with his dad that he thinks of himself as tall from then on.

Integrated Language Arts Experiences

- Before reading one of these stories, remind children of the book, *Are You My Mother?*, which most young children have heard. It is a classic "I Have A Problem" book, so children will recognize other books of the same form. Ask children for a quick retelling of that story so they remember that the bird had fallen from a tree and lost its mother. It approached everything in its path and asked the famous question. Finally, it found its mother.
- After reading one of these stories, draw a large comparison chart on paper, overhead transparency, or the chalkboard to compare the story to *Are You My Mother?* The chart might look like this:

Title	Are You My Mother?	(One of the books discussed here)
Character with problem		
What is the problem?		
Who does the character ask for help?		
Who gives him help?		
How does he solve the problem?		

The children and teacher together will complete the chart and hang it for future reference.
- Make other "I Have A Problem" books available for children to read and compare to these two books.
- Group compose a "problem" story using a character with a problem and three or four other characters who try to solve the problem. Write it and hang it for children to use as a model. With children in groups of five, have each group write another "problem" story to share with the class and to display for all to read. These stories may be illustrated, written in big book format and bound into a class book.

Literature Approaches
- Provide circle time for groups of six to eight children to sit together and discuss the story. The topic for this discussion: Who I ask for help when I have a problem. (personal experiences)
- Children may complete this cloze story to see a framework of the "I Have a Problem" text:

    (Name of character)_____ had a problem. His or her problem was that _____

    _____
    He or she went to see _____ to ask for help.
    _____ said, "I can't help you but maybe _____ can." So _____ went to see _____. He or she said, "I can't help you but maybe _____ can." So __ _____ went to see _____. He or she said, "I can't help you but maybe _____ can." (Name of character) _____ said, "I know what he/she would say and that is what I am going to do." (literary conventions)

- Make a list of possible problems that animal characters could have. For example: Alligator—toothache; Elephant—ears too big for a spring hat. (literary processes)

Story Branches

Pip's Magic
- Pip was a chameleon. Children find out how many colors chameleons may change into. Use a reference book to find the answer. They may draw a picture and write a sentence about chameleons.
- Allow them to make torn paper and collage illustrations for a story.

Hilda Hen's Search
- As a class, make a list of good places for Hilda to build her nest. Each child may write her a letter and tell her where he or she thinks she should lay her eggs.
- Teacher will ask children: What would you do if she made her nest in your playhouse? Write her a letter and tell her how you feel about that.
- Find the letter and the sound that Hilda begins with and then look for other words in the story that have the same beginning. Make a chart showing all of these words.

Hue Boy
- Say to the children: Select one of the suggestions made to Hue Boy and plan how to tell him that it won't work. Be sure you know why.
- Children may add to the story and write or tell a friend what they think his father told him later as they talked.

Story Grammar

The framework of "story" consists of a goal or objective sought by the character and the subsequent efforts to reach that goal. As stories grow more complex, goals change and subplots evolve as attempts are made to reach the goal or solve the problem. It is good for children to experience stories with a simple grammar or framework as they begin understanding types of structure. A text with a simple story grammar will reveal a goal, several attempts to achieve the goal with results of each attempt clearly shown, followed by a successful attempt and the resolution of the plot.

Hodges, M. (retold by). 1980. *The Little Humpbacked Horse.* Illustrated by Chris Conover. New York: Farrar, Straus, and Giroux.

Summary. In this Russian tale, there is an old man who has three sons: Danilo, likeliest to succeed; Gavrilo, unnoticeable; and Ivan, a fool who sleeps on the stove. There are two stages in the story, and with either stage, the structure of story grammar is evident.

In the first stage, something is trampling the wheat, so the father sends his sons one by one to watch and find out what is happening. The first two sons fall asleep, but Ivan sees a white mare with a golden mane. He jumps on and rides her, and she tells him to let her roll in the dew for three mornings and she will produce three horses for him after which she must be turned loose. He does as she requests. Two of the foals are beautiful enough to belong to the Tsar's horses and the third is humpbacked, so Ivan keeps this one. In the second stage, Ivan finds the feather of a firebird and is told by the Humpbacked Horse not to take it, but he does. Ivan sells the two beautiful horses to the Tsar and becomes master of the stable. In that role, he has to meet the Tsar's requests three times. It is only with the help of the Humpbacked Horse that he is successful.

Tsar's requests: 1. Bring me a firebird.
2. Capture the Tsarvena for the Tsar to marry.
3. Jump into a tub of ice-cold water, then boiling water, and then boiling mare's milk.

Ivan does these things with the help of the horse and eventually marries the beautiful girl and becomes the Tsar.

Waddell, M. 1988. *Can't You Sleep, Little Bear?* Illustrated by Barbara Firth. Cambridge, MA: Candlewick.

Summary. Big Bear and Little Bear live and play together during the daylight. At night, they go to the Bear Cave. Big Bear puts Little Bear to bed and settles in to read his Bear Book. Little Bear can't sleep, so Big Bear brings a lantern to light a little area of the cave. He does this three times, getting a larger lantern each time. Finally, Little Bear tells Big Bear that he is afraid of what is outside because it is dark out there. Big Bear takes Little Bear in his arms and they walk out to see the biggest lantern of all—the moon. Little Bear goes to sleep in Big Bear's arms.

Doherty, B. 1994. *Willa and Old Miss Annie.* Illustrated by Kim Lewis. Cambridge, MA: Candlewick.

Summary. A sensitive story with which children will identify as it treats losing friends and finding strength within one's self to look for other ways to fill a gap. When Willa moves to a farm, she leaves behind her very best friend. It is hard at first, but eventually she meets Miss Annie, an elderly neighbor, and animal friends who help her feel needed again.

Integrated Language Arts Experiences
- After reading one of the stories, web the concept of "friend" with the children. Include as many of their ideas about friendship as they have and then ask for names of characters in stories they have read who are true friends.

- Children may select a character from a story or someone whom they know and write about why that person is a good friend.
- A Good Friend bulletin board may be started for children to place their papers describing good friends. The characters in the story should find their way to the board also.
- In groups, have children identify the goal of the main character and talk about whether or not it was reached.

Literature Approaches
- Show children a list of the parts of story grammar: goal or objective, attempts to reach the goal, results of each attempt, final attempt, and resolution to the goal. (literary convention)

The list may look like this:

Goal or Objective	Character knows what is wanted
Attempt	Result of attempt
Another attempt	Result of attempt
Another attempt	Result of attempt
Final attempt	Result
Resolution of problem	Ending

- As children retell the story in their own words, other children will point out which part of the story grammar is being told.
- Children write a story using the story grammar form with a goal from their own lives that they have obtained. (For example, if they wanted a bicycle, they may have first asked Gramps and then asked Dad and finally were told that they could carry out the garbage for six months to earn one. (personal experiences)
- Revise and edit the story to be published in a class newspaper. (literary processes)

Story Branches

The Little Humpbacked Horse
- As a class, compare this story to other folktales where the number three was a special number. Talk about or draw the story if there had been four brothers or four horses instead of three.
- Students may draw pictures of the three tasks Ivan had to accomplish. They may also write a thank-you letter from Ivan to the Humpbacked Horse for his help.
- Use this lesson as a springboard for a mini-lesson on compound words. Other words that may be used are: sunshine, horseback, folktales, daylight, firebird.

Can't You Sleep, Little Bear?
- The teacher will call attention to how the author writes the name of Little Bear when he is calling him by name. His name is written and followed by a comma. Children may practice writing to friends and adding a comma following their name. For example:
Little Bear, why can't you sleep?
John, may I borrow a pencil?
- They may write or draw a picture about how someone helps you get to sleep when you are afraid of the dark.

Willa and Old Miss Annie
- Children draw pictures of the three animals that helped Willa get over her loneliness.
- Provide stuffed animals or puppets and an opportunity for children to dramatize the story with a friend.
- Discuss with children the title that is in front of Annie's name (Miss Annie). As a group, make a list of titles. Children may practice reading and writing the titles.

PRIMARY RESOURCES: EXPOSITORY TEXTS

Sequence

The primary function of expository text is to provide information. It is from this perspective that sequenced text in this form shows the chronology of the information presented. Some types of information rely more on sequence than others, so within the expository structure, some texts use sequence and others do not.

Cobb, V. 1989. *Writing It Down*. Illustrated by Marylin Hafner. New York: Lippincott.

Summary. Do you want to draw a picture or write your name? This book tells you how to do it and gives some background on tools needed for writing or drawing. With text and cartoon-like illustrations, the history of paper is told in sequence, as are the steps in making paper by hand. Ballpoint pens, pencils, and crayons are also traced from their beginning.

Gordon, G. 1993. *My Two Worlds*. Photographs by Martha Cooper. New York: Clarion.

Summary. Told in first person by Kirsy Rodriguez, this sequenced text tells of Kirsy and her sister's trip to the Dominican Republic for Christmas. The entire

Structures 65

family is introduced, the girls go shopping, they board the plane, and fly to Puerto Plata. Their grandparents are waiting for them as are other family members. Kirsy finds out what Dominican children do to help their parents. Christmas Day is a special treat with extended family. The next day they visit a beach and have their hair braided and beaded. Kirsy turns eight years old there and they celebrate her birthday. The next day, they must return to her home in New York City.

Kuklin, S. 1992. *How My Family Lives in America.* **New York: Bradbury.**

Summary. There are three children in this text who tell how their families share traditions from both America and another country. The children, who each have one parent born in another country or another culture, are proud of customs and heritage from both worlds. Their daily lifestyles are sequenced with special attention to favorite foods. Their parents came from Senegal, Puerto Rico, and Taiwan.

Integrated Language Arts Experiences
- Prior to reading the story to the children, ask them to tell how to make scrambled eggs from beginning to end or how their families spend New Year's Eve from five o'clock in the afternoon until midnight. Take their ideas and sequence them in a linear fashion to show the meaning of sequence.
- Read one or more of the stories to the children. During a second reading, ask them to listen for words that indicate sequence.
- List sequence words on a chart and group write a story telling how to do something from beginning to end. Children will copy the story and keep it as a model for sequence. They may practice handwriting with the sequenced story.
- Children will retell the text in numbered sequence. The teacher may ask, "What happened first in this book?," or "What happened next?," or "How do you know that was the next thing to happen?" The retelling may be repeated so everyone has a chance to tell a portion of the sequence.
- Provide a portion of one of the stories on overlay or duplicated pages so children who can read the text will have an opportunity to see the sequenced text.

Literature Approaches
- Have children fold sheets of newsprint so there will be eight vertical "windows" on the page. Children may draw lines on the creases to see the windows more clearly. Have them start on the far left window and

draw eight pictures or write descriptions of eight steps to share some kind of information with others. (personal experiences)
Suggestions:
    What my family does on _____ (holiday).
    Saturday breakfast at our house.
    It's bath time.
    It's bed time.
- Have them write or make pictures to show how to cook or make something: hot dogs, peanut-butter sandwiches, deviled eggs, s'mores, a picture made with crayons, a Valentine card. The text should be "how-to-do-it" rather than a story. (literary conventions)
- Add these words to reading and writing vocabularies as appropriate for the grade level: first, second, third, fourth, fifth, sixth, seventh, eighth, ninth, tenth, then, next, so, after, when, finally, last. (literary processes)

Story Branches

Writing It Down
- Have children use the steps to homemade paper-making as a class project and make paper for a journal.
- Guide children as they write and illustrate a "how-to" book on a subject that they know. Some suggestions: making peanut butter sandwiches, making roads in a sandbox.
- Have children use crayons and colored chalk for illustrations and then compare the two media.

My Two Worlds
- Have children select a holiday in their family and write how it is celebrated.
- Have them write or draw about a trip they have taken away from home. Ask them to make sure they show the first thing they did, then next, and so on.
- As a class, look up the Dominican Republic on a map or atlas and see how far it is from the school.

How My Family Lives in America
- As a class, prepare a cookbook showing each family's favorite foods.
- Have children ask their parents and grandparents where they were born. Prepare a map and place dots to show family origins.
- Some children may draw a series of cartoon blocks showing their family doing something together as the children in the book did with their families.

Cause and Effect

Expository text frequently seeks to explain events or functions and in doing so describes the cause and its subsequent effects. Cause and effect form is easily recognizable, so students may use the form in their own writing. Environmental issues are often discussed through cause and effect texts as are social issues related to human interactions or motivations.

Watson, N. C. 1990. *The Little Pigs Puppet Book.* Boston: Little, Brown.

Summary. Because it is raining and the three pig brothers can not go out to play, they decide to make puppets. The first pig plans to make a sock puppet, the second pig starts his with a cardboard tube, and the third pig wants to make a jaw puppet. The directions for making each of these puppet types are given in the book. When they finish their puppets, they, of course, want to perform with them. They write a script and begin rehearsal. They need a stage, so they build one, and, of course, a stage calls for scenery. A stage, a script, and puppets require music, programs, tickets, and refreshments. The performance is splendid, and they are looking forward to another rainy day.

Leigh, N. L. 1993. *Learning to Swim in Swaziland.* New York: Scholastic.

Summary. The eight-year-old author's life is changed because her mom and dad take her to live in Swaziland. Throughout the book she describes how the move has affected her life. These are some of the ways: when you cross the equator, the seasons reverse; school begins in late January; the night sky is different with different constellations; bathtubs drain counterclockwise north of the equator and clockwise south of the equator. She also gives much information on the country of Swaziland, explaining how to tell children from adults—children have their heads' shaved—and how to tell boys from girls—girls wear skirts and boys wear pants. Children there make their own toys because there aren't any toy stores. They walk to school because there aren't any school busses. She tells how the families live in a bunch of huts called a homestead. Because the husbands have many wives and many children, there is a husbands' hut, a wives' hut, and a children's hut. The author also tells a Swazi folktale about why animals behave as they do. She concludes the book by telling why she had to learn to swim in an old pool left from British colonial days: the rivers and lakes are full of crocodiles, snakes, and snails that make you sick.

Barrett, J. 1984. *Animals Should Definitely Not Wear Clothing*. New York: Atheneum.

Summary. Different cause and effect situations are shown on each page, each from the stem of the title: Animals should definitely *not* wear clothing. . . . The animals for whom the results are clearly shown in humorous drawings are the porcupine, the camel, the snake, the mouse, the sheep, the pig, the hen, the kangaroo, the giraffe, the billy goat, the walrus, the moose, the opossum, and the elephant.

Integrated Language Arts Experiences
- Before reading the books to the children, draw a chart on the board or an overlay and make two columns: Cause and Effect. In the cause column write "somebody pushed me"; in the effect column write "I fell down." Then add another line so the chart will look like this:

Cause	Effect
Somebody pushed me.	I fell down.
I smiled at my friend.	My friend smiled at me.

  Continue adding to the chart with children's suggestions. When you read the text to them, ask them to listen for things that made other things happen (causes) and what happened (effects).
- After the children have heard the text or parts of it several times and have enjoyed it, give each a prepared sheet of text to read. It may be a portion of the text or the whole thing. In partners, have them identify all of the causes and effects found in the text. Through whole group, list them again and talk about how the authors write about cause and effect and the kinds of words they use to show it.
- As a class, make a list of cause and effect words to use and to look for in reading. Some examples: because, so, when, if.
- Children select from these topics or one of their own and write a cause and effect paragraph with expository text:
  Manatees and boats

Structures 69

Elephants and their beautiful tusks
Hens and their chicks
Dogs and cats

Literature Approaches
- Say to the students: Draw a picture about something that you did that caused something else to happen. After the picture is complete, buddy buzz with a friend about the experience. (personal experiences)
- Have children read from a teacher-prepared selection of expository text books and find those that have cause and effect information in them. They may be displayed at a Cause and Effect Fair. At the fair, books may be displayed; drawings of cause and effect and excerpts from texts that show cause and effect may be copied and shown. (literary conventions)
- Children read three cause and effect books and compare how they are alike or different, using a comparison chart.

Title of Book	Book 1	Book 2	Book 3
Used cause and effect words			
Showed pictures of cause and effects			
Actually said that one thing caused another.			

Story Branches

The Little Pigs Puppet Book
- Children may make puppets by the directions in the book.
- The teacher may orchestrate this experience: On a rainy day, start the things the little pigs did and see if each thing that caused them to produce a play will happen to you.
- This story offers an excellent opportunity to reinforce the /p/ sound with children who are learning the sound-letter correspondences. Have children find or think of other words that begin with the same sound. Make a word wall or a collage of pictures.

Learning to Swim in Swaziland
- As a class, write a letter to Nila Leigh through her publisher at Scholastic. See if she still lives in Swaziland. Ask her questions about her life there now.
- At home, children should examine their bathtub drain and draw a picture of the way it swirls as it empties. (See if it differs from Nila's.)

Animals Should Definitely Not Wear Clothing
- Children may write a story or draw a picture about one of the animals that did wear clothing.
- They may draw pictures of the animals in and out of their clothing and place the pictures on a cause and effect chart.
- Practice writing sentences with and without the words "not" in them. Help children see what happens to the meaning of a sentence when "not" becomes a part of it.

Problem-Solution

Problems that affect groups of people in the world are often discussed in expository texts with reports of various attempts to solve the problem. Sometimes the solution will be reported in this type of text, while other times the solution will remain unknown. The problems are easily identified in this text type.

Machotka, H. 1993. *Outstanding Outsides.* New York: Morrow Junior Books.

Summary. The outside covering of animal bodies is the subject of this book for young children. The problem is stated on an introductory page: How do animals' outsides help them live in their worlds? Each animal is shown on two open pages; the first showing a close-up view of the animal skin, fur, skeleton, scales, feathers, and shells while the second page gives the recognizable photograph of the animal with text on its covering. Animals shown are: tarantula, shark, frog, snake, turtle, bird, and bear.

Berger, M. and G. Berger. 1993. *The Whole World in Your Hands, Looking at Maps.* Illustrated by Robert Quackenbush. Nashville: Ideal Publishing.

Summary. In this book, the reader is instructed to pick up a world map and then is told, "Now you've the whole world in your hands." But how do you use the information in your hands? How do you read the map? This books is a step by step guide to solving that problem. An interactive book with questions and directions, it begins with a map of a child's room within the map of the whole house. Next is a map of the community and it expands into the city, the state and the United States. Continents and the world follow with simple directions and activities to promote use of the map.

Hughes, M. S. and E. T. Hughes. 1986. *The Great Potato Book.* **Illustrated by G. Brian Karas. New York: Macmillan.**

Summary. The problem is: What can be done with a potato? It is the world's most important vegetable. Information is given on its relatives, such as the tomato, eggplant, petunia, and tobacco. Its greatest enemy, the Colorado Potato Beetle is continuously being battled. Ways to grow potatoes in a pot or in a garbage can are shown. Questions that are answered in this book are:

> Why are potatoes such good body fuel?
> How can you use the peelings, too, for body fuel?
> How were French fries named?
> What are some ways to cook them?
> What other values does the potato hold?
> What is the history of the potato, and in what parts of the world was it found?
> How has the potato been played with?
>
>> One potato, two potatoes . . .
>> Potato sack races . . .
>> Passing potatoes on a spoon . . .
>> Jump rope rhymes . . .
>> Potato festivals . . .
>> Potato songs and stories . . .

Integrated Language Arts Experiences
- Remind the children of "I Have A Problem" stories read earlier and ask if they remember some of the problems encountered by the characters. Draw a circle on the chalkboard and write "problem" inside. Lead the children to suggest that they could web ways to solve the problem. They could try the web with a problem like: why do animals need outside coverings?; how do you find where you are on a map?; or how many things can you do with a potato? The web will provide the background setting for the reading of one or more of the texts.
- Read the texts or portions of the texts to students. Following the reading, ask if students heard any other solutions beyond the ones they had thought of prior to reading the text. Include those ideas on the web.
- Have students draw a vertical line in the middle of a page of newsprint and write a question for a problem on the left and draw a picture of at least one solution on the right. When finished, the children will share in groups.

Literature Approaches
- Show children how using the problem-solution form of text will assist them in writing factual reports. As a group, write a report on the uses of tomatoes. Even without research, children will brainstorm a list of uses such as tomato juice, tomato ketchup, pizza sauce, spaghetti sauce, sliced tomatoes on hamburgers, and diced tomatoes on tacos. From their list, show them how to write the problem in a question form and then to write the solution using all of the items in the brain stormed list. (literacy processes)
- Children learn to use the card catalogue or the computer data base to locate books that will answer questions they have about certain issues or problems. Guide them toward thinking of questions they would like to have answered and then begin the library experience of using data retrieval. (personal experiences)
- After children have used the library services to find books on problems of interest to them, help them determine those books that are designed to discuss problems and solutions. (literary conventions)

Story Branches

Outstanding Outsides
- Children may write sentences about the animals in the book with this stem: The _____ (name of animal) needs _____ (his outside covering) because _____.
- Make a group big book called *More Outstanding Outsides*. Using additional animals and their outside coverings, draw pictures and write labels of their outside coverings.
- Find other words that have the word "out" in them and make an "out" booklet.

The Whole World in Your Hands, Looking at Maps
- Either as a class or within groups, decide on a trip that would be fun. Draw a line on a flat map from where the group is to where they will travel. Make a list of the cities they will go through on the way.
- Provide time for children to practice finding north, south, east, and west on the map.

The Great Potato Book
- Plan a big potato party for the class. Use potatoes at the party, such as serving potato chips, making potato print invitations, and having potato sack races.

- Make a papier-mache potato head and set him at the audio tape player. Invite children to talk at the listening post to Mr. Potato Head and tell him about their problems.

PRIMARY RESOURCES: POETRY

Rhyming

There are many forms of rhyming poetry. Some forms found in this unit are two-line couplets, three-line triplets, four-line quatrains, and many combinations of these types of rhymes.

Field, R. 1993. *If Once You Have Slept on an Island*. Illustrated by Iris Van Rynbach. Honesdale, PA: Boyds Mills Press.

Summary. This illustrated picture book of a single poem has a rhyming structure and extensive imagery in the words. It brings you to an island for a summer visit and makes you believe that you will never be the same again.

Johnston, T. 1990. *I'm Gonna Tell Mama I Want an Iguana*. Illustrated by Lillian Hoban. New York: Putnam's Sons.

Summary. This book is a collection of funny little poems, many with rhyming patterns, that reflect things that children must think about. Some of these topics are: potato eyes, walking on the ceiling, the zoo, the vet's office, grandma with her hair down (Rapunzel), and the comforting feeling of a night light.

Integrated Language Arts Experiences
- The teacher may give groups or pairs of children a book of poetry and ask them to look at the words and find words that rhyme. (Dr. Seuss books are good for this experience.) For younger children, they may match pictures of words that rhyme.
- Each child may have a set of rhyming words to illustrate and label with the two rhyming words.
- Bring in a large refrigerator box and cut a hole in it for a door. Cut windows and have children paint it. It may be called the "rhyming room." Allow two to four children at a time inside the box to post their rhyming words. Cushions may be brought in for children to sit on as they earn the privilege of sitting in the rhyming room and reading poetry.
- Read some of the rhyming poems to children after they have had some experience with rhyming words. Duplicate some of the poems for the overhead projector and invite children to read along.

- As a group, brainstorm and list on a chart other rhyming words from the poems in this cluster of books. Allow children to select others to illustrate and place in the rhyming room.
- Encourage children to read and write rhyming poetry. On the outside walls of the rhyming room, display children's poetry.
- Each morning begin the day with poetry reading and encourage children to volunteer to read their own poetry.

Literature Approaches
- As children listen to the selected poetry for a second time, ask them to sketch their thoughts about the poem. Allow for sharing of these thoughts in small groups or as a whole class. (personal experiences)
- As a group, compose and chorally read a rhyming poem. Note with the children the names of the two, three, or four line rhymes. (literary conventions)
- After reading poems for pleasure, select some that show the use of commas in sequence. Teach a mini-lesson on the correct way to use commas in sequence. (literacy processes)

Story Branches

If Once You Have Slept on an Island
- Say to the children: Draw about a time you visited an island or a time you visited a grandparent or friend during the summer. How were you different when you returned?
- Have them find the words that rhyme in this poem.
- Find words that begin with the blend /sl/ and keep a word bank of these words.

I'm Gonna Tell Mama I Want an Iguana
- Have children draw a picture to show Mama's answer. As a class, write a response poem about it.
- Have each child pick a favorite poem; copy it in large letters for a chart pad and illustrate it.
- Provide children with a mini-lesson on the "ing" missing from "gonna." Have them listen to each other for the clear pronunciation of the "ing" sound.

Just for Fun

Fun poetry is just for fun!

Nichols, B. P. 1983. *Once a Lullabye.* Illustrated by Anita Lobel. New York: Greenwillow.

Summary. In this very repetitive song poem, the lyrics are repeated with minimal changes as different animals are substituted. Young children will love the consistency of the verses as they move from "Once I was a little horse,

> baby horse, little horse,
> Once I was a little horse,
> NEIGH, I fell asleep."

to a little cow, goat, sheep, pig, dog, cat, mouse, owl, crow, duck, chick, frog, fish, bee, fly, boy, and girl. The onomatopoeic responses of the animals will also make this pleasurable for young children. The illustrations are detailed and delightful.

Merriam, E. 1988. *You Be Good, I'll Be Night.* Illustrations by Karen Schmidt. New York: Morrow Junior Books.

Summary. Funny little poems that contrast cups and saucers, trees and pears, corn bread and biscuits, boys and girls, and east and west are found in this book. It is full of fun poetry for young children.

Bennett, J., compiler. 1991. *A Cup of Starshine.* Illustrated by Graham Percy. San Diego: Harcourt, Brace, Jovanovich.

Summary. These are rhymes about people and things that are important to young children. Some titles are: "This Tooth," "Granny, Granny, Please Comb My Hair," "Skipping Rhymes," "Dragonfly," "Fireflies," "Camel," and "Elephant." Illustrations are of crayon and are simple yet very appealing.

Integrated Language Arts Experiences
- The teacher will read the titles of several poems and children may select one title to illustrate before hearing the poem. The children will know that the poems are "funny," so their illustrations may also be funny.
- The children will listen to the teacher read the selected poems. On the second reading, when a child hears a poem for which he or she has illustrated the title, the illustration should be brought up to share with the class.
- After listening to the poems, children will write about how their predictions were close to or far away from the meaning found in the poem.

Literature Approaches
- After hearing a poem a couple of times, children will plan hand motions to go with it while they read or hear it read. (personal experiences)
- Children will find pictures from magazines that remind them of something in the poem. All pictures may be pasted onto brown paper to make a collage of the poem. (literary conventions)

- As a class, compose a "Just for Fun" poem; revise and edit it and copy on a chart to go on the wall. (literacy processes)

Story Branches

Once a Lullabye
- Assign animal parts to children who will sing the animal call at the appropriate place in the book.
- Have children think of other creatures and make the sounds they would make before going to sleep.

You Be Good, I'll Be Night
- As a class, find other things that go together, such as good and night, cup and saucer, and pears and tree; add verses to the original poem.
- All together, create a rhythm to accompany one or more of the poems in this book.

A Cup of Starshine
- Make a group list to add to the actions from "Monday Morning." Make a chart of all of the words that would fit in this poem. (action verbs)
- Provide opportunities for children to skip rope to the skipping rhymes in the book.

INTERMEDIATE RESOURCES: NARRATIVE TEXTS

Cumulative

Cumulative texts have an add-on feature in which every character or event may be added to the next one. In some tales, each character or event is mentioned again as part of the solution. In the old folktale *The House That Jack Built*, the accumulation is repeated throughout the text: for example, "This is the dog that chased the cat that ate the rat that lived in the house that Jack built" and so on.

Wood, A. 1984. *The Napping House*. Illustrated by Don Wood. San Diego: Harcourt, Brace, Jovanovich.

Summary. In the napping house, there accumulates a snoring granny, a dreaming child, a dozing dog, a snoozing cat, and a slumbering mouse, until a wakeful flea bites the slumbering mouse, that wakens the cat, dog, child, and granny. The house then is no longer a napping house. This story is also available in big book format from the same publisher.

Taylor, C. 1992. *The House that Crack Built*. Illustrated by Jan T. Dicks. San Francisco: Chronicle Books.

Summary. In this parody of the old cumulative folktale, *The House That Jack Built*, various players in the drug world are shown as they are related to "crack" cocaine. The large house with its swimming pools is shown in the illustration with the text, "this is the house that crack built." The house is followed by the man who lives there, the soldiers who guard him, the farmers who work in the fields, the plants grown by the farmers, the drug, cocaine, made from the plant, the street where it is sold, the gang that uses it, the cop on the beat, the boy feeling the "heat," the crack itself, the girl smoking it, her baby who is hungry, and all the tears shed because of it. As each character is introduced, the others are carried cumulatively in the text. An afterword provides information on the book and addresses of drug service organizations.

Aardema, V. 1981. *Bringing the Rain to Kapiti Plain*. Illustrated by Beatriz Vidal. New York: Dial.

Summary. In this cumulative story told in poetic verse, Ki-pat helps end a drought on the Kapiti plain. As he stands on one leg looking at the big, black thunder cloud, an eagle drops a feather, which Ki-pat uses with his bow to pierce the cloud and loose the rain. The text and illustrations show the accumulation of the cloud, the dead grass, hungry cows, Ki-pat, who owns the cows, and the eagle, whose feather turns the story around.

Integrated Language Arts Experiences
- Prior to reading one of the selections, read a few lines from a cumulative tale, such as *The House that Jack Built* and *One Fine Day* by Nonny Hogrogian, or *Drummer Hoff* by Ed Emberley. List the basic characters on a chalkboard and assign groups of students to respond with their character's text. The lines are easily learned even without the words in front of them. The entire story may be read in a few minutes by the group with assigned participation.
- Note as one of the selections is read that this story is also of the cumulative format. If possible, provide multiple copies for students to read.
- Provide many opportunities for reading the text in a variety of ways with different students reading parts, with choral readings, with puppets made of characters and objects, or a readers' theater.
- Group write a cumulative tale with this core: This is the class that read the most books. It may expand to the grade level, the school, the city, the state, the country, the world, and the universe.
- Pair students for collaborative cumulative story writing. Provide ways for them to read their stories aloud and display them.

- Edited stories should have standard punctuation, language usage, and spelling.

Literature Approaches
- Students talk in groups about a time when a chain reaction occurred in their lives and one event caused another to happen. If students are unclear about the cause-effect relationship of the characters and events in cumulative tales, provide the book *Why the Chicken Crossed the Road* by David Macaulay for them to read and discuss. (personal experiences)
- Have students collect as many cumulative type books as possible, identify, and sort the different forms. There are some forms that repeat the core line with every additional event ("the house that Jack built"); in other stories, the cumulative effect is not seen until the turning point of the story when everything reverses (*One Fine Day*). There are still others that imply the cause-effect relationship but do not include it in the text as repetition *(Why the Chicken Crossed the Road)*. Label the types and provide areas for those types of stories to be placed when found. (literary conventions)
- Use excerpts from one of the cumulative texts to show how strings of text such as these may be punctuated. Compare the punctuation of some of the texts and generate class rules for the use of commas and semi-colons with texts that have embedded clauses. (literary processes)

Story Branches

The Napping House
- In this book, there is the dozing dog. The other characters are described but not with alliteration (use of same letter for both object and its describer). Have students make alliterative labels for the other characters. Use the thesaurus to find labels that keep the same meaning as the ones in the book.
- Have them write the script for what Granny said to the child after they woke up and found the bed broken.
- From scenes in this book, have students write sentences using adjectives, verbs, and adverbs. For example, the dutiful dog dug quietly.

The House that Crack Built
- Allow time for students to react to this sensitive material. Provide thought questions for them to consider in small groups and later to bring their thoughts to the whole class for discussion. Questions might be: How many other people are affected by this problem? How might the

contagiousness be stopped? How can you avoid getting caught up in this trap?
- Ask officers and personnel with drug abuse and prevention programs to meet with the class and answer questions.
- Allow time for personal journal entries in response to this story.

Bringing the Rain to Kapiti Plain
- As a group or as individual research projects, find more about the Nandi tribe in Kenya. Some students might create a mobile representing this culture and its tale.
- Provide time for students to compare Ki-pat to other cattle herders they have read about. As a class, make a Venn diagram to show the similarities and differences.

Cyclical

Cyclical stories are those where the character begins at one place and goes through some experiences only to come back to the beginning.

Van Allsburg, C. 1981. *Jumanji.* Boston: Houghton Mifflin.

Summary. In this cyclical tale, two children find a game and decide to play it when their parents are gone for the evening. It has some strange directions, and the children discover that once begun, the game must be finished, and someone must reach the golden city of Jumanji! As they start the game, they soon realize that whatever is on the card played actually materializes in their living room. First, a lion appears on the piano and chases Peter into a bedroom, where Peter slams the door and leaves him. They continue playing and other zoo animals, a monsoon, and a safari guide also appear. As a volcano is erupting molten lava in the living room, Judy rolls a shortcut and reaches the city! Instantly, everything clears, and they run to the park to leave the game right where they found it. To their amazement, the house is back to normal when their parents return, and as they stare out the window toward the park, they see two boys running through the park carrying the game box. It will start all over again soon.

MacLachlan, P. 1994. *Skylark.* New York: HarperCollins.

Summary. In this sequel to *Sarah, Plain and Tall,* told by Anna, whose father had married Sarah in the first book, the family is still living on the prairie. Their problem is an old one for the farmers of that era: lack of water. Slowly the family cuts back on many necessities of life, such as mopping the dust covered floors and taking baths. Meanwhile, Sarah's aunts from the seaside in

Maine continue writing about their storms and their rainy afternoons. Anna and Caleb take pleasure in small wonders of life that continue, however, such as the impending birth of a calf and kittens. A devastating fire burns down the barn, and the well is nearly dry when Sarah takes Anna and Caleb to Maine for a visit. The question is: Would Sarah, who is much like the prairie skylark who flies around the skies but never really lands on the ground, come back? Her name is not written in the land as are Jacob's, Anna's, and Caleb's. Just before time to return to school, when Caleb is missing his father very much, Jacob appears one day on a sand dune. It has rained; the barn has been rebuilt; the kittens have been born; and it is time to go home. When they reach their prairie home, Sarah, who has told them that they too would have a baby in the spring, writes her name in the dirt with a stick. They are all home!

Cherry, L. 1994. *The Armadillo from Amarillo.* San Diego: Harcourt, Brace.

Summary. An adventurous Armadillo sets off from Amarillo, Texas, to see the world. His travels take him to San Antonio and several other Texas cities. Upon meeting up with an eagle and flying on its back, he sees the Texas plains and New Mexico. Flying higher and higher, they are able to see Cape Canaveral and a rocket that has just taken off for the moon. They fly up to the rocket, are taken aboard and look back to see not only other states, but other countries in the world. They realize the chain of universe to world to earth to country to state to city to home, and that is where they go—back to Amarillo.

Integrated Language Arts Experiences
- Prior to reading one of the selections, read to the students *Rosie's Walk* by Pat Hutchins, which begins and ends in the barnyard. Point out that stories that begin and end in the same place or with characters completing a cycle and others getting ready to begin the same cycle at the end of the story are called cyclical stories. Ask them to look for cyclical stories in the ones they read over the next few days.
- After students have read one of the stories either independently or as shared reading with multiples texts, ask them to show ways the cycle might be shown to others (for example, a circle on the board with excerpts that show how the story begins and ends; a flannel board circle showing symbols of the story; a dramatization of text with beginning and ending emphasized).
- Give a scenario for a drafted short story. For example, the dog finds a bone in the yard, has an adventure with the bone, and in the end finds another bone in the same yard. Have half the class write about the cyclical plot and have the other half end the story without finding

another bone. After a short period of time for drafting, have students orally share their stories to compare sequential stories with cyclical ones.
- Some students may want to revise and edit their stories while others may elect not to carry it beyond the draft stage.

Literature Approaches
- Students may select a character from the story and let him/her know that they know how the character feels. They may share some personal experiences in their writing that reflect some of the character's emotions also. (personal experiences)
- As a class, make a card file or data base of all the cyclical books you can find. Record the title, author, and what makes the story cyclical. (literary conventions)

Story Branches

Jumanji
- As a response project, suggest that students make a game board on a file folder or poster board as they imagine how Jumanji must have looked. Write game cards to go with it.
- They may also write a letter to the two Budwing boys. Will they warn them about the game or not?

Skylark
- Read the first three entries in Anna's diary (pages 1, 7, 13) to the students and have them predict what the story will be about.
- Later, say to the students: Reread the diary entries and select one around which you will create another story, either about the Witting family or other characters.
- Have them draw a large circle and make lines on it like a cut pie. Inside in the top pie slice, draw a picture or write a few words to describe what happens in the beginning of the book. With each succeeding pie slice, fill in the story with pictures or words until the last slice completes the cycle and the family is back home on the prairie.
- Write some diary entries from first person perspective using first person pronouns.

The Armadillo from Amarillo
- Students may draw a picture of an armadillo and research its habits and habitat.
- As a class, create a map showing where the armadillo traveled in the United States.

- Provide a mini-lesson on generalizations regarding syllables breaking between double consonants. Have students find other words with double "l" and check to see if the syllables are broken between those letters also.

Problem-Solution

In stories with the problem-solution text form, the problem is easily identified and consumes the characters throughout the story. The characters may solve the problem themselves or seek help, but the seeking of help is not as prominent as in the "I Have A Problem" stories for the primary grades.

Young, E. 1992. *Seven Blind Mice.* New York: Philomel.

Summary. In this simply written and illustrated book based on an ancient fable lies great opportunity for discussion of problem-solving. It is a major problem encountered by seven blind mice to determine what the strange creature is by their pond. Each mouse feels a different part of the animal and has a different perspective on what it might be. For young children, the days of the week and the colors are also significant. For use with older students, the focus may be on conclusions drawn by the various mice as they worked together to solve the problem.

Barrett, M. B. 1994. *Sing to the Stars.* Illustrated by Sandra Speidel. Boston: Little, Brown.

Summary. How a young violinist overcomes the fear of playing on stage in front of an audience is the problem in this story. The solution, involving an old man who is trying to help Ephram with his problem, is satisfying.

Penn, M. 1994. *The Miracle of the Potato Latkes, A Hanukkah Story.* Illustrated by Giora Carmi. New York: Holiday House.

Summary. Tante Golda shares her wonderful potato latkes with her friends in Russia until a drought limits her potatoes. She always makes the latkes for the first night of Hannukah, and this year, she has only one potato. What happens to solve her problem is a miraculous story.

Integrated Language Arts Experiences
- Prior to reading one of the selections, ask the class a question that reflects a problem for them. Some examples might be: How can we reduce the noise in the cafeteria? How do you go about finding the right book in the library? What would you do if we ran out of art supplies this year at school? Gather responses from the children on solving the problem.

- Read aloud or provide copies for students to read one or more of the selections. Stop early in the story and ask students to write the problem on a card. Stop periodically and ask them to write solutions to the problem as they hear clues to them in the story.
- Following the reading, discuss the problems and solutions as a whole class, examining different view points as they arise.
- Through group dictation and negotiation, compose the problem and a simplified statement of the solution. Have children write the problem and solution on sentence strips or chart pad and display in class.
- For independent writing, ask students to use the same problem and solution and write a different story.

Literature Approaches
- Invite students to write "imaginary" problems and possible solutions. Students will use their own personal background for writing these stories and will relate to the feeling of problem-solving without disclosing how close the problem is to personal experiences. (personal experiences)
- Select several stories with the problem-solution format along with some that do not focus on a problem and ask students to sort them as problem books or nonproblem books. (Most stories have a problem, but it will be obvious that concept books, travel books, information books, and many biographies are not based on a problem-solution.) (literary conventions)
- Make a list of all books found in the card catalogue or the computer data base that have the word "problem" in the title. Place the list on a chart for all to see.

Story Branches

Seven Blind Mice
- Use a "feely box" to examine objects and try to decide what they are. Make this box a class project and challenge children to bring in objects to place in the box. Of course, all objects must be approved by the teacher.
- Have students experiment with art illustrations, using a black background and brown paper bags cut and pasted as collages to depict objects and characters.
- Give them an opportunity to write a concept story using colors, days of the week, or numerals. Then illustrate it and share it with a kindergarten class.
- Look at irregular ways of making nouns plural, such as from mouse to mice, man to men, goose to geese. A collection of irregular plurals might be helpful to some students.

Sing to the Stars
- Say to the students: Write about a time when you were afraid to do something in front of others. Tell how you overcame that fear.
- Have them compare Ephram and the old man in a comparison chart. Hang the chart in the classroom.

The Miracle of the Potato Latkes, A Hanukkah Story
- As a class, survey the students to discover the names used for "aunt," "uncle," "grandmother," and "grandfather." Make a chart to show the results.
- Have students ask aunts and grandparents for a recipe for potato latkes and plan to make them at school.
- Review the use of titles before people's names. Find those that have abbreviations and learn to spell the abbreviations.

Story Grammar

The framework of "story" consists of a goal or objective sought by the character and the subsequent efforts to reach that goal. As stories grow more complex, goals change and sub-plots evolve as attempts are made to reach the goal or solve the problem. It is good for children to experience stories with a simple grammar or framework as they begin understanding types of structure. A text with a simple story grammar will reveal a goal, several attempts to achieve the goal with results of each attempt clearly shown, followed by a successful attempt and the resolution of the plot.

O'Brien, A. S. 1993. *Princess and the Beggar*. New York: Scholastic.

Summary. In this adapted Korean folktale that takes place in the walled city of Pyung-yang in Korea, the sensitive princess, as a child, sees a child beggar named Pabo Ondao and takes pity on him. She weeps at his plight and is chastised for it. Later, her compassion grows, and she frequently cries over tender subjects. One day her father, in disgust, says she should marry the beggar Pabo. Later when her father turns her out of his home because she will not marry his choice, she goes to Pabo and marries him. She teaches him to read, write, ride, and write poetry. He is able to impress the king without the king knowing who he is. When it is revealed that Pabo and his wife are really the king's daughter and her husband, the king takes them back in again.

Sutcliff, R. 1993. *The Minstrel and the Dragon Pup*. Illustrated by Emma Chichester Clark. New York: Candlewick.

Summary. In this tale with strong story grammar is a traveling minstrel who finds and loses a dragon pup. His attempts to regain his pet, and the resulting events, make this a fine story for youngsters.

Aardema, V. 1993. *Sebgugugu the Glutton, A Bantu Tale from Rwanda.* Illustrated by Nancy Clouse. Grand Rapids: Willia B. Eerdmans Publishing.

Summary. This ironic tale of how a greedy man brings on his own sorrow is a tale in which attempts to reach a goal and the consequences of each attempt are clearly shown. Sebgugugu has a wife, two children, and a cow. He interprets a bird's song to mean that if he kills the cow, it will be replaced with a hundred cows. He is greedy, so he kills the cow in spite of his wife's requests that he not do so. In a series of events, he calls on the Lord of Rwanda, Imana, to help and is given food with directions regarding the source of the food. In each case, he clearly disobeys Imana and is punished. The last punishment may be disturbing to some students (his wife and children disappear), so discussion of the resolution of the story will be important.

Integrated Language Arts Experiences
- A review of story grammar prior to reading the text will help students recognize the importance in a story of: a goal or objective, attempts to reach the goal, the consequences of each attempt, and the final resolution. Make a chart of these dimensions of story grammar and have it in view of students as they read or listen to the story selection.
- Select one or more of the stories for students to read or listen to and structure the first reading of the story for pleasure.
- In subsequent readings, have students in groups determine the dimensions of the story grammar and complete charts giving the information. Groups may share information and their perspectives as they determine the story grammar.
- Students select a character and write a description of that character on a strip of poster board. Students will hang the description around their necks and mingle with other students who also have described a character. It will be each student's task to identify as many characters as possible during a time period.
- Rewrite the character description using additional adjectives and descriptive language. Look at the text of the story read and find examples of descriptive language as a model.

Literature Approaches
- As a class, identify a helper and a hurter among the characters in the story. Make a chart comparing the two and showing what each has done

to help or hurt. Compare the helpers and hurters to others you have read about in previous stories. (personal experiences)
- Students may write a thank you letter to the helper and a scolding letter to the hurter. (literary processes)
- Have students outline the story grammar in another folktale that they have read. They may retell a folktale changing it to reflect a simpler story grammar. (literary conventions)

Story Branches

The Princess and the Beggar
- As a class, make a collection of folktales from the Orient. Compare them for theme.
- With a partner, compare this story to *Cap o'Rushes*. Write about how the father felt in each case when he saw his daughter again.
- Review adjectives with this story and have students write descriptive terms for each character in the story.

The Minstrel and the Dragon Pup
- Students may make a Lost Dragon poster for Lucky.
- In their writing logs, ask them to describe how Lucky and the Minstrel felt when they were reunited. Compare that to how the king felt when his son woke up.

Sebgugugu the Glutton, A Bantu Tale from Rwanda
- As a group or for an individual project, compare Sebgugugu to Anansi in *Anansi Finds a Fool*.
- Have students talk and then write about Sebgugugu's punishment. Was it too severe? Did it free his family or punish them too? Do you think he learned a lesson? Why or why not?
- Review knowledge about word pronunciations when a vowel is embedded between two consonants, as in Seb. (It is usually a short vowel sound.) Review the generalization about the pronunciation of a vowel when it is the end of a syllable and preceded by one consonant (gu). (It is usually pronounced as a long vowel.)

INTERMEDIATE RESOURCES: EXPOSITORY TEXTS

Sequence

The primary function of expository text is to provide information. It is from this perspective that sequenced text in this form shows the chronology of the information presented. Some types of information rely more on sequence than others, so within the expository structure, some texts use sequence and others do not.

Russell, M. (adapted by Ginger Wadsworth). 1993. *Along the Santa Fe Trail.* Illustrated by James Watling. Morton Grove, IL: Albert Whitman.

Summary. In this sequenced text, Marion Russell, a seven-year-old girl, travels with her mother and brother to New Mexico on the Santa Fe Trail in a wagon train of 500 covered wagons. The daily hardships, the beauty of the nature along the way, and the encouragement and support from each other are shown clearly as she carries the reader progressively over the trail. Text to support the sequence includes: "After my stepfather's death . . . , when school closed in the spring of 1852 . . . , after a few days . . . , each noon . . . , at sunset . . . , after the evening meal . . . , after about a month . . . , as we continued . . . , after we had traveled . . . , we were a bit over two months . . . , when the mules had rested . . . , as darkness deepened . . . , in a few days. . . ."

Cuneo, M. L. 1993. *How to Grow a Picket Fence.* Illustrated by Nadine B. Westcott. New York: HarperCollins.

Summary. The directions are clearly stated for how to grow a picket fence. Find a spot, study the path, and pick a basket of sticks are the first few directions, complete with illustrations. What you need to complete the task is described in terms of gloves, nourishment and protection for the sticks. When they mature, they may be taken to the fair for a first prize ribbon. A tongue-in-cheek "how-to-do-it" book just right for children who have a well-developed sense of humor.

O'Kelley, M. L. 1983. *From the Hills of Georgia, An Autobiography in Paintings.* Boston: Little, Brown.

Summary. The events of a family's life, the seasons of the years, and memories of growing up are all found in sequenced text and paintings done by the author that reflect on her life. As a young girl growing up in Georgia, she recaptures the daily activities and the ongoing cycle of life in this beautiful book that may be shared with others but will be treasured as an independently read jewel.

Integrated Language Arts Experiences

- Draw a timeline on the chalkboard and remind students that when things happen in a sequence, they can be charted on a timeline. Write days of the week on cards and tape to the timeline in various spots. Ask students to remember events from the class that could go with each day. Show them that the information is sequenced because it is in chronological order.

- Read one or more of the texts, either as a read-aloud or have the students read in multiple texts or copied selections.
- As a group, have students retell the text as it is written on an overlay or chart. Give opportunities for group reading and rereading of the retold text.
- Have students identify words and phrases that give clues to the sequential nature of the text. Have students list these words and phrases in their writer's notebook to use as they write sequential text.
- In writer's workshop, require one final piece of writing in sequence. This piece will be drafted, revised, edited, and polished over a period of days or weeks and will be submitted for evaluation on classroom or individual grading criteria.

Literature Approaches
- Students write an autobiography in expository text. It should be written in third person with an objective viewpoint, giving the sequenced information in order of its happening. (personal experiences and literary processes)
- Using selections from one or more of the texts, students identify sequential language and record it in the writer's notebook. Compare the author's language to the sequential language used by the students as they retold the text and also copied in their writer's notebook. It is hoped that some of the same language will be found in both sources. (literary conventions)

Story Branches
Along the Santa Fe Trail
- As a class, look for other stories about adventures on the Santa Fe Trail. Make a classroom collection so students may easily read them.
- During social studies instruction, find the trail on a map and see how many states it crossed.
- Students may draw pictures or write about sunsets on the Trail, leapfrog and dare base on the Trail, or births and deaths on the Trail.
- Find other words in which the /e/ in Santa Fe is pronounced as an /a/. Look up the word origins and find if all of these words have roots with the same language.
- Students may read Franck's *The American Way West* (1991, New York: Facts on File), adapted from *To the Ends of the Earth* by Irene Franck and David Brownstone to research trails in other parts of the country.
- If parts of historical roads or trails are in existence today near the reader's area, a field trip would be worth the effort.

How to Grow a Picket Fence
- Students may write a script for telling someone how to do something. Tell them to notice the verbs (action words) that you use as you give directions. After writing the script, make a list of the verbs. Did you frequently begin the sentence with a verb? Notice how that was done in this book.
- Have them rewrite the directions for growing a picket fence in sequence by numbering each step and listing them on a chart. This activity may be done by small groups or the entire class as a group collaboration.

From the Hills of Georgia, An Autobiography in Paintings
- Say to the students: Remember an event in your life that you would like to have painted. Paint it and write a label for it as Mattie O'Kelley did in her book.
- As a class, find all the paintings in the book where you can identify the season. See how many years are shown in these paintings. Compare results with others to see if there is consensus.
- Review past, present, and future tense verbs as you note the language in this story and as students write about events in their own past history.

Cause and Effect

Expository text frequently seeks to explain events or functions by describing the cause and its subsequent effects. Cause and effect form is easily recognizable, so students may use the form in their own writing. Environmental issues are often discussed through cause and effect texts as are social issues related to human interactions. Sometimes it is a stretch of the imagination to realize how an event can cause various effects.

Carr, T. 1991. *Spill! The Story of the Exxon Valdez.* **New York: Franklin Watts.**

Summary. The factual story of the ill-fated oil tanker that grounded and broke open, spilling thousands of gallons of oil onto the waters and shores of Alaska is told. The cause of the accident is deliberated, as well as the effects on the environment and on the lives of people involved. Color photographs are as vivid as the text in describing the serene beauty of the area and the horrible aftermath of the spill.

Arnold, C. 1993. *On the Brink of Extinction, The California Condor.* **Photographs by Michael Wallace. San Diego: Harcourt, Brace, Jovanovich.**

Summary. This book clearly points to the causes—hunting, poisoning, and habitat destruction—of the near-extinction of the California condor. The hopeful aspect of the text is another cause-effect story: Because of the efforts of personnel and volunteers at the Los Angeles Zoo and the San Diego Wild Animal Park, there is hope for reestablishing this great flying bird into the wild.

Pinkney, A. D. 1994. *Dear Benjamin Banneker*. Illustrated by Brian Pinkney. San Diego: Harcourt Brace.

Summary. Because Benjamin Banneker, a black boy growing up in the mid-1700s is free and has never been owned by another man, he is able to ask questions and wonder about things in the world. Because he is a farmer, he has to work long, hard hours to produce tobacco. He is interested in astronomy, and he teaches himself about the subject at night, as he studies the sky and all of its objects. Because he is a black man, he has difficulty convincing a publisher to publish his almanac for farmers. Because there are others who have faith in the abilities of black people, he receives assistance and finally has his almanac published. Benjamin Benneker knows that many black people would never be able to use his almanac because they cannot read, therefore, he writes to President Thomas Jefferson. He reminds Jefferson that it is he who wrote that "all men are created equal." Jefferson's answer, which comes as a result of Benneker's letter, indicates that he hopes with time the situation will change. Benneker never sees the Black people given their freedom, but he is a cause to that effect.

Integrated Language Arts Experiences
- Before beginning the study of expository cause and effect text structure, read the students the book, *Animals Should Definitely Not Wear Clothing*, by Judi Barrett. After the first two or three pages, ask them to predict what the effect will be of each animal wearing clothing. They will enjoy the story and the pictures, and their awareness of cause and effect will be heightened.
- Provide multiple copies of the texts, selected copies of segments of the texts, or read some of the text aloud to the students. If selected texts are given to groups, provide time for group share back so the entire class will have access to the total text.
- Following reading, allow students time to react to the texts. All texts have the potential for raising interest in the subject areas, and the need for whole class discussion will be felt.
- If groups have read different texts, each group may make a preliminary presentation of either the cause or the effect and the class members may prepare questions related to the issue. Times may be set aside for the exploration of the causes and effects of the issues brought forth in the reading.

- Students should be encouraged to engage in additional research on the topics, finding contemporary information in newspaper files or library vertical files and finding historical information through following clues in the author's notes.
- Writing a cause-effect piece of work in expository text should be an assignment for a grading period. Issues related to social studies or science are usually appealing to students and rich with opportunities for authentic learning.

Literature Approaches
- Finding an issue that the student is really interested in and will be persistent in researching is important because to write in cause-effect expository text, students must have content knowledge. Spend time exploring issues, giving issue interest inventories, and providing time for students to discuss their potential issues with peers. When they finally decide on an issue for reading and writing about, there will be a personal interest in it. (personal experiences)
- Provide practice sessions when cause-effect text is read, examined, and dissected for language and paragraphing practices. Mini-lessons work well with this approach, followed by students practicing the writing with partners or in groups. (literary processes and literary conventions)
- Publish pieces of work on cause and effect on a bulletin board or in a newsletter. (literary processes)

Story Branches

Spill! The Story of the Exxon Valdez
- Students may make a map of Prince William Sound in Alaska where the Valdez collided with a reef. Show the before and after effects of the collision.
- As a class, collect a list of effects related to the disaster: the gallons of oil that were spilled, the miles of coast that were spoiled, the different forms of land and air life that were destroyed, and the forms of sea life destroyed.

On the Brink of Extinction, The California Condor
- Find a corner in the classroom and mark a space on the floor with masking tape that is large enough for a condor to sit with wings spread. Note the size to the students. Within the space on the floor, arrange books and reports that have been written about the condor. Make it a "condor corner" for reading.
- Make a chart of all the known causes for the near extinction of the condor. Make another chart of all the known remedies to help stop the extinction.

- Prepare a mini-lesson on the different spellings of the same sound: -tion and -sion, as in extinction and extension.

Dear Benjamin Banneker
- Students may find out where the Banneker-Douglas Museum and The Friends of Benjamin Banneker Historical Park are located. Write for more information on his life and accomplishments.
- Students may read Banneker's letter to Jefferson very carefully and rewrite it in contemporary language (how we speak today).

Problem-Solution

Problems that affect groups of people in the world are often discussed in expository texts with reports of various attempts to solve the problem. Sometimes the solution will be reported in this type of text and other times the solution will remain unknown. The problems are easily identified in this text type.

Foster, J. 1991. *Cartons, Cans, and Orange Peels, Where Does Your Garbage Go?* New York: Clarion.

Summary. The problem is stated in the title of this book, although the problem is larger than just where garbage goes. Addressed in this book are the problems of how much garbage our cities are collecting, the aggravation caused when animals get into garbage before it is collected, and how garbage differs depending on its composition. The solutions are abundant in each of the 11 chapters as dumps, landfills, incinerators, recycling, and hazardous waste procedures are explained. A glossary helps with the different terms, and sources for more information are valuable.

Aaseng, N. 1989. *The Problem Solvers, People Who Turned Problems into Products.* Minneapolis: Lerner Publications.

Summary. This collection of short essays on problem solvers shows how John Deere solved the problem of rich soil that could not be plowed, how and why an automatic dishwasher was invented, how Gerber baby foods came about, what problem resulted in the creation of Polaroid cameras, and how the water-injection inventions of Rachele Jacuzzi made the word "Jacuzzi" a household name. All of these conveniences that we take for granted came from someone's problem.

Fraser, M. A. 1991. *On Top of the World, The Conquest of Mount Everest.* New York: Henry Holt.

Summary. It takes "eight months, an army of men, and three tons of supplies" to get Edmund Hillary and Tenzing Norgay to a point 1,100 feet below the summit of Mt. Everest in 1953. There have been many problems and more to come as they face the torturous last thousand feet to become the first people to stand on the highest mountain in the world. Their problems and solutions as they climb the final summit are graphically described and illustrated in this inspiring book.

Integrated Language Arts Experiences
- Before reading any of the texts, brainstorm with students on types of problems that might be found in expository texts. List some and survey students for types of problems and solutions they would like to read about.
- The teacher will segment selected texts or sections of the book and give to different groups to read. Upon finishing the reading of the text, ask them to determine the major problem in their section and the solutions given in the text. If using either *The Problem Solvers* or *Cartons, Cans, and Orange Peels,* chapters may be given to small groups to read for later discussion and sharing.
- Students will study the different ways authors present a problem. Have different groups make a model to show that approach. For example, in *Cartons, Cans, and Orange Peels,* a scenario is described at the beginning about garbage piling up on the sidewalks and dogs getting into it. In some of the chapters of *The Problem Solvers,* background is established before the problem is stated. In *On Top of the World,* the problem is implied, but only stated as a hope: "In the morning, they hoped to be the first ever to climb the highest mountain in the world—Mount Everest."
- Give students encouragement and opportunities to imitate the approaches and styles of these writers in composing problem-solution texts.
- It is obvious that in these materials, there are innumerable ways to integrate subject matter beyond the language arts. Because the focus of this book is on integrating language arts through literature, however, restraint has been applied, and teachers will be expected to make their own content connections. And they are abundant!

Literature Approaches
- Ask students to consider objectively a time when they had a problem and found a solution to it. Give them opportunities to talk or write about their experiences and to formulate what they thought the problem was and how it was solved. (personal experiences)
- Have students practice writing in expository style by writing a paragraph describing the problem and another paragraph explaining the solution. (literary conventions and literary processes).

Story Branches

Cartons, Cans, and Orange Peels, Where Does Your Garbage Go?
- As a class, decide on ways to help educate the public about recycling. Make posters showing what can be recycled and post them in local grocery stores.
- As individual projects, students may make a list of possible solutions to the garbage problem. Write to your city administrators with suggestions.
- Review use of punctuation and when to use question marks, exclamation points, and periods.

The Problem Solvers, People Who Turned Problems into Products
- As a class, make a bulletin board of problem solvers. Draw pictures and write reports on the accomplishments of the problem solvers in this book.
- Have a projects notebook for the class, suggesting problems that might turn into products if given enough time and energy. For homework assignments, have students spend time thinking, writing, or experimenting with some of the problems and possible solutions.
- Review ways to make nouns plural: add s or es, unless the noun is irregular. Use words from the book for examples.

On Top of the World
- Students may draw a scale map comparing the highest mountain peak near their home to the 29,028-foot peak on Mount Everest.
- Students may identify problems Hillary and Tenzing face in the book. List them with their solutions.

INTERMEDIATE RESOURCES: POETRY

Rhyming

Merriam, E. 1985. *Blackberry Ink.* Illustrated by Hans Wilhelm. New York: William Morrow.

Summary. This book is full of delightful rhymes that are fun to read and say, great imagery, and typical topics of interest to curious youngsters. Some of the topics are dogs, cats, pizzas, monsters, and the washing machine. There are three poems in the book that will be particularly appealing to students in elementary grades. They are Dirty Bertie, who needs a bath, Xenobia Phenobia, who hates everything, and Bella, who has a new umbrella.

Siebert, D. 1988. *Mojave*. Paintings by Wendell Minor. New York: Crowell.

Summary. In a moving display of paintings and clustered couplets, this book tells the story of the Mojave Desert. Beginning,

> "I am the desert.
> I am free.
> Come walk the sweeping face of me."

This poem invites readers to experience vividly the words while savoring the majestic illustrations. Topics continue with a windstorm, dust-devils, long-eared jackrabbits, tortoises, ravens, and many more natural features and habitats for other creatures.

Dickinson, E. 1978. *I'm Nobody! Who Are You?*, *Poems of Emily Dickinson for Children*. Illustrated by Rex Schneider. Owings Mills, Maryland: Stemmer House.

Summary. The illustrated poems in this book reflect the innermost thoughts of most children—in the 1800s when they were written and today! Although some readers may need to refer to the glossary found in the back of the book, the images and emotions should be obvious to modern children.

Integrated Language Arts Experiences
- Make a chart of the poem selected so students can follow as it is read by the teacher the first time. Students may join in on subsequent readings.
- Group write an answer to the poem.
- Have half the class read the original poem while the other half will read the answer.
- Allow students to make copies of the poem on charts and illustrate parts of it.

Literature Approaches
- Read from the books to the students, and immediately following the reading, ask them to respond to the poem by talking and listening in their poetry circle, consisting of four to five students. Suggest that they discuss what the poem reminds them of in their own lives. (personal experiences)
- After hearing several selections, have the students pick a favorite or a least favorite and try to transact with the author. Have them imagine they are asking the author these questions, predicting what the author would have said (literary conventions):

Why did you write this poem?
What do you want me to remember about it?
Why did you pick a rhyming scheme for the poem?
Was it (or is it) your favorite?

- Have students practice reading for fluency and interpretation. Have them read it as they think the author once read it. (literacy processes)

Story Branches

Blackberry Ink
- Students research to find out how to make other "inks" with fruits and tree barks.
- They may write other poems such as the rhyming "Dirty Bertie."
- Expand vocabulary with a word splash! Students think of all the compound words they can and list them on the chalkboard within five minutes. The words may be copied onto cards to be used on a bulletin board.

Mojave
- Students may make sound effects of the desert to record and play while the poem is being read.
- As a class, find the Mojave Desert on the map. See how far it is from the school's location.
- Using the dictionary, find other words in which the /j/ sounds like an /h/. Determine if the words are related to a specific language.

I'm Nobody! Who Are You?, Poems of Emily Dickinson for Children
- Have students search for more information about Emily Dickinson and her poetry.
- They may illustrate a poem using crayons as were used in this book.
- Following the reading of this poem, conduct a mini-lesson on sentence combining in which students are shown ways to combine short, choppy sentences into more complex ones. The example may be used: I'm nobody, but who are you? or If I am nobody, then who are you? Other combinations may be used also.

Just for Fun

Laan, N. V. 1990. *Possum Come a-Knockin'*. Illustrated by George Booth. New York: Alfred A. Knopf.

Summary. In this hilarious and wonderfully rhythmical narrative poem, the family is at home doing what they always do when a possum comes a-knockin' at the door. Through extensive use of repetition and much predictability, the poem becomes a participation activity that will captivate children of all ages.

Eliot, T. S. 1990. *Mr. Mistoffelees with Mungojerrie and Rumpelteazer.* **Illustrated by Errol LeCain. San Diego: Harcourt, Brace Jovanovich, and New York: Farrar, Straus and Giroux.**

Summary. Two narrative tales from *Ol' Possum's Book of Cats,* these two endearing poems will soon be memorized by children who will sing them. Some children will have seen the Broadway show, *Cats,* and all will be captivated by the escapades of the "The Original Conjuring Cat," Mr. Mistoffelees, and the notorious Mungojerrie and Rumpleteazer. Illustrations are an added pleasure in this book.

Evans, D. (compiler). 1992. *Monster Soup and other Spooky Poems.* **Illustrated by Jacqueline Rogers. New York: Scholastic.**

Summary. The spookier the better for most children, and this book fits the bill. They are spooky in a fun way! For example, the power shovel is compared to a dinosaur; Halloween poems and illustrations are abundant; and dragons and other monsters fill the soup bowl.

Integrated Language Arts Experiences
- Poll the students to determine how they feel about humorous poetry. (It is usually a strong favorite.) Ask students to bring in their favorite "fun" poems. Read some of them to the class.
- After establishing that "fun" poetry is fine to read in school, read from the selections in this cluster. Make copies and read the selections chorally.
- Have them write a "funny" description of something they heard in a poem. Post it on a "Fun Poems" bulletin board along with a copy of part or all of the poem.
- As a class, examine the poems to see how they are punctuated. Compare punctuated poems to unpunctuated ones (those of e e cummings, for example).

Literature Approaches
- After reading the book or selected poems, students may draw, describe in writing, or physically show facial expressions to represent characters from the poems. Their interpretations of feelings will be evident. (personal experiences)
- Students may copycat one of the poems with the purpose in mind of creating a "funny" poem. (literary conventions)

- Have them practice these language arts support skills:
    Use of "ing" verbs; list them and add the missing "g" (*'Possum . . .*).
    Use of colon to indicate dialogue instead of quotation marks (*Mr. Mistoffelees . . .*).
    Use of quotation marks to indicate dialogue: ("Bedtime Stories" in *Monster . . .*).

Story Branches

Possum Come a-Knockin'
- Students may take character parts and dramatize this poem while other children read it aloud.
- Others may plan some movements to accompany each "verb" in the poem.

Mr. Mistoffelees with Mungojerrie and Rumpelteazer
- Listen to the recording of these poems on the *Cats* tape. Sing along with the tape and learn the words.
- Students may write their own poem about a mischievous cat or other animal.
- Encourage students to make up their own combinations of sounds that produce such wonderful names as the ones given these cats. Insist that students place vowels and consonants appropriately to be able to pronounce the words in English.

Monster Soup and other Spooky Poems
- Say to students: Find a favorite monster and write your own poem for fun.
- Have them use a Venn diagram to compare the power shovel to a dinosaur.
- Allow time for them to find some fun poems to read to the class on Halloween day.

Nonconforming

Poetry that does not fit the mold of "poetry" is sometimes called nonconforming poetry. It includes free verse and poetic narratives that depend greatly on the placement of the text on the page for their poetic appearance.

Garland, S. 1993. *The Lotus Seed.* Illustrated by Tatsuro Kiuchi. San Diego: Harcourt, Brace.

Summary. This free verse, first person narrative tells of a grandmother watching the emperor of Vietnam cry as he loses his throne. As a remembrance of him, she plucks a lotus seed from the imperial garden. Years pass and she grows up and marries, only to see her husband go off to war. Finally war comes to her door, and as she runs, she grabs the lotus seed along with her children. They sail on a tiny boat and arrive in another country with big cities and skyscrapers. She raises her family while working day and night and reminds her children of the story of the emperor and the lotus seed. One night, one of her grandchildren finds the seed and plants it near her onion patch. She cries and won't eat or sleep for a while. Then one day, the lotus plant emerges with a beautiful blossom. She is happy again. When the plant turns to a seed pod, the grandmother gives each of her grandchildren a seed descended from one in the imperial garden.

Kroll, V. 1994. *The Seasons and Someone.* Illustrated by Tatsuro Kiuchi. San Diego: Harcourt, Brace.

Summary. In this poetic narrative of a year with an Eskimo family, the stem of "what will happen when . . ." is used to set the stage for each season. Because of an old Eskimo tradition, the girl in this story refers to herself as "Someone" or "Somebody." Her daily life, with the small pleasures of buds on berry bushes and her closeness with the wildlife, is shown in beautifully illustrated oil paintings. The words of the story are descriptive and laden with meaning. Students will enjoy the description of sucking the liquid from an Eiderduck's egg and eating berries and whipped blubber.

Thomas, J. C. 1993. *Brown Honey in Broomwheat Tea.* Illustrated by Floyd Cooper. New York: HarperCollins.

Summary. Sensitive poems told from the eyes and hearts of African-Americans, their beauty is found in the words as well as the messages that touch the human spirit. These poems are for mature readers with pride in their heritage and family.

Integrated Language Arts Experiences
- For a glance at cultural diversity, use all three books as examples of how cultures are shown through their poetry. Divide the class into three groups and ask each group to find poetry from the culture selected by the group. The three books represent these cultures: Vietnamese, Eskimo, and African-American.
- Give each group one of the books and ask them to prepare the reading and sharing of the book with the class. Encourage them to read chorally the assigned parts in order to share the books with the class. Several readings of each book will be appropriate.

- Compare illustrations of the three books. (Two are by the same illustrator.) Use a comparison chart to contrast the illustrations. Write about how they make you feel.
- List "Things We Know" about the culture from each book. Make a list of questions that arise from the readings. Students may select questions to answer from other readings. Their research products may be displayed.
- Compare the narrator of each story. Give the narrator a name and describe his or her character.

Literature Approaches
- Have students write in personal literature logs regarding the feelings evoked from these books. (personal experiences)
- Students may write to one of the characters and tell the character how they feel when they read the book. (personal experiences)
- Students may compare the way the text looks in the three books. Try writing some poetry patterning after each of the three styles. (literary conventions)
- Students may draft, revise, and publish some nonconforming poetry. (literacy processes)

Story Branches

The Lotus Seed
- As a class, find a seed pod from a flower or vegetable (peas or beans) that has pods and break it open to see the seeds. Plant them and nurture the flower. Imagine that it is a lotus plant.
- Students may research and find out why the lotus flower is special in Vietnam.
- Say to students: Think of a time when you left something behind and wanted a reminder. Did you bring something with you? Write a story about it.

The Seasons and Someone
- After a second reading, have students search for a page of text that provides the greatest imagery for them. They will try to decide how the author makes the pictures so vivid. Then have them try to write a paragraph that is similar to one in the book.
- As a class, make a collage of all the animals and wildlife mentioned or shown in the illustrations in the book.
- Research and find out what the foods are like that Somebody and her family ate.

Brown Honey in Broomwheat Tea
- After discussion, students may write a metaphor for what they could be called after reading what the narrator's mother and father call her. (Her mother called her "brown honey in broomwheat tea" and her father called her "sweetwater of his days.")
- Say to the students: Select one poem and read it over and over until you can read it with all the feeling in your heart.

CHAPTER 4

Themes

For decades, teachers have used various forms of theme teaching. Simply stated, themes are concepts around which the curriculum evolves. Themes may be structured around curricular subject areas, such as "explorers," "communities," or "transportation;" themes may be based on broad, integrated concepts, such as, "things that move" or "helping others;" there may be holiday or cultural themes; and sometimes themes are designed to allow students to concentrate on the characteristics of an affective focus, such as "patriotism" or "happiness." The focused theme may examine a person's life, a place, an event in history, or the characteristics of a single concept.

Themes may be broad, as in a nine-week unit, or they may be as narrow as a set of three or four experiences for students concentrated around a single idea. These experiences may be accomplished in a few days. Sometimes single idea themes may be presented alone. Such is the case when children take special interest in a topic that is not part of the curriculum but one that should be developed because of their motivation.

The themes in this chapter, with the suggested integrated activities, are focused on a specific concept. Related to the recommended literature, there are different approaches to the concept. There are suggestions for integrating the language arts with the theme, recommendations for expanding literary appreciation, and specific ideas for branching into a deeper experience with the books. Teachers using the ideas will decide how much of each theme to use, how it fits into a larger existing unit or broader theme, or how several themes may be combined into an expanded study.

Themes

The nine themes found in this chapter include book clusters and activities for both primary and intermediate grade levels. The suggestions for primary grade levels are found in the beginning of the chapter and the book suggestions and activities for intermediate levels follow. When beginning a theme, teachers may wish to scan the books and suggestions for both primary and intermediate levels as they plan ways to meet the needs of children at varying stages of development. Although the activities are written with age ranges in mind, it is likely that many of the books and some of the activities will easily transfer across all levels of childhood.

PRIMARY RESOURCES

Kaleidoscope

Teachers often begin the school year with a theme aimed at respecting the individuality of each child and appreciating that child's contributions to the whole. Each activity in this theme study should afford an opportunity to reinforce the idea that each person is unique and special.

Keller, H. 1993. *Harry and Tuck.* **New York: Greenwillow.**

Summary. Beginning when they are infants, Harrison and Tucker Taylor, twin boys, communicate to each other and for each other and do everything together. When they go to school, they are separated and soon become individuals: Harry and Tuck. There is a nice feeling of growing up in this simple story for young children.

Carrick, C. 1993. *Two Very Little Sisters.* **Illustrated by Erika Weihs. New York: Clarion.**

Summary. From the historical fiction genre, this story is about two real sisters—Lucy and Sarah Adams—who are midgets. They live in the late 1800s and early 1900s. They have a wonderful childhood, and when they are teenagers, P. T. Barnum asks them to join his circus. They do not like being called midgets, so they leave the circus, take singing and dancing lessons, and begin performing in music halls. Later they return to their parents' home and turn the house into a tearoom, where they entertain and serve guests. The house, built in 1727 by a relative of our sixth president, John Quincy Adams, still stands today in Massachusetts.

Polacco, P. 1992. *Mrs. Katz and Tush*. New York: Bantam Doubleday Dell.

Summary. Mrs. Katz, an old Jewish widow, is sad that she will have to be all alone for Hanukkah and Passover. Larnel, an African American neighbor child, finds a cat and brings it to her; she calls it a good Yiddish name, Tush, because the cat has no tail and all one can see is her tush. Larnel visits almost every day, and Mrs. Katz tells him about her life in the Catskill Mountains and about Jewish traditions. They also play with Tush. Tush disappears one day, and Larnel's father and two neighbors find her and bring her home. Larnel helps her celebrate Passover. The next morning, Mrs. Katz calls Larnel and tells him that the angel of death has passed her by, but the angel of life has not. There are four new kittens with Tush, and now Mrs. Katz is a bubee.

Integrated Language Arts Experiences
- Bring kaleidoscopes for children to manipulate and enjoy. After several experiences with the kaleidoscopes, suggest to the children that the class is like a kaleidoscope. Lead them to recognize this metaphor by asking and talking with them about these questions:
What does a kaleidoscope show?
Would any color or design be the same if it were all by itself?
What does it take to make a beautiful picture in the kaleidoscope?
How is our class like the kaleidoscope?
- After children see the cover or the first page of one of the books, ask them to guess what the people are like in the story. Make a list of their ideas. They will probably include things like little, big, child, grown-up, happy, sad, funny, wanting something.
- Read the story aloud and show the pictures. Give each child a character to listen for when the story is read the second time. (Many children will have the same character.)
- Children draw their own character showing something about the character that is special and unique: what the character liked; the way the character acted, looked, or talked; or what the character wanted.
- They may write or dictate a sentence or story about the character and how he or she was alike or different from another character in the book.
- As a class, make a kaleidoscope bulletin board and display the pictures and writing about the characters.

Literature Approaches
- After reading several books to children representing various cultures and lifestyles, ask students to select a character and compare their own life and personality to the character's by drawing their own pictures on one side of the page and the character's on the other. Show how they are alike and different. (personal experiences)

Other suggested books are:
Johnson, A. *Tell Me A Story, Mama*
Garland, S. *The Lotus Seed*
Kuklin, S. *How My Family Lives in America*
Gordon, G. *My Two Worlds*
Franklin, K. *The Shepherd Boy*
Binch, C. *Hue Boy*
Penn, M. *The Miracle of the Potato Latkes*
- Have children make character webs to show everything known about each character. Include how they looked, what they liked to do, what they wanted, and inferred or stated personality traits. (literary conventions)
- Develop a word wall of vocabulary used in the story. Each child may find one word used in the book to write on a sentence strip and place on the word wall. (literacy process)

Story Branches

Harry and Tuck
- Have children bring baby pictures to school and show how they were alike or different from Harry and Tuck.
- Have children write about if they would like to have Harry or Tuck for a friend and why (or why not).
- They can make a Venn diagram and compare Harry and Tuck.
- Children may practice writing each other's names.

Two Very Little Sisters
- After listening to the story, children will draw pictures of how the little sisters' lives were alike or different from their own. One side of the drawing paper will be labeled Alike and the other side will be labeled Different. From the individual pictures, brainstorm a class list of ways the sisters are alike or different from children of today.
- Children may find other picture books about the circus. Write a sentence or a story about why the sisters did not like working and living in the circus. Have them tell a buddy if they would like living in the circus.
- They may compare the way the sisters dressed to how girls of today dress and draw pictures of how they are alike and different.
- Students may expand their vocabulary by using the word "very" in several ways. Allow them to dictate their own use of the word in a sentence written by an adult.

Mrs. Katz and Tush
- The teacher will make a chart listing every child's pet and the pet's name. Each child may draw a picture on the chart of his or her pet.

- If there are Jewish children in the classroom, have them share information on Jewish holidays. Make a chart of all holidays celebrated by each family represented in the class.
- Have children draw a picture or write a sentence about how they imagine Mrs. Katz and Larnel talk to each other when he comes to visit.
- Practice writing a letter to someone with the title of Mrs.

Changes

By looking at changes in the lives of literary characters, children may find ways to cope with changes in their own lives.

Kachenmeister, C. 1989. *On Monday, When It Rained* . . . Photographs by Tom Berthiaume. Boston: Houghton-Mifflin.

Summary. In this sequential essay of days of the week, a young child's normal, everyday activities and the emotions they produce are simply stated and shown in black and white photographs. "On Monday, when it rained," his mother will not let him play outside and take his new red bike to a friend's house, so he is "disappointed." So it is with each day of the week as he feels embarrassment, pride, fear, anger, excitement, loneliness, and wonderment. Young children will have experienced similar events and will know the feelings expressed in this book.

Lewin, H. 1992. *Jafta, the Homecoming.* Illustrated by Lisa Kopper. New York: Knopf.

Summary. In this simple story, a South African family has been separated because the father has been away in a city working while the mother and children live in the village. Things are changing now in the country, and Jafta's father is coming home. Jafta's father misses the big storm, Nomsa's wedding, the wounded hawk, and the dog when she is a puppy. The anticipation grows as they await his arrival. And they are happy when he comes.

Ransom, C. F. 1993. *We're Growing Together.* Illustrated by Virginia Wright-Frierson. New York: Bradbury Press.

Summary. When a little girl's mother remarries, a new life is begun for the family. Howard, her new daddy, her mother, sister, and the little girl who tells the story move to a house in the country where they have pigs, a garden, and big woods nearby. She asks Howard how long they will live there, and he answers, "Forever." As a year passes and they celebrate birthdays, she learns to write her name, she meets a new grandmother, and gets a kitten for Christmas.

Themes

She learns to accept the changes in her life and looks forward to Howard being her daddy forever.

Integrated Language Arts Experiences
- The teacher will have a flannel board face with movable features so the facial expressions may change. Prior to reading one or more of the stories, children will have experiences changing the face as a group and then as an independent activity at a center.
- Prior to reading any of the stories, children may be asked to talk about the meaning of the word "change" and to give examples of how people and their lives change.
- Children will make pop-up characters representing themselves in some kind of change: change to a different house, change to a different city, change from baby to school-age child, change from living with mom to living with mom and dad. Two drawings representing the child as he was and as he was after the change will be drawn and cut out. A file folder will be snipped from the fold at two different places in the form of a triangle making sure that the points of the triangle do not meet so the triangle is not completely cut out. The snipped area may be pushed forward and the cut-outs pasted on them. When the file folder is open, there is a 3-D effect showing changes in this child's life. The cut-outs may be folded so the file folder may be closed and filed away.
- Read one or more of the stories to the children for their pleasure.
- Ask children to locate changes in the story or stories. List them on a chart or chalkboard. Read them chorally as a list.
- Children will write a description of (or label) the changes they drew on the pop-up cut-outs under each picture and decorate the file folder.
- Give children a sample of their handwriting from earlier in the school year. Have them copy the sample in today's handwriting and see how they have changed.

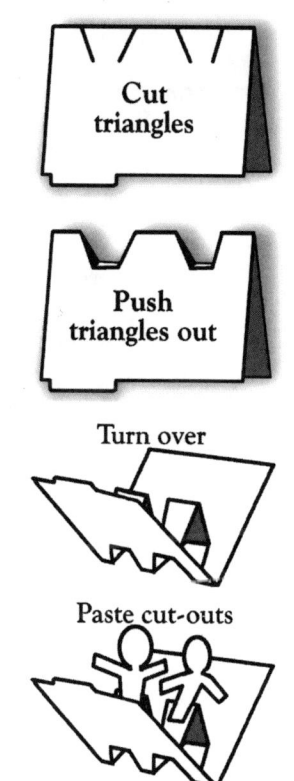

Literature Approaches
- Children will select one story from those read and will write or dictate an event the story reminded them of in their own lives. Talking about this experience before they begin will help them think of how they have had similar experiences. (personal experiences)
- Children look at pictures in the books and notice how the pictures, as well as the text, tell the story. Have them draw a picture that also matches their dictated or written event. (literary conventions)
- Children and teacher will look at book titles and talk about the purposes and uses of book titles. Then each child will write a title for his or her event and picture, capitalizing letters correctly and underlining. (literary processes)

Story Branches

On Monday, When It Rained
- Children will group write another story about each day of the week using the same format, "On _____ (day of the week), when _____, we _____." Continue with a sentence about the event and conclude with: "I was _____." For example: On Saturday, when we went shopping, we ate at a restaurant. I had a hamburger. I was stuffed.
- Each child will select one picture of the boy's face and list words to describe his expression. A picture may be drawn of the expression and displayed with the list of words.
- Have each child think of a time when he or she experienced one of the emotions in the book. Have the child pose with that expression and take a photograph. Let each child write his or her own story to go with the photograph.
- Provide tactile experiences for children to write and read the days of the week. Some media for these experiences include writing in shaving cream or sand, writing in crayon over screen wire, or writing or tracing over sandpaper.

Jafta, the Homecoming
- Children may draw a picture of a homecoming; they may write a sentence or a story to go with the picture and tell who came home and how people felt.
- Children will make four boxes on a piece of drawing paper and in each box, draw a picture and label something that the story tells that Jafta's father missed by being away from home.

- They may make a welcome home sign as Jafta might have made if he had had crayons and a big piece of paper.
- As a class, examine the letters of Jafta's name and sound each syllable as it is pronounced. Teachers may help children use the strategy of sounding out the letters to be able to say or write a word.

We're Growing Together
- Children will draw pictures or write sentences about things that this family does that their family also does. (Maybe they visit grandmother and pet the kittens.)
- They will draw pictures or write sentences on the back side of their paper about things this family does that are different from what their family does.
- Provide opportunities for children to look at seed catalogues and decide what they would want to plant in the spring. Make a spring garden at school.
- Introduce children to the contraction for "we are." Follow with a language experience chart in which children volunteer sentences to be written that begin with the contraction "we're."

Beginnings and Endings

There are beginnings at the beginning, middle, and end of many experiences. Often endings are really beginnings. Recognizing beginnings and endings often leads to more satisfaction with a story and better understanding of it.

Thomas, A. 1993. *Wake Up, Wilson Street.* **New York: Henry Holt.**

Summary. A grandmother, Nana, and her grandson, Little Joe, are the first ones up in the mornings on Wilson Street. They have to be quiet and not wake Mommy and Daddy. Nana makes hot cocoa and Little Joe gives each cup a marshmallow. As they watch the morning appear, they see birds from their window. They also watch the paper boy toss the morning paper to their door. They watch the neighbors rise and begin their morning activities: getting the paper, feeding the ducks, opening the produce market, and delivering the milk. They watch a neighboring artist get ready to paint in the morning light. They watch another neighbor begin washing his car in the coolness of the morning. Soon Mommy and Daddy come downstairs to join the "early birds" for breakfast.

Franklin, K. 1992. *The Old, Old Man and the Very Little Boy.* Illustrated by T. Shaffer. New York: Atheneum.

Summary. The old, old man, whose hair is the color of clouds, whose face is as brown as the garden, and whose feet are wide and tough, sits on a stump and watches the villagers pass each day. A very little boy stops and talks to him, brings him a sweet potato to eat, and listens to his stories. The little boy finds it hard to believe that the old man had once been a little boy, and the old man loses a silver tear as he thinks back onto his boyhood days. Years pass, the old man dies, and the little boy grows up, marries, and has children. Eventually, he, too, becomes an old, old man and sits in the village watching the younger generation walk past him. He, too, tells a very little boy about his childhood, and he also loses a silver tear as he thinks of the years gone by and the old, old man from whom he had learned that within every old man, there is still a very little boy.

Williams, V. B. 1981. *Three Days on a River in a Red Canoe.* New York: Greenwillow.

Summary. Told both as a narrative from the perspective of a child and as a "how-to" book on camping and canoeing, this book has a succinct beginning and ending and lots of fun in between. It is the story of how a child's mom, her aunt, and her cousin pool their money and buy a red canoe and then plan and make a three-day trip down the river. The needed supplies are listed as well as shown in use along with recipes, maps, rope knots, and directions for setting up a tent. Specific wildlife species and other facts of nature are interwoven into this delightful account of an unforgettable experience.

Integrated Language Arts Experiences
- The teacher may prepare the children for thinking about the theme of beginnings and endings by asking them to suggest as many ways as they know that signal the beginning of a story. Suggestions such as these may be listed on a chart or chalkboard: "One time," "once upon a time," "one day," "it was a fine day when. . . ." Then have them tell story endings, such as "and they lived happily ever after," or "and that's the way it was."
- On a line of magnetic tape placed across the chalkboard, ask children to dictate where a story's beginning might take place if the story were to stretch across the line. Follow through with suggestions for where the ending would be shown. Using the line, show them how the beginning and ending of other things might be shown there too. For example, the beginning of the day (morning) could be written on the chalkboard at the left side. The ending of the day (dusk) might also be written on the other side. Explore other concepts with beginning and endings and write the words on the board under the beginning or the ending of the line. Some concepts to consider are young people and old people, beginning

and ending of the school day, beginning and ending of the lunch period, and beginning and ending of vacation and trips.
- Read one or more of the stories to the children.
- Have the children retell the story while the teacher takes dictation and places their sentences at the appropriate places along the magnetic line, representing the beginning and ending of the story.
- Children may copy sentences from the retold story onto construction paper. These papers may be laminated and students may hang them with clothes pins from a clothes line in the classroom, practicing sequencing the story from beginning to ending. If more than one story is used with this theme, color code the construction paper so that all pages of a story are one color, giving children clues to help with the sequencing.

Literature Approaches
- Set up a storytime dramatization center and place one or more of these books in the center along with props for inviting dramatization. (personal experiences)

   1. Coffee pot, packets of hot chocolate and marshmallows, morning paper, bathrobes, slippers.
   2. Stool for sitting, silver tear, cloud white wig, sweet potatoes, clock, calendar.
   3. Cardboard canoe, life jackets, camping equipment, such as cooking gear and tent.

- Using pictures or sentences on strips, have several familiar story parts mixed up on a table. The children's task will be to sort the stories and sequence them from beginning to end. Use old favorites such as Cinderella, Snow White, or the Three Pigs or use stories recently read by the children. (literary conventions)
- Give each child a paper with a thick horizontal line across the page. Retell one of the theme stories and ask children to draw pictures or write a few words to describe the beginning and the ending of the story. (literacy process)

Story Branches

Wake Up, Wilson Street
- Group write a story using either the name of the street the school is on or the name of the school itself (*Wake Up, Gateway Elementary School,* for example). If children write about the things that happen in the early morning hours on the street where they go to school, they may include neighboring houses where people live whom they know or buildings on the street such as a post office or bank or gas station. If writing about

early morning activities at school, children might focus on who gets there first in the morning and the roles that different people play to get the school started each day.
- Children may tell or write about a time they were "early birds."
- After looking at the illustrations of Wilson Street, children might draw their own street and label the houses or other buildings.
- Have children talk about when they capitalize nouns (When they are proper or when they begin sentences).

The Old, Old Man and the Very Little Boy
- The children will sit in a circle and tell what they know about an old person who may have told them stories of long ago. The teacher may take dictation and record children's comments.
- Using a paper plate with hands connected with a brad (like the face of a clock), children will make a picture of the old man and one of the young boy and paste one to the hour hand and one to the minute hand. They need to be connected to the brad separately so one can catch up and move beyond the other. As the story is reread, children may move the dials representing the old man and the boy as the boy is portrayed as becoming an old man and another boy is taking the young one's place.
- Teacher and children should bake and eat sweet potatoes as the story is read again.
- As a class, look carefully at how the adjectives are used in this title to express intensity as well as contrast. Young children may also think of contrasts and how describing words can help clarify the contrasts. Other possibilities include "the long, long snake and the very short boy"; "the big, big dog and the very smart cat."

Three Days on a River in a Red Canoe
- Children may draw pictures or write about a trip they have had when they planned everything they would do each day and made lists of what they needed to bring. If any has not had such a trip, they may draw a picture or write a story about a trip they have taken and how it would have been different if they had planned as the characters in this story planned.
- Children may look at the pictures in the book and decide which animals the story characters saw on the trip that they would also like to see. Then they may draw their pictures.
- As a group, cook fruit stew and dumplings as directed in the book.
- Provide a mini-lesson on how phrases such as "on a river" or "in a canoe" tell where something happens. Children might also read *Rosie's Walk* for

another look at such (prepositional) phrases. Children may draw pictures to illustrate or write phrases showing where things happen.

Surprises

Surprises create excitement and that is just what children like in their stories. Sometimes surprises are problems; sometimes surprises are solutions; but almost always surprises are fun!

Neville, E. C. 1988. *The Bridge.* Illustrated by Ronald Himler. New York: Harper & Row.

Summary. A little boy, Ben; his parents; his dog, Chowder; and his rabbit, Rhubarb, live in the country across a bridge that calls out "rattle-rattle-rattle" when cars go over it, alerting everyone in the house that someone is coming. Ben loves to watch machines of any kind and is always excited when the bridge announces someone is coming. He watches the oil tank truck deliver heating oil and hears the bridge call out with a "crack" when the truck crosses. On the return trip, the bridge cracks enough to drop the tanker into the creek below. Ben and his mother call for help and soon an empty tanker is filled with the remaining oil, and a tow truck pulls the tank truck out. The question remains: How will the bridge get fixed? The next day, Ben goes to watch a bulldozer and a backhoe clear the creek of boulders and insert a culvert to form a bridge. It is great to watch, but Ben realizes quickly that the new bridge does not make noises to announce anyone's arrival. He and his mother creatively rig a cow bell on an old broken rake and attach the rake to a plank from the old bridge. Sure enough when Ben's daddy comes home, the bridge says, "ringle-dingle-dingle." It is not the same sound but it serves the same purpose.

Denslow, S. 1993. *Bus Riders.* Illustrated by Nancy Carpenter. New York: Four Winds Press.

Summary. Louise and Warren climb on the school bus each morning and are greeted by Lee, the jolly driver. The children tell him stories, and when they are almost ready to stop for the Pickles family, they each guess which of the Pickles' dogs will be first on the bus. Warren wins as he guesses that Fly would be the first one on and is told that a candy bar is his prize, which he can retrieve it on the way home. But when they board the bus in the afternoon, a woman named Thelma is driving. She tells them that Lee has had a gallbladder attack and will be out for three weeks. Warren does not get his candy bar, and Thelma spends the next week yelling at the Pickles because their dogs are out of control. The next bus driver is Willie, who wears tank tops, shorts, and sandals and doesn't allow the dogs to play. The Pickles children quickly begin wearing the same clothing as Willie. Next, Mr. Dodd, the assistant principal takes over, and the dogs have to remain tied. When Lee returns, Warren gets his candy bar and the games begin again as before.

Fuchshuber, A. 1988. *Giant Story, A Half Picture Book*. Minneapolis: Carolrhoda Books.

Summary. Half of the story is about Bartolo, the giant, who is afraid of everything. He even hides from deer, and one day he gets stuck half in and half out of a cave while hiding from a bird. He wants a friend more than anything else but is too afraid of everything to make friends. He runs and runs and finally lies down in a meadow and wishes for a friend. Lying there, he feels something warm and soft in his hand. And therein lies the surprise in this book. It is a half book, because the other side, upside down is a *Mouse Tale* about a mouse who is not afraid of anything, and for that reason, she has no friends either. She lies down for a rest and finds that when she awakes something is gently stroking her fur. Who could it be?

Integrated Language Arts Experiences
- Prepare children for the reading of one or more of the stories by bringing in a gift wrapped box and asking them to guess what might be inside it. (A toy bridge, a toy school bus, and a toy giant would be appropriate for the "surprises" inside the package.) Let children write their suggestions on Post-its or squares of scrap paper that may be pasted to the box. Put the box on display and announce the day and time for the opening of the "surprise box." Because the suggested toys inside the box are related to the three stories in this cluster, include as many as are appropriate. After the opening of the box, the toys may be placed on a shelf near the books for children to handle as they reread the story or stories.
- There are surprises in each story, so children may be asked to listen for them as the stories are read aloud or as copies of the text are provided for children to read either as a group or independently.
- Make a group chart listing all the surprises the children can find in one or more of the stories. Examples include the noise the bridge makes, the truck crashing through, how the bridge "made a noise" after its repair; the dogs crashing onto the school bus, different drivers, who won the treats; that a giant was afraid, that a mouse was not afraid, how the mouse and giant met.
- Have children select a surprise, draw a picture of it, and then write a label, sentence, or story about the picture. Pictures and writing will be displayed on a bulletin board or wall near the surprise box.

- Select sample sentences from children's writing about the surprises, and with children's permission, recopy them as standards for handwriting copying practice.

Literature Approaches
- Have children think about a time they were surprised by something that happened or by someone who visited them at home. Provide magazines for them to find pictures to represent the surprises and allow them to tear or cut the pages for a "surprise collage." They may paste torn or cut paper on construction paper to make a picture and then write about it. (personal experiences)
- Lead children in a discussion on what surprises them in stories. Have them think of several stories they have recently heard or read and then talk about how the author writes to surprise the reader. In the stories in this cluster, they might talk about how the author of *The Bridge* surprises the readers with the truck crashing through the bridge and with the way they make a bell for the bridge. In *Bus Riders,* children might find the dogs on the bus surprising and the whole book of the *Giant Story, a Half Picture Book* is rather surprising. After this discussion of how writers write surprises, the class may create a class "surprise story" on chart paper. The stories may be typed or printed and duplicated for each child to take home to read to his or her parents. (literary conventions)
- Before the printed copies of the story are taken home, have children read the story chorally as others follow on their own papers. Then break into pairs and have each partner read the story once or twice to the other partner. Encourage the children to read with feeling because it is a surprise story! (literacy process)

Story Branches

The Bridge
- Provide an opportunity for children to listen to their environment and decide what words can describe the sounds. Make pictures of the places and the sounds. Examples are sounds at the school bus ramp, sounds on the bank of a stream or creek, sounds under a tree where birds are nesting, cafeteria sounds before the children start eating.
- Children may draw pictures of different types of trucks and machines in the story. Dictate to the teacher or write what each does.
- They may build a bridge in a shoebox and add a bell that will ring when the bridge is crossed. Popsicle sticks may be used for the bridge.
- Find other words that begin the with blend /br/. Make a bridge on a bulletin board and write the words on the bridge.

Bus Riders
- After talking about their own experiences, have children write their adventures of riding a bus to school. If any have not had that experience, they may write about riding another form of transportation when there were other people involved.
- As a group, identify the dogs on the bus by matching their names and pictures. Students may find the characteristics of each breed of dog and write a sentence or paragraph about each. Make a booklet about dogs.
- Let the children vote on which of the bus drivers they would rather have and write to Louise and Warren telling them why.
- Begin looking at ways to make words plural by examining the word "riders" with and without the "s."

Giant Story, A Half Picture Book
- Children may write another story about other things the giant might be afraid of and how he reacts when seeing them.
- As a group, retell the story of what would have happened if the giant and the mouse had met each other while they were awake.
- Children may make a picture book with two characters who meet in the middle as in this book.
- Find other words that begin with the same sound and letters found at the beginning of giant (gem, gym, and giraffe, for example).

Perspectives

Recognizing different people's opinions and trying to understand how others might view an issue or an event is important.

Raschka, C. 1993. *Yo! Yes?* **New York: Orchard.**

Summary. With large print and one or two word phrases on each page, along with simple illustrations, this is a well-told story of two boys of different ethnic backgrounds meeting and becoming friends. On the first two pages, an African-American boy takes a stance and says, "Yo!" to the lighter-skinned boy on the facing page who says, "Yes?" Through a series of similar exchanges, they begin communicating. It is soon clear that both boys need a friend, and so they become friends with each other. "Yo! Yes!"

Babbitt, N. 1994. *Bub or The Very Best Thing.* **New York: HarperCollins.**

Summary. Sounding much like a fairy tale, this story begins in the castle of the king and queen with an argument between the two of them. The king feels the queen gives their son, the prince, too many toys, and she in turn feels that he gives the prince too many lessons. They both agree that they want the best for him but are not sure what that is. The king wants to find the answer in books, so he and the prime minister set about looking for the answer, and the queen and the prince do also in a different way. They ask the nursemaids, one of whom says the very best thing is vegetables and the other says it is sleep. Then they ask the gardener who says it is sunshine; next the court musician answers, "songs." The lord and lady recommend that they talk to him and listen to him. When the queen and prince find the king and ask if he has found an answer, his answer is much like hers: "They all say something different." Then they ask the cook's daughter who suggests they ask the prince. He says, "bub." The king and queen decide that someday he will explain what "bub" means, but the cook's daughter already knows that "bub" is really "love."

de Paola, T. 1993. *Tom.* New York: G. P. Putnam's Sons.

Summary. Tommy is named for his grandfather, Tom, so his grandfather asks him to call him Tom instead of Grandpa. Tommy's family visits his grandparents every other Sunday and Tom and Tommy read the comics, act out a funny poem, and laugh and giggle until his Nana scolds them. In winter they go down to the cellar and shake and sift ashes to have ready for the next snow. Tom then tells Tommy stories. Other times, they sit in the yard and look at puppies. Tommy visits other times too and sometimes goes to visit at the grocery store they operate. He helps put up cans and watches Tom butcher meat or chop off chicken heads and feet. Once Tom gives him a chicken head and tells him to go home and plant it and it will grow into a chicken bush. Tom also teaches him how to pull the tendons in chicken feet and make them move. When Tommy scares little girls with the moving chicken feet, he is sent to the principal's office and has to take a note home to his parents. The next weekend his grandfather says they will think of something else to do.

Integrated Language Arts Experiences
- Ask the children if they always agree with what everybody says. See if any of them can remember a time when they did not understand what someone else did or wanted to do. Then after a while, they might have gotten to know the person and they could understand each other's opinions. Tell them you are going to read them a story and the people in the story do not always see things the same way. In *Yo! Yes?* two boys look and talk differently at first, but then become friends; in *Bub,* everyone has a different opinion about what is best for the prince; in *Tom,* a grandfather and a grandson stand two generations apart and young Tommy doesn't always understand his grandfather's perspective.

- Read one or more of the stories to children. Ask the children to retell the story in their own words while the teacher takes dictation on a chart or overlay. As a group, revise and edit the story to make it say what the class wants and write a line or two on each page of chart paper. Have at least eight to ten pages so the children may illustrate the story in groups of two to three. Have the class read their own story frequently as a choral reading. Laminate the completed big book and hang in the classroom for independent reading.
- Suggest to the students that they might like to make a classroom big book of the original story (of one of stories in the cluster). To do so, they need to write to the publisher of the book to get permission to use the author's words in their big book. Publishers' addresses are listed below. After obtaining such permission, groups of children may be assigned to copy the text, to replicate the illustrations (or draw their own), and to make a title page and cover for the big book. As they work on the book, give them many opportunities to read the text aloud as a group, read it independently, or read with partners.

G. P. Putnam's Sons
200 Madison Avenue
New York, New York 10016

HarperCollins Publishers
10 E. 53rd St.
New York, New York 10022

Orchard Books
95 Madison Avenue
New York, New York 10016

- To help children understand the concept of "perspectives," as a class write a story using the following frame:

    _____(character) thought the best way to make a puppy happy was to _____. (His or her) mother thought the way to make the puppy happy was to _____, but (daddy) thought they should _____

The story may continue with as many characters and different opinions as the class wishes.

Literature Approaches
- Direct the children to draw a picture about a time when they had an opinion that was different from someone else's. Have them make a line

Themes

through the middle of the page and show what they thought on one side and what someone else thought on the other side. (personal experiences)
- Guide children as they look at pages in the books in this cluster and see how the pictures match the story. Look at how the boys are on different pages in most of the book of *Yo! Yes?* In *Bub,* when the text is about a character, that character will be shown on the page. Have children write or dictate text for each side of the picture chosen, making sure that the text matches the pictures. (literary conventions)
- Children will copy the text for the pictures in their best handwriting on sentence strips and attach to the pictures. (literacy process)

Story Branches

Yo! Yes?
- Direct the children to draw some pictures showing how they and a friend met and became friends.
- Children may also draw pictures showing how body language can tell what one is thinking. Have them hold up their pictures and let others guess what they are really saying with the body positions and facial expressions.
- Provide times for children to read the book aloud to a friend.
- Children should write one sentence and use an exclamation point.

Bub or The Very Best Thing
- Make a classroom chart showing the people who were asked the question on the left and what their answers were on the right. Give children opportunities to illustrate the chart.
- Give children opportunity to look closely at the small pictures of the dog on pages where there is text. As a class, write a story about the dog's adventures.
- Bake muffins and eat them with strawberry jam just as the king, queen, and prince did.

Tom
- Children may draw or write a story about visiting their grandparents.
- Take a field trip and visit a butcher shop and see how meat is ground, chopped, and prepared. Then come back and draw a picture or write a sentence about what a butcher does.
- Have a class discussion on what Tommy did with the chicken head and chicken feet. Was his grandfather playing a joke on him? Why did the teacher get mad when he tried to scare her with the chicken feet? Did he get what he deserved by having to go see the principal and then take home a note? What will his grandfather think of next?

- Reinforce the way we write proper nouns with capital letters to begin the word.

Considering Others

Someone with a giving nature who considers others, helps others, and puts others before self is a theme found in much of the literature for children. It is a value that may be taught through modeling and demonstration. I hope these stories will hit the mark!

Zolotow, C. 1987. *A Rose, a Bridge, and a Wild Black Horse.* **Illustrations by Robin Spowart. New York: Harper and Row.**

Summary. A child's love and dedication to his sister is shown in this gentle book of few words and impressionistic illustrations. The little brother tells his sister he will break rocks in half for her, he'll bring her a wild black horse and he'll tame him for her to ride, he'll bring her a stone from a mountain top and coral from the sea, he'll do her arithmetic and take her for a ride in a fast moving car, and he'll build her a bridge and bring her a rose. Then he'll find an animal friend to accompany them while they explore.

Schick, E. 1987. *Art Lessons.* **New York: Greenwillow.**

Summary. This is a gentle book about Adrianne, an artist who offers to teach a boy to draw. She shares with the boy what she has learned. In her studio, they "look and draw, look and draw." Adrianne takes him to the zoo, and he draws a tiger while she draws flowers. The next time they return to the zoo, he knows why she drew the flowers; the tiger is still there, but the flowers are gone. They walk to the river and watch reflections. At the park, the boy is sad and does not want to draw. She tells him that artists draw when they are happy and when they are sad. He draws a sad picture. At the art museum, he learns that it is all right to copy pictures because that is one way to learn how to draw. They make pictures on napkins at the ice cream shop and take a long walk on the way home.

Sanders, S. R. 1989. *Aurora Means Dawn.* **Illustrated by Jill Kastner. New York: Bradbury Press.**

Summary. In this beautifully illustrated book set in 1800, the Sheldon family, which includes parents and seven children, travel with two oxen and a wagon from Connecticut to Aurora, Ohio. They are met by a fierce thunderstorm and barely have time to unhitch the oxen and find protection. Huddled under the wagon in the mud, they stay all night. The next morning, it is clear that they are trapped, with many fallen trees in the path of the wagon. Mr. Sheldon decides to walk to Aurora and get help to cut their way out. When he reaches Aurora, no one is there, so he walks to the next village and finds eight men to come help free his wagon and his family. They arrive at Aurora as the sun is setting. The parents snuggle their children in the base of a hollow sycamore tree for the night and wait for dawn to see their new home.

Integrated Language Arts Experiences
- Ask students, "If someone said to you that he or she would like to help you with your chores at home, what would you ask this person to do?" Take their suggestions and then turn the question around and ask, "If you could help someone else, whom would you help and how?" Make an experience chart listing what they would like to do to be helpful and considerate.
- The making of the chart can expose the children to the use of contractions, such as "I'd" for I would or "I'll" for I will. Write the contractions as a pattern and later return to them for instruction in contractions.
- Read one or more of the stories. Make another chart of all the helpful things they can remember from the story or stories. Hang the charts and use them frequently for choral reading.
- Help children decide what they can do to be helpful at home and at school. As a class, group-write a pledge to be considerate of others and helpful when possible. Children may copy the pledge in their best handwriting and paste it to construction paper that has been rolled from both ends to resemble a scroll. It may be tied with a ribbon and taken home.
- Videotape children being helpful and play the videotape on Friday afternoon for the children to see.

Literature Approaches
- Make a vocabulary wall that shows words and phrases children have found that may be used to describe helpfulness and consideration of others. These books and others may be placed on a table under the wall where children can use them to search for words that writers use. (literary conventions)
- Have children write thank you notes to people who have been considerate to them as a class or as individuals. Thank you note paper may be cut to fit the correct size envelope and children may decorate the note cards with crayons or markers. (personal experiences)
- One or more of the books in this cluster may be recorded on tape and left with the book at a listening post. (Permission from publisher needs to be

obtained for tape recording.) Children may independently use the earphones to listen to the story and follow it in the text. (literary processes)

Story Branches

A Rose, A Bridge, and A Wild Black Horse
- Have children decide what they would like to give their brother or sister and draw a picture of it. Write on the bottom of the picture what it is.
- The teacher may laminate all pictures from the preceding activity end-to-end and place them on the floor, while the children walk from one end to the other on top of the pictures, reading the things they would give their siblings.
- Children may write a thank you note from the little girl in the story to her brother. Thank him for everything in the story he gave her.
- For children who are ready to use commas in sequence, this story is a good example to call to their attention as a model.

Art Lessons
- Provide an opportunity for children to look for a long time at a "single red flower in a glass vase, on a yellow mat" and then draw it as Adrianne and the boy did.
- Encourage children to find pictures at home and at school that have been drawn with reflections in water and then try to copy some of them.
- Children may group write a letter to the little boy's mother telling her what he has learned from Adrianne.

Aurora Means Dawn
- Have children imagine what it would feel like to ride in a covered wagon as they moved from their home to another home in the wilderness where few people lived. Have them draw a picture of their house and of the Sheldons' house in Ohio.
- As a group, make a list of things the children would take with them if they had to move.
- Children may write thank you letters to the men who helped pull the Sheldons' wagon from the mud.
- Expand vocabulary by showing students how to find word origins in dictionaries. (This activity will not be appropriate for all children.)

How Much Courage Did It Take?

Courage comes in many forms and is needed in varying amounts at different times. Characters who exhibit courage are found among all ages, sexes, and kinds of creatures. Stories of courage instill hope and a sense of justice in the readers. And who knows how such a story might influence children's lives?

Cole, S. 1993. *The Hen That Crowed.* Illustrated by Barbara Rogoff. New York: Lothrop, Lee, and Shepard Books.

Summary. Mr. Goodhart, a farmer in Bean Blossum, where roosters are not allowed because no one wants roosters crowing early in the morning, buys four chicks at the feed store. Henrietta, Geraldine, Clara, and Charlene are their names. Soon there is a problem with Charlene; she doesn't lay eggs like the rest of the hens and she starts crowing. Mr. Goodhart tries several ways to keep her from crowing, but she always crows anyway. Eventually, Mr. Goodhart realizes that Charlene is a rooster and tries to chop off her head, but he can't make himself do it. Instead, he ties a kerchief around her eyes to keep out the sun so she won't crow at sun-up. That doesn't work and tying her in a cloth bag doesn't work either. Then he locks her in a dark shed. She waits all night for the sun to come up as she looks through a peephole knot in the wood. Finally, it is bright and she starts crowing; actually it is one o'clock in the morning, and she is crowing at a fire—not the sun. The town loves her then because she has saved the town of Bean Blossum from burning. Then they decide that roosters should be welcome in Bean Blossum.

de Beer, H. 1992. *Little Polar Bear and the Brave Little Hare.* Translated by J. Alison James. New York: North-South Books.

Summary. In this large print text, the story is told of Lars, the polar bear, and a little hare named Hugo. Lars rescues Hugo from an icy hole, and they play together after that. Because the little hare is afraid to slide down a steep slope, Lars calls him a scaredy-hare. They are far from home when it begins to snow, and again Lars comforts the little rabbit as they make a pile of snow to be their home for the night. Even though Lars is not secure in the dark, he doesn't let Hugo know it. The next morning, a loud noise from a car traveling to the research station awakens Lars. He finds Hugo hiding in the snow and again calls him a scaredy-hare. Lars talks Hugo into going with him to the research station, where they find some leftover vegetables and have a picnic. Lars decides to go down to the roof of the research station and look around. While he is there, he leans too far into the window and falls inside the research station. His only hope is for Hugo to rescue him. Hugo is so frightened but he gathers enough courage to kick snow through the window and distract the man inside, while Lars escapes through the open door. They both run as fast as they can. Later Lars told Hugo that he is very brave. Hugo says he just did what he had to do, but Lars never calls him a scaredy-hare again.

Wetterer, M. 1990. *Kate Shelley and the Midnight Express.* Illustrated by Karen Ritz. Minneapolis: Carolrhoda.

Summary. This easy, 48-page story is about Kate Shelley, who is born in Ireland in 1865 and comes to America with her parents and four brothers and sisters. They settle in Iowa near a railroad line, and her father works for the railroad until he dies a dozen years later. This story is about Kate's bravery when, during a raging storm, the bridge breaks and the train goes down in Honey Creek near her house. In spite of her mother's objections, she takes her father's old railroad lantern and goes out into the stormy night. As she reaches the site where the train has crashed, she hears voices and finds two men still alive. She tells them she will go for help, and she knows she must warn the station to stop the midnight express. Because of high winds, she crawls over the Des Moines River bridge and finally reaches the station. The man there telegraphs the next station to warn the incoming train and the message gets through, although it is the last one sent before the lines go down under the storm. Through Kate's heroism, the two men in Honey Creek are saved and the midnight express is warned that the bridge is out.

Integrated Language Arts Experiences

- Before beginning this theme, have children list all they know about "courage" and list all questions they have about it. Post their "know" list and their "question" list so all can refer to it as the books are read and experienced.
- It is recommended that the theme study begin with one or more of the animal stories that reflect courage. The teacher may read aloud the *Hen That Crowed* or children may assist in the reading of the easy reader, *Little Polar Bear and the Brave Little Hare*. Discussions will follow on the bravery of the animal characters, how the children know they were brave, and how brave they were. Characters, in these books and others the children have read, may be ranked according to which had the most courage. Children will disagree and express different opinions when considering what took the most or least courage. They should be encouraged to have an opinion and accept others' opinions also.
- Children may participate in making a "courage quilt" in which each child will select a character from literature that has shown courage and represent the character with a drawing on a quilt square made of construction paper or of fabric. Paper squares may be illustrated with any art medium, but the fabric squares will require fabric paints. The paper squares may be laminated. Squares may be stitched together with yarn or sewing thread to make a full size quilt for a wall hanging. Children may do much of the sewing (under close supervision).
- The third book, involving the bravery of a young girl, may be read independently by some children or read to the class by the teacher. Following the completion of the reading or hearing of the story, the teacher might lower the lights and close the blinds, play a tape of howling wind and rain, and reread excerpts of Kate's experience as she crawled

over the broken trestle to be able to warn the oncoming train of danger. Have children talk about how much courage it would take to do that. Then give them paper and tempera paints to depict Kate in the story. Keep the tape playing while they paint.
- In a follow up session, have children write what they think Kate's thoughts were as she was out in the weather that night trying to save lives. Display their writings and their paintings near the courage quilt.

Literature Approaches
- Ask children to write a story about someone they know who did something that required courage. It may have been when a parent went into a dark room, when someone petted an animal, when someone helped another who was having difficulty, or when someone stood up to a bully. Children may dictate to adult volunteers or aids, or they may write their own stories. (personal experiences)
- Select an excerpt from one of the stories and copy it onto an overhead transparency without any punctuation. Show it to the children and have them practice reading it without punctuation. Add punctuation and have them read it again. They should begin to see the reasons for using punctuation. Ask them to look at their writings and decide if they are punctuated correctly. (literacy process)
- Display on a card the word, "where" and ask children if they can answer the question asked by the word in the story or stories read. As they give answers to "where" the story happened, write them on other cards and attach them to the "where" card with string that is run through holes in the bottom of each card. Punch holes in the top of the "where" card and attach it to another larger card to hang above it. The larger card should read: Setting. Help children see that the setting is where the story takes place. (literary convention)

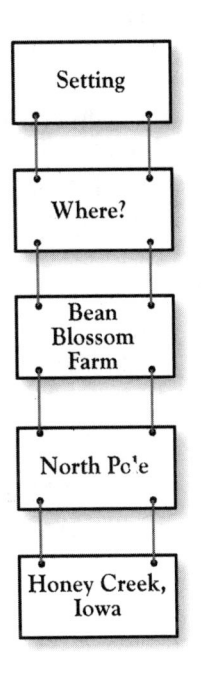

Setting
Where?
Bean Blossom Farm
North Pole
Honey Creek, Iowa

Story Branches

The Hen That Crowed
- Children may make a clothes hanger mobile of Bean Blossom and hang cut-outs of the four new chicks from strings on the hangers.
- They may paint a mural showing the ways Mr. Goodhart tried to keep Charlene from crowing.

- As a class, decide on a new name for Charlene.
- Prepare a mini-lesson on the digraph /ch/. Have children find other words that begin with the same sound combination.

Little Polar Bear and the Brave Little Hare
- Directions for reading pairs: With a friend, practice reading this story with one person reading one page and the other reading the next page until it is finished.
- Have children find out how big polar bears and rabbits at the North Pole are and draw a picture of Lars and Hugo, showing the differences in their sizes.
- Children may write about why Lars or Hugo was brave.
- Rhyme with words "bear" and "hare" and look at the different spellings for the same sound: ear or are. Have children find other words that are spelled as each of these words is spelled.

Kate Shelley and the Midnight Express
- Have the class involved in a bulletin board book report on this book. Display a map showing where Kate's family had come from (Ireland) and where they settled in this country (Iowa).
- Several children may draw pictures of the night the train went into the creek. Others may draw pictures of Kate going for help. The pictures should be part of the book report.
- Directed writing directions: Write or draw about a time that you did something that scared you but that you knew you had to do. Share it with your friends or the class.

Family and Friends

Little in this life is more important than "family and friends," so it is fitting that a literature theme be devoted to such stories with related experiences. Family and friend affection is world-wide and all people can relate to this theme, particularly with so many definitions and configurations of the meaning of "family" and of "friend."

Lewin, H. 1983. *Jafta's Mother.* **Illustrated by Lisa Kopper. Minneapolis: Carolrhoda Books.**

Summary. Jafta, a South African child, describes his mother in this book in ways that young children will understand. When he wakes in the morning, she has prodded the fire, bringing the "smoky smell of food" to his nostrils and making him want to get up. She is there working all day long, making his life more comfortable. She can storm when needed but more often sings. After supper, there are stories and talk of today, yesterday and tomorrow. Then she puts him and his brothers down to sleep.

Russo, M. 1992. *Alex Is My Friend.* New York; Greenwillow.

Summary. Alex is a little boy with a problem that keeps him from growing; Ben, a year younger than his friend, Alex, tells the story. Alex has to have an operation so he can begin to grow normally. Ben learns to accept Alex and his problems and to be sympathetic and helpful.

Zolotow, C. 1993. *Peter and the Pigeons.* Illustrated by Martine Gourbault. New York: Greenwillow.

Summary. Peter loves pigeons; he loves their sounds, their colors, the way they move their wings, and how they twitch their beaks when he feeds them peanuts. His father takes him to the zoo to see which of the animals he likes best. As each animal is described, Peter's father thinks that animal might be Peter's favorite. But Peter decides that he likes pigeons best because they are the animals he knows the best.

Integrated Language Arts Experiences
- Children will make a "Family and Friends" book that will be bound with spirals when the theme study is complete. Each child will be asked to bring to school a picture of his or her family. That picture will be mounted on the cover. The teacher should bring a camera to school and take pictures of groups of children who work well together. Have them developed with several copies of each photo so children may have them to mount on the back cover as "friends." The first half of the book will be about "family" and the second half about "friends."
- By reading all the books listed in this cluster to the students or having the students read them, they will find stories about a mother, a father, and friends, both animal and child. After the reading or hearing of a story, ask children to draw or write a few words that describe the friend or family member in the story; on the back side of the same paper, draw or write a few words to describe their friend or family member. Look for ways they may be alike or different.
- After each reading session, have children work on their family and friends notebook. Suggestions for pages are:
  1. a list of family members;
  2. drawings of what the family enjoys doing;
  3. a drawing or a photograph of the family pet (which is also a friend);
  4. a list of all friends;

5. a drawing of the child and friends playing their favorite games;
6. a back cover that shows a photo or drawing of friends.

- For children who are writing thoughts (as opposed to drawing pictures or writing labels), show them how a complete sentence is written with a capital letter for the beginning letter and punctuation at the end. Guide each student, as at least one sentence is correctly written.

Literature Approaches
- Invite family and friends to class for a "family and friend get together." Children will share their finished books with family and friends. The children will serve refreshments and will have a thank you card for each visitor that says "Thank you for being my family" or "Thank you for being my friend." Refreshments may be planned and made by the children. Some suggestions are: Friendship punch (make it by any recipe and call it "friendship punch"); Family favorites (children bring recipes for favorite finger foods or nutritional snacks that may be prepared in the classroom). (personal experiences)
- Ask the children why they think these books were written. Take their suggestions and make them into a chart on reasons to write a book. (literary conventions)
- Encourage each child to write a story about a family member or friend. Remind them that everyday events are those that make good family and friend stories. Help with taking dictation when needed or assisting in editing with these novice writers. (literacy processes)

Story Branches

Jafta's Mother
- Mother is described "like the sun rising in the early morning," "like the sky, she's always there," "she cools us as the rain does." Children may pick one of the descriptions and tell why it describes Jafta's mother. They may also tell a buddy or write it on paper. Some may also wish to draw a picture, too.
- Have the children look at the pictures of either waking up in the morning or going to bed at night and tell how Jafta's life is similar or different from theirs. Write about it or draw a picture.
- Have the children find South Africa on a map so they can see where Jafta lives. As a group, find out how many miles Jafta lives from their state.
- For those children ready to use possessives, use the title of this book as a model for the singular possessive.

Alex Is My Friend
- After children have heard the story, reread it to them and then take their dictation as they generate sentences like the title of the book. Some examples are: Dolly is my doll. Petey is my dog. For independent writing, children may be encouraged to write the name of their friends using the same form as the title of the book. Allow them to write as many sentences as they wish.
- Make get well cards for Ben to send to Alex.
- As a group, list reasons why Ben is a good friend to Alex. Post the list so children may be reminded of what makes a good friend.

Peter and the Pigeons
- Group discuss the way the author describes the pigeons. Have the children find an animal to observe. They may look at the way it looks, sounds, moves, and eats. Then write about it as the author of this book has written about pigeons.
- Have children find the words used in this story to describe each animal and write those descriptions on sentence strips. (Examples are "huge and golden lion"; "delicate, flowing-tailed red fox"; "striped ponies" (zebras); "soft, lumbering, white polar bears"; "shiny black bodies and small whiskered, pointy faces" (seals); "huge, wrinkled hippopotamus"; "great gray elephant with a long trunk and gentle eyes.")
- They may draw pictures of the descriptions.

Comparisons

With this theme students have a wonderful opportunity to read similar books and make judgments regarding comparable aspects. Comparative thinking is a necessity for daily life and can be demonstrated and practiced well with the plentiful examples found in children's literature. Such a theme could easily integrate math, science, or social studies.

Daly, N. 1992. *Papa Lucky's Shadow*. New York: Margaret K. McElderry Books.

Summary. Papa Lucky, once a great dancer, lives with his daughter and granddaughter, Sugar. He brings out the old dancing shoes and begins practicing again. Sugar practices with him and likes it when he dances to "Me and My Shadow," and he lets her be his shadow! He dances for coins on the street, while Sugar collects the change and a few bottlecaps that ended up in the hat. Papa Lucky is happy when he can buy Sugar's mother a new iron. When they go to the Pensioners' Club meeting, Papa Lucky lets Sugar dance as his shadow. They never tell her mother that Sugar is dancing, too!

Ackerman, K. 1988. *Song and Dance Man*. Illustrated by S. Gammell. New York: Knopf.

Summary. Grandpa, who used to be a vaudeville dancer, puts on a show for his grandchildren in the attic while grandma prepares supper. They are fascinated with his old clothes and hats they find in a leather-trimmed trunk and with the cloth he calls a shammy, which he uses to shine his shoes. He sings, dances, does magic tricks, and tells jokes until grandma calls them to supper. He tells his grandchildren on the way down the stairs that he wouldn't trade a million of the "good old days" for the days he spends with them.

Fox, M. 1990. *Shoes from Grandpa*. Illustrated by P. Mullins. New York: Orchard.

Summary. A cumulative tale, this story takes place at a family barbecue. In the story, Jessie's grandfather gives her a pair of new shoes, and everyone else gives her something to go with them. From socks, to a skirt, a blouse, a sweater, a coat, a scarf, a hat, and mittens, Jessica is completely wardrobed, except for the one thing she really wants—a pair of jeans. The repetitiveness of the cumulative phrases makes this book fun for children and easy to read chorally, even without the text.

Integrated Language Arts Experiences
- Although the other themes in this chapter have been designed for teacher selection of one or more of the three books recommended in a cluster, this theme, by virtue of its topic—comparison—is designed for all three books to be read and experienced.
- *Papa Lucky's Shadow* may be read aloud by the teacher to all students. Before reading the book, note that Papa Lucky is a grandfather who tap dances and that his granddaughter, Sugar, tells the story. Ask the children to listen for how Sugar became Papa Lucky's shadow.
- Children will need time for reactions to the story, so story-talk may follow with designated groups first reacting to the story on an emotional level and then selecting a character for further discussion. The teacher will model this story-talk prior to the first time it is used, allowing children to see how she emotionally reacts to a story, i.e., "I thought about my grandfather when I heard this story." The teacher will also model character discussions; an example could be, "I'd like to talk about Sugar's mother, because I think she might have worried about Sugar going out with her grandfather."

- Students can pair-read *Song and Dance Man*. Introduce children to another grandfather who also tap dances. Show them the cover of the book and call attention to the name. Hold up *Papa Lucky's Shadow* along side *Song and Dance Man* and discuss similarities and differences in the grandfathers and in what they are doing. Multiple copies of the book, *Song and Dance Man*, are needed for children to read this story. One book for every two children will be sufficient. With an advanced primary classroom, children may first read silently, allowing plenty of time for the reading. If the children are not able to read the story, the teacher may read it aloud while children follow along and read silently, or students may be paired so that one of the team can read aloud and the other follow with a marker. This story gets better with each successive reading, so even if the first reading must be done aloud by the teacher, follow-up readings may be done with pairs reading silently. Many opportunities are present in this story for expressive reading.
- A comparison of the two grandfathers and their tap dancing experiences is a natural opportunity for writing. As a guided group experience, the teacher may begin a comparison chart:

Story	Grandfather's Name	Description	Where He Danced
Papa Lucky's Shadow			
Song and Dance Man			

- Following group completion of the chart, children may be asked to write something in their reading/writing log about the two grandfathers.
- *Shoes from Grandpa*, a cumulative story, may be shared as a choral reading after the teacher has read it to them first. Children will be interested in the sound and repetition of the language and will enjoy repeated readings.
- Students may create comparison charts of the three grandfathers, three granddaughters, or three pairs of shoes.

Literature Approaches
- Children compare one of the characters in one of the books to someone they know. It may be a comparison of their own grandfather to one in a story, it may be a comparison of one of the children, or it may be a comparison of what they do when they visit a relative or friend. They may draw pictures or write about their comparisons. (personal experiences)
- Guide children as they read a series of cumulative stories to children including one or two that are not cumulative. Have them then decide

which ones are cumulative and make a chart of titles of cumulative tales. (literary conventions)
- Place the collection of cumulative tales on a reading table with a check off chart listing every child's name. Every time a child reads one of the cumulative tales to another child, the reader checks in the "read" column and the listener checks in the "listen" column. (literacy processes)

Name	Title	Times Read	Times Listened

Story Branches

Papa Lucky's Shadow
- Show the children a pair of tap dancing shoes. Let them feel the taps and hear the click, click sounds they make. Find out if any of them are tap dancers. Find out if any of their parents or grandparents are tap dancers. Write an experience story, dictated by the children, based on what they found out in the survey.
- One concept that may need clarifying for some children will be the "Pensioners' Club," probably called the Senior Citizens' Club in many neighborhoods. If possible, arrange for the children in the class to visit during one of the meetings of the Senior Citizens' Club. Often the elderly are thrilled to have young visitors. The children might plan their own songs or dances for the senior citizens.
- Read the poem, "My Shadow," by Robert Lewis Stevenson, to the children and encourage them to imagine how it might sound if someone sang and danced the poem as a song.
- This book title may also be used as an example of the singular possessive for those children who are ready to use such mechanics in writing.

Song and Dance Man
- Give children opportunities to write stories and draw pictures of experiences they have had with their grandfathers.
- Colored pencils may be used to create artwork similar to that in *Song and Dance Man*.
- Stage the housekeeping play area as an attic and fill it with a trunk and dress up clothes from the vaudeville days. Rotate children through the

center over the period of a week, giving all an opportunity to pretend they are in the grandfather's attic.
- Invite children to make a joke book with other silly poems and jokes that the Song and Dance Man would like. Leave the joke books on a special shelf in the classroom for others to read.

Shoes from Grandpa
- For a second reading, pass out prewritten strips containing the phrases that tell what different family members are giving Jessica; these phrases are repeated throughout the story, so children will listen for the phrase, hold up the strip and chorally read that part of the text. Several readings will allow children to become familiar with the sequence of the phrases and a variety of patterns of choral reading may result.
- Write a letter from Jessica to family members telling them what she really wants.
- Make a collection of cumulative stories and place them on a shelf that reads: Cumulative Stories. Encourage children to read the stories to each other during paired reading time. Some books to have available: Hogrogrian's *One Fine Day*, Wood's *The Napping House*, the folktale *This Is the House that Jack Built*, and Brett's *The Mitten*.
- Make a collection of other words that begin with the /sh/ digraph. Find pictures or write the words and place them on a word wall.

INTERMEDIATE RESOURCES

Kaleidoscope

Included in this unit are concepts of individual differences, special talents, acceptance of differences, and the celebration of diversity. Such a celebration begins with children accepting other children and recognizing the value of different viewpoints and different accomplishments, noting likeness and differences in cultures, and knowing that variations, along with similarities, contribute to the kaleidoscope of life.

de Paola, T. 1991. *Bonjour, Mr. Satie.* New York: Putnam's Sons.

Summary. Rosalie and Conrad, kittens, wait for their uncle, Mr. Satie, to arrive, following a visit to Paris with his rat friend, Ffortusque Ffollet, Esq. When they arrive, they tell of their latest adventures in Paris with many first name acquaintances, such as Pablo (Picasso) and Henri (Matisse). There is some competitiveness between the two artists as each has his own following. The paintings are hung on different walls, and Mr. Satie is selected to judge them. The differences in the two styles of painting are very obvious; it is clear that some people like one and some people like the other. Finally, Mr. Satie tells the crowd that to compare the works of these two artists would be like comparing apples and oranges. So the contest is a draw! After the story, Mr. Satie and his friend give the kittens their gifts from Paris—paint sets—and they all set out to paint.

Park, B. 1983. *Beanpole*. New York: Knopf.

Summary. Lillian Iris Pinkerton, who turns 13 on her birthday, is taller than anybody else in her grade at school, and she is very self-conscious about it. Through her first person narrative, Lilli tells the reader about her birthday wishes and how one by one, she attempts to make them come true. Two of the three are accomplished, and she feels pride in herself regarding her attempts for the third wish. Learning to accept herself and her abilities are the focus of this book about a witty, sensitive individual.

Spinelli, J. 1990. *Maniac Magee*. Boston: Little, Brown.

Summary. Jeffrey Lionel Magee, later to be known as Maniac Magee, starts life with good parents and a good home. When his parents are killed in a trolley accident and he is sent to Pennsylvania to live with an aunt and uncle who despise each other, his life takes a downhill spin. He lives with them for eight years and then runs away. His experiences as a homeless child, as a talented athlete, as an expert knot unraveler, and as a warm-hearted youngster, who judges people for who they are rather than where they live or what they have, are unforgettable.

Integrated Language Arts Experiences
- Bring kaleidoscopes for students to view and to make a list of other things that are like kaleidoscopes: anything that fuses to make a better product than could be made individually or with everything exactly alike. The aspect of symmetry in a kaleidoscope allows students to consider likenesses as well as differences. It is hoped that they will conclude that as a group they are much like a kaleidoscope, with everyone contributing many different things, while at the same time there are some strong similarities among the individuals.
- Books may be read to the students or they may read in pairs or independently. Provide each student with a "character notebook," and at the end of each reading session, have students pick a character and complete one of the following:
    Write an entry describing the character.
    Make a character map (a map to the person's character by drawing the character and determining places on the character where traits

are found). For example: near the heart, one might write the word, sensitive or cares for... (another character); or to the side of the hand with an arrow drawn to the hand one might write, "could unravel any knot."

Make a character report card by determining several areas to be graded and by giving the character a grade on each area. For example, B. B. Appleton from *Beanpole* might be graded on dancing, talking, and bragging.

- Students may share character reports in small groups or with the whole class. The procedure must be structured so that students who disagree regarding a character's traits might have an opportunity to read from the book to show why he or she disagrees, and the one who made the assertion about the character may also show passages from the book to support the opinion.
- Reports may be edited for standard spelling, punctuation, and usage, rewritten, and placed on a display board.

Literature Approaches

- Following the reading of one or more of the stories, students will write of a personal account of when "being different from" or "being like" someone else made them feel uncomfortable. (personal experiences)
- Using their previous knowledge of round characters (fully developed characters who change during the story) and flat characters (those who stay the same and whom we never really get to know), compare two characters in a story or characters across stories and show the difference between round and flat characters. They should be able to see that readers are able to identify with characters and recognize their likenesses and differences when they are fully developed. (literary convention)
- The culminating activity for this theme may be a choice of one of the following:

    Survey the class and determine likenesses and differences in several areas, such as: favorite book titles, favorite genres of books, favorite television programs, favorite foods, favorite restaurants, and others as students suggest. Compile the results on bar graphs and display them in the room.

    Make symmetrical designs of different colors and shapes, overlapping them to represent a kaleidoscope for a bulletin board. Obtain a picture of each child who will list special things about himself or herself. The pictures will be mounted on top of the colored designs to show the class kaleidoscope. Each child's written work should be edited for standard mechanics. (literacy processes)

Story Branches

Bonjour, Mr. Satie
- Students may identify the characters who were guests at the art exhibit. They can find their names in reference books and determine how they might have know Picasso and Matisse. They may also collect information and place it in a class scrapbook.
- The teacher may borrow prints of these artists' paintings from the public library and hang them in the classroom. Find other examples of their work in books and art museums.
- Students may write another adventure for Mr. Satie. They might select another time period and include the popular personalities of that day as was done for this story.
- Make a collection of foreign language expressions and phrases that may be displayed on a bulletin board.
- The teacher may check to make sure all students are correctly using abbreviations for titles and can spell them.

Beanpole
- Students may make a character report card on Lilli's best friends, Belinda and Drew. Use criteria for the grades, such as: true friend, dependable, supportive, fun, or other criteria considered important for friendship.
- They may list all the characteristics of Lilli that make her someone they would want as a friend. (Does her height matter?)
- Students may write a letter from B. B. Appleton to Harold Dunbar telling him how he felt after taking the money for dancing with Beanpole.
- Make a collection of compound words and display them on a word wall or a notebook of compound words.

Maniac Magee
- As a class project, students may make a class book on the heroic feats of Maniac Magee. Pairs of students may select one of his accomplishments and illustrate and write about it.
- Talk about these questions in a "grand conversation":
  1. How did Maniac feel about the line between the East and West Ends of town? How do you know?
  2. In what ways did Maniac manipulate Grayson? How did Grayson profit from his acquaintance with Maniac?
- Students may compare characters in this manner: select two characters and draw a circle to represent each character. By connecting the two circles with arrows, show how each character felt about the other. The

point of the arrow should be directed from the person who expresses the feeling. For example: Maniac *envied* > Amanda.

Changes

Students may recognize through these books and activities that growth comes through change and that change is not always easy and sometimes hard to understand. They may identify with characters who change from the beginning to the end of the book; they will certainly note that life is not static.

White Deer of Autumn. 1992. *The Great Change*. Illustrated by Carol Grigg. Hillsboro, OR: Beyond Words Publishing.

Summary. Wanba, a nine-year-old Native American girl, asks her grandmother questions about life and death as they fish for food. They are careful to return to the water those fish they do not need and to save all parts of the dressed fish for further use. They watch the pelicans fly around and also use fish as their life support. Wanba asks her grandmother why the fish have to die and is told "so the Circle of Life is never broken." On the way home, they stop for a rest in a circle of palms, and a caterpillar crawls on grandmother's arm. The grandmother uses the caterpillar and, ultimately, the butterfly to again exemplify that life is full of changes. Wamba is told that dying means change. Closer to home, they stop by the corn rows to empty their sacks of fish remains for corn fertilization. Wamba then asks if her grandpa's body is also returned to the earth as the fish are. Her grandmother explains that his body is now a part of the earth, but his "special part" is still a part of everything around them. When asked if they will ever see Grandpa again, the grandmother tells Wanba to close her eyes and see if she can see him. The old woman says, "There is no death in the Circle of Life, . . . only the Great Change."

Godden, R. 1992. *Great Grandfather's House*. Illustrated by Valerie Littlewood. New York: Greenwillow.

Summary. Keiko, a seven-year-old Japanese girl who was large for her age, comes to Great Grandfather's house in the country to stay while her parents are in England. Her six-year-old cousin, Yoji, who is small for his age, is also there. There are extreme contrasts in the children. Yoji is quiet and loves nature. He has friends among the animal and bird world, like the titmouse and the frog, and he can entertain himself with homemade toys and quiet walks and talks with nature. Keiko is the opposite; she is spoiled with many toys and has a rough and loud manner and little respect for her elders. Through a series of ups and downs, Keiko develops some of the quietness of her cousin.

Although she saves his life and that of the titmouse, she is susceptible to falling back into her old ways. Her initial response to Great Grandfather's house is that she does not like it and does not want to be there. In the end, she really likes it there and wants to be quiet and at peace with nature as her Great Grandfather, Old Mother, and Yoji seem to be.

Wisler, C. 1993. *Jericho's Journey.* New York: Lodestar Books.

Summary. In this story that takes a pioneer family through great changes from Tennessee to Texas in 1852, Jericho, who is small for his age, finds ways to contribute to the family's goal of reaching Texas safely. The story is told from Jericho's point of view and deals with the closeness of a family that has experienced much love as well as tragedy, the harshness of life on the trail, the tenacity to trudge on even in the greatest of perils, and the small pleasures of life like a warm meal, a witty remark (and there are plenty of those), or a face lick from a collie. Though the trials are abundant, the family reaches Texas to find a house already built and supplied, ready to be a home.

Integrated Language Arts Experiences
- Write the word Change in a circle on the chalkboard and ask students to brainstorm what the word means and to give examples of change. After exhausting the webbing process, ask students to select one of the words or phrases on the board and transfer it in good handwriting to a sentence strip so the entire web may be attached to a wall.
- One or more of the books in the cluster may be read aloud or assigned as paired or individual reading. It is suggested that *The Great Change* be read aloud to the group as a whole, followed by discussion. These issues will probably arise: talking to grandparents about death and dying, environmental issues, death of wildlife as part of chain of life, and questions on various groups' beliefs regarding death and life after death. Students should be permitted to explore these issues as a literature discussion group without the teacher's participation except to keep the discussion moving. The question for a focus may be: How is the word "change" used in this story and what does it mean?
- One or more of the chapter books may be assigned as paired or individual reading, or the teacher may choose to read aloud. Before and after each chapter, students should have an opportunity to write in a journal, reacting to the story, and then discuss the events from the story. Journal sharing may be optional as children feel like sharing their thoughts.

Literature Approaches
- Students may relate to one of the changes experienced by a character and compare that character's change to something they have experi-

enced. For example, Keiko's changes began when she went to live with a grandparent; some children may relate to this experience. Jericho's change, on the other hand, began when the whole family moved from Tennessee to Texas. Many may have had an experience in moving from one state to another. Have them write in their journal, write for sharing, or write a personal piece that they choose not to share. (personal experiences)
- Have students search texts of stories to find examples of how characters change; for example, Keiko was a selfish, loud child in the beginning and later became quieter and more giving. Students may work in pairs and share their findings orally with another pair. (literary conventions)
- Have students identify excerpts from the stories that support the changes they have noted. Then have them copy the excerpts into their journals, giving appropriate credit with bibliographic information and page numbers. (literacy processes)

Story Branches

The Great Change
- Students may make a list of things they like to do with their grandparents. They may be asked to list some of the questions that Wanba asked her grandmother that they might like to ask theirs.
- Have them find examples of descriptions in the text. Then they may read them to a friend who has his or her eyes closed and can try to imagine what is being described. Try to write something descriptive.
- Students in the class may find other books written by the author and compare them to this book. Are there other metaphors of life such as the Great Change and the Circle of Life in his other books? What are they?

Great Grandfather's House
- Have students show changes in Keiko's character from the beginning to the end of the story. Make a chart, a timeline, or a sequential narrative to show how she becomes different.
- They may build a boat like Yoji's and see if it will float.
- Students may pretend it is six months after Keiko left and she is writing Yoji to tell what she has been playing with at her home. Has she really changed or slipped back to her old toys and rough manners?
- Check students' accuracy in using singular possessives and use the title to this story and the next as springboards to a review of the generalizations.

Jericho's Journey
- As a class, find east Tennessee and Texas on a map. Students then may skim the book during a second reading to find the names of towns and rivers the family traveled through and across on their trip. They may make a road on a bulletin board to show the trail of the Wetherby family.
- Students may determine ways that life was different in Texas than it had been in Tennessee.
- In chapter 5, there was a discussion about why the family had to trade their paper money for gold. Jake said, "Most of these farmers and traders can't read. They can recognize coins by color and size, but they wouldn't know a twenty-dollar bank note from a newspaper" (p. 55). Discuss with a group or a partner what Jake meant and how what he said might apply to today's world.
- As a class, compare the /j/ sound found in the title of this story to the soft /g/ sound found in words like gym and giant. Deduce some generalizations for spelling when these words are heard and not seen. For example, if someone read a story about Jericho, how would he or she know to spell it with a J or a G?

Beginnings and Endings

Through the books in this theme, students may recognize the ambiguity of beginnings and endings. Many facets of beginnings and endings are found in children's stories—sometimes symbolic and sometimes real.

Crespo, G. (retold by). 1993. *How the Sea Began.* **New York: Clarion.**

Summary. In the retelling of this Taino myth, Yaya, his wife, Itiba, and their son Yayael live on a mountain, and there are no seas. Yayael is a gifted hunter who can always bring home food even when others come home empty-handed. One day when he is hunting, he recognizes an approaching hurricane, so he hides his bow and arrows and tries to reach his home safely. The storm destroys much of the village, and sadly, Yayael does not return. His father later finds his bow and arrows and places them in a gourd hanging high in their hut for his spirit to find. The villagers soon become hungry because no one can bring in game quite like Yayael had. His father, out of desperation, takes down Yahael's bow, and as he does, the gourd dumps nice, fat fish on the floor. They are delighted and cook them quickly. The next day, the men go to the fields and leave some young boys to watch the gourd. They become hungry, tip it, and find more fish. They cook and eat them, and as they try to replace the gourd, it falls to the ground and breaks open. As it does, water rushes from the gourd and continues flowing until the villagers' mountain top becomes an island. From then on they have all the fish they care to eat.

Foreman, M., and R. Seaver. 1991. *The Boy Who Sailed with Columbus.* Illustrated by Michael Foreman. New York: Arcade.

Summary. In this fictionalized picture book based on research by the authors, Leif is a Viking child raised by the friars in a monastery in western Spain, who is invited by Christopher Columbus to sail on the first voyage to the East by way of the West. Leif is a singer who sings the *Angelus* every evening on the Santa Maria.

The factual history is retold of the three ships sailing toward the Canary Islands where the Pinta's rudder is replaced and then toward the western sunset in search of a route to the eastern lands of Japan and China. Leif is one of the duty boys who turns the half-hour glass and records the time as quickly as the last grain of sand pours from it. His is a serious job because navigation of the ship depends on accurate time keeping.

After 10 days on the seas, they run into seaweeds that even have live crabs running on them. They pass through the weeds, which are interpreted as a sign of land; other signs are noted also, but each leads to disappointment as the days pass, and the sailors become more and more discontented. They even talk of mutiny, but their choices are limited as they do not have provisions for the return trip. Columbus, himself, sees the first light from land, and the next day it is confirmed that they have reached "tierra."

Columbus and a party including Leif land and are met by naked natives. The land is claimed for the king and queen of Spain and is named San Salvador. Over the next few weeks, they explore islands and meet other natives, whom Columbus calls Indians because he thinks they have reached the Indies. Leif is disturbed to realize that Columbus has taken several Indians against their will and plans to take them to Spain as proof of his discovery. The pain of an Indian father's face, when his family has been taken aboard without him, haunts Leif for the rest of his life. The father comes aboard willingly, choosing to live his life as a slave with his family rather than to see them leave without him.

On Christmas Eve, disaster strikes, and in this story, it is the fault of Leif, who has been ordered to take the tiller while the helmsman sleeps. Leif, too, is tired and lets the ship run into a reef. Many of the supplies and the men are rescued by the sister ship, the Nina, but the Santa Maria is lost, and the Nina is too small to carry all the men back to Spain. Columbus orders 35 of the men to remain on the island until he returns with another ship. Leif is ordered to stay as punishment for sleeping at the helm. From that point, his life changes dramatically.

He is stolen away by a group of Indians and eventually taken to an old man named Two Moons, who names him Morning Star. He becomes the eyes of the blind Two Moons and learns the ways of the Arawaks and Secotans. He later becomes the medicine man for many tribes, marries Wild Sage, and has three sons. One day in his old age, the Spaniards' ships return, and he takes his family and moves to another part of the island.

Schlein, M. 1991. *I Sailed with Columbus*. Illustrated by Tom Newsom. New York: HarperCollins.

Summary. In this fictionalized novel, also based on factual information regarding Columbus' first voyage to the new world, Julio is a 12-year-old orphan raised by the friars in a monastery on Canary Island, where Columbus repairs the Pinta before embarking. He is taken on as a ship boy because he can read, write, and sing the chants needed for each half-hour turn of the ampoletta (the sandglass) and for each morning, noon, and evening. Events of this story are comparable to those in *The Boy Who Sailed with Columbus,* as both are based on facts of the voyage. This book carries Julio along with Columbus through March 13, 1493, when Julio stays in Lisbon, looking for a ship to the Canary Islands, while Columbus in the Nina sails for Seville. The two boys in the books are about the same age and have the same job on the initial voyage, but their stories are very different as the books progress. Comparisons are abundant, and each has its own strengths.

Integrated Language Arts Experiences
Because these stories are related, it is suggested that the Taino myth be used with at least one of the other books and that the myth precede the reading of the story of Columbus. It was the Taino whom Columbus encountered when he landed in the new land. This story may have been known to those natives who first set eyes on Columbus. That, in itself, constitutes a beginning and the beginning of an ending.

- Ask the students for examples of beginnings and endings and ask them to decide whether the Taino myth was a story of a beginning, an ending, or both. Read the story to the students and have them discuss it with a reciprocal questioning technique. Group students by fives and ask each group to meet immediately after hearing the story to talk about it and its deeper meanings. Following discussion, they will generate two questions they believe reflect the central themes of the story and will have an opportunity to ask them in a large group discussion to follow. All members of the group will record the questions and come to the large

group prepared to ask their groups' questions. Two of the five will be called on to ask the questions and to respond to the answers given by other classmates.
- Following the discussion, students will record thoughts in their literature log for future reference.
- One or both of the Columbus stories may be read next and may be read independently by the students or with oral reading by the teacher and selected students who have had a chance to preview the story and become familiar with it before reading aloud to the class. With either book, prepare students for the reading by helping them remember what they know about Columbus and his first voyage to the New World. Remind them that the Taino were the natives he met. As students read or listen to the story, ask them to think of the theme and consider "beginnings and endings" in the story.
- Ask students to list all beginnings and all endings related to the story. (The trip had a beginning and ending; the New World had an exploration beginning; the life of the Tainos had the beginning of an ending; the Santa Maria had an ending.) Beginnings and endings may be shared, and kernel thoughts may be used in writers' workshop for other stories.
- Following completion of reading the story, have the students complete timelines for the life of the boy who sailed with Columbus. If both books are read, have half the class each make a timeline and share them.
- Discussions and journal writing or essay writing on Columbus's voyage as it impacts our lives even today are necessary with either book.

Literature Approaches
- Students may describe the part of the voyage they would have liked best or worst if they had sailed with Columbus. After editing and getting the paragraph to say what they want to say correctly, they may rewrite it and mount it on blue construction paper cut in the shape of sea waves. Post the paragraphs on a bulletin board. (personal experiences)
- Students may reread the beginning or ending of one or both books on Columbus. If reading both books, make a drawing or collage of each beginning or ending and place them back to back on a sheet of construction paper that you can hang with string from the ceiling. Both sides (both stories) are visible by twisting the construction paper. Place each boy on his side of the paper. If only one book is read, one side of the paper may show the beginning while the backside shows the ending of the story. (literacy conventions)
- If both books are read, use a Venn diagram to compare and contrast the two boys whose fictionalized stories indicate that they sailed with Columbus. Following a group effort in the comparison, ask each student to

select a comparative or contrastive feature and compose a paragraph on the similarities or differences of that feature in the two characters. (literacy process)

Story Branches

How the Sea Began
- As a class, list all the beginnings and endings in this story. Individual students may write about what the Taino villagers' lives may have been like after the beginning of the sea.
- Students may speculate on what might have happened to Yayael. They might find another beginning for him and continue his story.
- Connect this theme to a social studies unit and have students research the Taino Indians and find out about their ending. Make a bulletin board that includes the beginning of exploration of the New World.
- Using the question of "how," determine when adverbs may be used. Use the question of how to develop some sentences with adverbs. For example: The sea began slowly.

The Boy Who Sailed with Columbus
- Provide opportunities for students to read other accounts of the Columbus voyage and compare the events of the journey to the new land with those described in this story.
- As a class, make a map of current lands in the Caribbean and try to locate places described in the book.
- Groups may investigate different native tribes mentioned in the book and those found in other sources; make a chart showing each tribe and where they lived.
- Use this title as a model for students writing about someone who did something. For example, they might write about The Girl Who Saved a Dog, The Boy Who Washed Dishes, The Teacher Who Went to School.

I Sailed with Columbus
- Students may compare the duties of Julio de la Vega Medina with those of ship boys in other stories of the times.
- They may also compare the writing style (diary format in first person) of this book to that of *The Boy Who Sailed with Columbus* (narrative in third person).
- Another comparison is to look at differences in maps in this book to contemporary maps of the same region. Make a chart of the different names for the same places.

Surprises

Students may find pleasure in reading about surprises as well as considering how the authors of these books write to build an anticipation for surprise.

Howard, E. F. 1993. *Mac and Marie and the Train Toss Surprise.* Illustrated by Gail G. Carter. New York: Four Winds Press.

Summary. Mac and Marie Fitzgerald, two African-American children, have a note from their Uncle Clem, who works in the dining room of the train that passes by their house. He says that he will throw a surprise from the train when it passes their house (which faces the railroad tracks near Papapsco, Maryland, on the Baltimore and Washington line) on a certain night. They wait for the train and the surprise is thrown out. They unwrap the big white package to find a seashell from Florida that has the sound of the ocean in it. Mac decides he wants to be an engineer on a train.

Alexander, L. 1992. *The Fortune-Tellers.* Illustrated by Trina Shart Hyman. New York: Dutton.

Summary. A young carpenter asks a fortune-teller for his future; the fortune-teller tells him he will be rich if he earns large sums of money, he will become famous if he becomes well known, and he will live a long life if he can avoid an early demise! The carpenter leaves but decides to ask more questions, turns around, and runs back in to find the room empty. In comes a lady. She thinks he is the fortune-teller who has changed from an old man to a young one, so he plays the role, letting her think he is the fortune-teller. He continues, earning much wealth and happiness, using the same ambiguous language he has learned from the old fortune-teller. Actually, the old fortune-teller has met with bad luck. He has been carted off from town only to be picked up by a giant eagle and dropped into a river, never to be heard from again. Much to the surprise of the carpenter, everything the fortune-teller predicted comes true.

Byars, B. 1993. *McMummy.* New York: Viking.

Summary. Batty Batson and Mozie Mozer are best buddies, but sometimes Mozie's look gets Batty into trouble. So it is that when Mozie most needs him to go with him to water the professor's greenhouse plants, Batty is grounded. Valvoline, the aspiring Miss Tri-County Tech, accompanies him instead and hears the McMummy humming. The bean pod (or is it a being pod) being grown by the professor is taller than Mozie and seems to have something captured inside—maybe a m-mummy. A storm rips the greenhouse apart, releasing the pod from its vine at the same time that Valvoline is competing in the beauty contest. She needs her mustard seed necklace to bring her luck. When the green pod strides on to the stage, people are frightened and surprised, but Valvoline finds her necklace and wins the competition. Later, while rummaging through the debris in the greenhouse (which the professor gave to Mozie), Mozie and Batty find two green seed pods. Guess what they intend to do with them.

Integrated Language Arts Experiences
- The teacher should write "talk teasers" on strips of paper and make sure that each literary discussion group in the classroom gets one strip for the beginning discussion. Suggestions for "talk teasers" are:
The best surprise I have ever had was . . .
The story I have read with the greatest surprise ending is . . .
The best surprise ending in a movie I have seen is . . .
I (love) or (hate) surprises because . . .
I like to surprise my _____ by . . .
When I am surprised, I feel like . . .
- The first two stories are picture books and may be read to the students or, with multiple copies of the text, students could read these stories in one class period. They might be read first as whole-class reading and then chapters of *McMummy* could be read.
- Dramatizations of one or more of the books will be appealing to the students. Different books or segments of the same book may be assigned to small groups for practicing the dramatization and later performing it for the other groups in the classroom. Students should be encouraged to use their own language rather than try to remember what a character said word for word. As they creatively dramatize the story, they demonstrate their comprehension.
- A tall, narrow wall or bulletin board might have the words Surprise Stories spelled vertically, and students could write titles of books that have surprise events on pieces of colored construction paper, taping or stapling around the words. Students could then use the suggested titles as recommendations for independent reading.
- Have pairs of students begin writing a story on any subject with any type of plot. Every two to three minutes, each pair will pass their story to the next pair, and that pair will continue writing the story until the signal is given again for the story to be handed on. These "rotated stories" should have surprise events as various authors had part in writing them. Oral sharing may complete this activity.

Literature Approaches
- Students may react to one or more of the stories with an entry in their literature logs. The entry assignment may be to compare the story with

another story that also has some surprise events. Have them assess the story in the cluster for the effect of the "surprise" and for overall enjoyability. (personal experiences)
- The teacher should draw an ascending line on the chalkboard to represent the rising action of a plot in a story. Then after the line has peaked, show it falling to show the resolution of a story. The teacher will think aloud as a demonstration of looking at the plot of a story. The teacher "think aloud" will help students see how she or he identifies the rising and falling actions in a plot. The teacher might begin with a well-known story such as *Peter Rabbit*. Point to various places on the plot line to show how the action climaxes when Peter is on the brink of being caught as he hides in a watering can. Following that point, the action declines as Peter finds his way home and into the sick bed. After this demonstration of rising and falling plots, have students in groups of four or five draw a plot line on a paper and make dots showing where various events in a story fall. Depending on the age of the students, they might draw the plot of one of the stories in this cluster. (literary conventions)
- Have each student design a story with a surprise event in the plot. Encourage students to edit and share their stories in a "Book of Surprises." (literacy process)

Story Branches

Mac and Marie and the Train Toss Surprise
- As a group, students may make a map of the states the train would pass through as it traveled from Washington, D.C., to Florida. Find the path of the Baltimore and Washington route to Florida.
- The teacher may suggest: Decide what you would like the "surprise" to be and rewrite the story with your own ending.
- Students may be asked to: write your own thank you note to Uncle Clem as if you were Mac and Marie.

The Fortune-Tellers
- Students may write a diary entry for the young carpenter who visited the fortune-teller on the day that he also became the fortune-teller.
- They could also write another adventure for the old fortune-teller who was never heard from again.
- In a group discussion, look at the conditional "ifs" in the messages given the carpenter by the fortune-teller. Then students may write his messages in more straightforward language, stating clearly what is meant.

McMummy
- Students may illustrate the M-mummy pod and show how its size compares to a 10- to 12-year-old child.
- They may grow several packets of vegetables and fertilize them regularly to see how large they will grow. Keep a log of the activities related to their planting and growth.
- Some students might enjoy drawing Valvoline in her beautiful sequined gown and then writing to her, giving her some tips on how to win the beauty contest.
- Use the phone book and several other alphabetical sources of information to determine the placement of Mc in alphabetical order. Does it come in exact order and precede the "Me" or is it placed by itself at the beginning or the end of the other "Ms"? (Note to teachers: The alphabetization will not be consistent in all sources, so check several references and allow students to generalize about the lack of consistency.)
- As a class, brainstorm other parts of names that at one time had relational meaning, such as "son" in Johnson, meaning "son of John," or "O" as in O'Neal, meaning "of Neal."

Perspectives

Recognizing that different people see things in different ways is a first step toward accepting others' views and beliefs. Walking in another's shoes for a mile spawns a broader outlook. That experience may be possible through these stories.

Drescher, J. 1993. *The Birth-Order Blues*. New York: Viking.

Summary. Millicent Brown, a reporter for *The Fast Flyer News* decides to survey her friends and determine how they feel about being an oldest, middle, youngest, or only child. She interviews Kim, an oldest child, Beth, a middle one, and Rollin' Ralph, a youngest. She also interviews Tony, an only child. She asks how they feel about being in that position, and then she asks if there was anything good about it. The results of her survey are published in *The Fast Flyer News* as "Magnificent Millicent's Birth-Order Blues Survey." The survey is found on the last page of the book. This book is illustrated with cartoons and dialogue balloons that tell the story.

Byars, B. 1992. *Coast to Coast*. New York: Delacorte Press.

Summary. Birch is a 13-year-old who worries about her grandfather, who seems to have lost his former zest for life since her grandmother died. She talks him into taking her with him and going on his lifelong dream trip: a flight from

South Carolina to California in a Piper Cub. They accomplish the trip, learn to understand themselves and each other better, and find satisfaction in what they have done. There is humor in the story and deep emotions, as they dig into the family's past history and work through their feelings.

Fleischman, P. 1993. *Bull Run.* Woodcuts by David Frampton. New York: HarperCollins.

Summary. In this unforgettable book, readers meet characters who experience the battle of Bull Run in various ways. There are a minimum of three entries for each character and as many as five to six for others. They tell from their personal perspectives how the war has affected their lives. Some of the characters are Lilly Malloy from Minnesota, whose brother Patrick runs away from home to join the army; Shem Suggs, a blacksmith, who joins the cavalry; Gideon Adams, a light-skinned Black man who joins the Union forces through a disguise; James Dacy, a sketch artist for the *New York Illustrated News*; Toby Boyce, an 11-year-old fife player who joins a Georgia unit; and other characters, all of whom are fictional except for General McDowell. A note at the end of the book lists Southern and Northern characters and the pages on which they speak.

Integrated Language Arts Experiences
- Citing an issue of importance to the students, such as abolishment of free reading on Friday afternoon or the enforcement of no talking in the cafeteria, have each student interview another student to determine the interviewee's opinion. Then have them switch roles. Each student will write a summary of how he or she perceives the perspective of the other person. The summaries will be shared in pairs as they assess each other on how well perspectives were represented.
- The first story in the cluster is a picture book and may be shared aloud by the teacher, followed by discussion and continued activities as suggested below in "Story Branches." The other stories may be read across several days in one or more of these reading modes: independently, in pairs, or with oral-shared reading by some of the students to the larger group. Spontaneous response discussions need to be held following each reading session to clarify questions and to allow verification of comprehension among students.
- Students should select a character from one of the stories and identify that character's perspective on an issue. They may compose a narrative from that character's perspective and show how the character feels through what they have that character say about the issue. For example, in *Coast to Coast,* it is clear that Birch believes the trip will give her

grandfather a new lease on life. A narrative that allows Birch to talk about this issue would show her perspective. Students may orally share the narratives without divulging the character's name and other students will determine who the character is and if they agree that the perspective is shown in the narrative.
- Students may revise and edit the perspective narrative and include it in a classroom notebook on "character perspectives."

Literature Approaches
- Have students draw a picture and then write a story using dialogue about an episode when they held a different perspective than someone else on an issue. Have them consider very carefully the dialogue for how they explained their perspective to the other person and how they reacted to that person's opinion. (personal experiences)
- Have students find a story told in first person. It will be told from a character's perspective and will use first person pronouns such as I, me, we, and us. (*Bull Run* is a good example of first person point of view.) Notice how the author lets the character give the reader information. Have them try writing a few paragraphs from first person point of view and let your character give the reader information. (literacy conventions)
- Take the first person narrative draft to author's chair for sharing. Ask other students if they can tell the perspective of this character by how it is written. (literacy processes)

Story Branches

The Birth-Order Blues
- Students will survey the class or the school to determine how the students feel about being the oldest, middle, youngest, or only child.
- Compile the results of this survey and share it in a class or school newspaper.
- As a class, sponsor a contest to determine the name of the school or class paper.
- Students may write and illustrate a story using dialogue balloons as used in this story.

Coast to Coast
- From the cities listed on the trip from South Carolina to California, students may select two or three and find notable landmarks that Birch and her grandfather might have seen while they were flying over the city. A mural might be made to depict the flight with different students contributing landmark symbols across the country.

- The book may be used throughout a study of United States geography. Other flight paths may be mapped out as plans are made for Birch and her grandfather to return to South Carolina by a different route. Students may determine miles, terrain they would have to fly over, and conclude a "best" flight path home.
- Students may dialogue with Birch and ask her questions or tell her their experiences with grandparents, with finding "family" secrets, or in taking trips with family members.

Bull Run
- Using the entries for various characters, have students select a character for a narrative story, filling in and completing the fragmented stories found in the book.
- By assigning reading parts by character, plan a readers' theater for this book. One fifth grade class might present it to other fifth graders.
- Students may research the battle of Bull Run and locate the geographical area and its landmarks on a map.
- Practice descriptive writing by using adjectives extensively in describing some of the characters in this book.

Considering Others

Characters with compassion and concern for others, both in humorous and serious form, are found in this theme. Students may recognize these characters as similar to many of their own friends and family members.

Steig, W. 1992. *Doctor DeSoto Goes to Africa.* **New York: HarperCollins.**

Summary. Dr. Bernard DeSoto receives a cablegram from Mudambo in Dabwan, West Africa, to come and relieve his toothache. Dr. DeSoto is a mouse dentist, and Mudambo is an elephant. The doctor is interested in going to Africa and in working on an elephant tooth. He and his wife reply favorably. "Let us go-oleo!" is her response. They take a ship and are met by Mudambo's brother, Adiba, who takes them to the Mudambo residence. Dinner is difficult because Mudambo is in such pain. Soon they begin work on his tooth and realize that they need tusk to repair the tooth. They decide to ask the museum for a piece of walrus tusk, and Adiba sets off to retrieve it. The DeSotos go to bed on a pin cushion, and during the night, a disgruntled rhesus monkey, Honkitonk, kidnaps Dr. DeSoto. He is paying the elephant back for a disagreement. The doctor is placed in a cage deep in the jungle, and in spite of the search efforts, he is not found. Finally in desperation, Dr. DeSoto gains enough strength to bend the cage ribs and escape. In utter exhaustion, he is discovered by a search party and is returned to Mudambo's house, where after recovering himself, he is able to fix the tooth. He and his wife enjoy more traveling before going home.

DiSalvo-Ryan, D. 1991. *Uncle Willie and the Soup Kitchen.* New York: Morrow Junior Books.

Summary. Uncle Willie meets the young boy after school and watches him until the boy's mother gets home from work. They enjoy each other's company as they laugh and play, although Uncle Willie is an elderly man. Uncle Willie also works in the local soup kitchen and tells the boy about how many people they fed that day. The boy is curious about why they need the soup kitchen and who goes there. He is told that "Sometimes people need help." People, like the Can Man who picks up cans in his shopping cart all over town, need help. The boys asks why the Can Man doesn't eat at home, and he asks where the Can Man lives. Uncle Willie doesn't know and tells the boy that the only requirement for eating in the soup kitchen is to be hungry. His mother, recognizing the boy's interest, suggests that he go with Uncle Willie next Monday when there is no school. On the way there, they stop at the meat market and are given two big bags of chickens. At the soup kitchen, the boy meets Underfoot, the cat, and several other people who are chopping vegetables, making fruit salad, slicing cheese, and preparing baskets of bread and peanuts. The workers, including Uncle Willie and the boy, eat first; then Uncle Willie yells, "Lunchtime," and the long line of people come in and are served plates of food. Soon the food is gone and Uncle Willie and the boy start home, playing their usual games.

Kherdian, D. 1989. *A Song for Uncle Harry.* Illustrated by Nonny Hogrogrian. New York: Philomel.

Summary. Petey is a 12-year-old boy living in Wisconsin in the 1930s; his family came from Armenia and still has other family members there. His dad's cousin, whom he calls Uncle Harry, lives down the street from his house and is Petey's favorite person in all the world. When Petey gets scratched and needs a bandaid or when he just needs to talk, he finds his uncle. Sometimes they ride around in a Model A car, but usually they go fishing. Sometimes Cousin Sam comes along. During World War I, Uncle Harry is exposed to poisonous gas, so he receives a disability pension and does not work. Uncle Harry has a special way of making one forget troubles, as when he teaches Petey how to tell time to keep Petey's mind off a cut finger. They take time to enjoy nature, observe bullhead fish and their babies, crack and eat sunflower seeds, and talk about Uncle Harry's sister, Zabel, who has just died in Armenia. He likens her life and death to the water in the river—a stream of possibilities that continues to run even when one cupful of water (such as his sister) is removed. Petey is surprised when his uncle disappears for a few days and returns from Chicago with Aunt Charlotte, his new wife. Petey's dad helps him realize that life changes and people have to change with it.

Integrated Language Arts Experiences
- Announce to the class that each student will be given the name of another student and it will be each student's responsibility to observe the student whose name he or she has received during the next four to five days and make notes of all the helpful things that person does or says. Then on Friday afternoon, the students will sit in a circle, and each person, in turn, will stand and validate the one who was observed by saying, "(Name) has been helpful and considerate of others this week. I saw (him or her). . . ." The students will then shake hands and both will sit down. By the end of the session, all children will have been validated for something, all will have had an opportunity to talk, to listen, to be recognized, and to recognize another. Each day the teacher will give mini-lessons on the types of things to look for in observations: holding the door for someone; saying, "thank you" or "excuse me"; answering a question for someone; helping someone find a page number, etc. The teacher will give mini-lessons on why the names must be kept secret until the afternoon of validations, how this activity can help people feel better about themselves, and why this is a serious experience and not one for ridicule.
- As students collect observational data on other students who are being helpful, they should be encouraged to keep their data in a private notebook, so they can remember it for the validation. The teacher may ask to see the notebook at the end of the week.
- If desired, the validation may continue for a number of weeks. Once students are accustomed to the process, they may begin making congratulatory cards or posters to promote the actions of their partners. Teachers must evaluate the benefits of continuing the validation project, although some teachers have found it helpful to continue though 25 to 30 weeks to allow each student to validate each student in the classroom and to be validated by everyone.
- Once students are into their observations and understand the relation of the activity to the theme study, one or more of the picture books may be read to students or they may read the books for later discussion. The first two books in the cluster are illustrated and demonstrate consideration of others clearly.
- Students in small groups may select one of the following response projects to be done with one of the books:
  1. Dramatize the story;

2. Make a TV roller story by summarizing and drawing pictures for the roller;
3. Make objects for a hanging mobile showing the characters.
- The teacher may conduct a mini-lesson on names and titles, using Doctor DeSoto, Uncle Willie, Uncle Harry, Aunt Charlotte, and others as examples. Abbreviations for Doctor, Mister, and Mistress may also be reinforced with this instruction.
- The third book in the cluster is a chapter book and will take several sessions for completion. The relationship between the boy and his uncle may be the point for discussions. A relationship web will be helpful to construct with the whole class. Students will be able to talk about how the boy helped his uncle and how the uncle helped the boy.

Literature Approaches
- Story starter for writing in the literature log: Write about someone who has helped you over the past years. This may be a piece of writing to share or one that remains private. (personal experiences)
- Using one or more of the books, have students find passages that are descriptive of the setting, the characters, or some events in the plot. Have them copy the passages and place them in a three-ring notebook that students may use as models when they get "stuck" in their own writing. Encourage students to imitate the way these authors have used description. (literary conventions)
- Ask students to look back through the writer's notebook or literature log and find a character, setting, or event that they may use for description. Have them try to write descriptively. They may later conference with the teacher on their description attempt. (literacy processes)

Story Branches

Doctor DeSoto Goes to Africa
- As a class, read a collection of William Steig's books and compare the characters, the language, and the fantasies. Make hanging book reports, so many of Steig's books may be viewed simultaneously.
- Discuss the possible responses of the museum when asked for a piece of walrus tusk. In the story, the museum was very accommodating in giving the dentist a piece of walrus tusk. How realistic would that request be today?
- Find West Africa on a map. Call several airlines to find how long it would take to travel there from the reader's area. Find out costs.

Uncle Willie and the Soup Kitchen
- Discuss the issue of homelessness, people sleeping on park benches, and why soup kitchens are needed. Follow the discussion with journal entries, giving children an opportunity to write down their thoughts about how people can help when others are in need.
- Have students calculate how much chicken soup, fruit salad, and bread would be needed to feed 120 people. Use the cafeteria staff as a resource. Decide how much would be needed to feed the number of people in your class. Prepare your own lunch one day using the soup kitchen's menu.
- Find out if there are soup kitchens in your neighborhood. As a class project, cans of food could be collected to donate to the kitchen.

A Song for Uncle Harry
- Students may write an acrostic poem (finding a word that describes the person for each letter in that person's name) about a favorite person who does things with them and listens to their questions and ideas.
- Students find Armenia on a world map and see how far it is from their hometown. Then find the state of Wisconsin and see how far Petey's family traveled to get there from Armenia.
- In a small group, talk about everything Petey learned from his uncle. Then have peanut butter and jelly sandwiches and roasted chestnuts or sunflower seeds for a snack.

How Much Courage Did It Take?

Courage comes in many forms and is found in various degrees. Sometimes, it is also misunderstood. There are some heroes in these stories whose motivation and magnitude of courage may be well debated.

Wisniewski, D. 1990. *Elfwyn's Saga*. New York: Lothrop, Lee & Shepard Books.

Summary. From Icelandic history and legend comes this tale of Anlaf Haraldsson and his band of weary travelers from the north. They land on the greenest valley of the land, aided by the Hidden Folk, but infuriate warriors led by Gorm the Grim, who are also trying to find this valley. Gorm curses Anlaf, causing Anlaf and Gudrun's beautiful daughter, Elfwyn, to be born blind. Unbeknownst to the ones around her, she is blessed and loved by the Hidden Folk, who secretly watch after her. On her tenth birthday, she is given a horse, and she rides over field and forest. On the evening of Elfwyn's birthday, Gorm pays a visit to the great hall and brings a gift to make amends for their past problems. It is a huge crystal that gives off a shining light. Only Elfwyn, who can not see it, is not impressed. All who look at the crystal remember something from their past that had not been attained, and they become unhappy. Each evening they view the crystal and begin expressing their unhappiness to others; they quarrel and fight. Even Anlaf does not have time for his daughter. Early one morning, she ties a rope to her horse and attaches it to the crystal. Although Gorm tries to stop her, she nudges her horse on, and the crystal topples and shatters. The glass blinds Gorm and chases Elfwyn as she rides through the night. The Hidden Folk once again rescue Elfwyn, and the glass plows into the mountain where the curse against Anlaf has been carved. In an instant, as the mountain and the curse are destroyed, Elfwyn's sight is restored, and she returns home to grateful and loving parents.

Cervantes, M. de. 1993. Retold and illustrated by Marcia Williams. *Don Quixote*. Cambridge, MA: Candlewick Press.

Summary. In this retelling of the well known story of Don Quixote of La Mancha, his horse, Rocinante, and his friend, Sancho Panza, several of their adventures are told with cartoon illustrations. Don Quixote's obsession with knights of old Spain and how he becomes a knight are told simply in text under which are humorous cartoons with dialogue that gives more insight into his eccentricity. Among the adventures recounted in this book are his many fights for the honor of Dulcinea, the giants seen by Don Quioxite, his bout with the windmills, and his search for a new helmet. The end of the book finds Don Quixote and Sancho Panza starting on yet another adventure.

Wisler, C. 1991. *Red Cap*. New York: Dutton.

Summary. Ransom J. Powell is 13 and very small for his age when he runs off to join the Union Army. One of his best friends has been killed and another has enlisted, when he finally left. He joins a Virginia regiment as a drummer. He endears himself to many of the soldiers as a fiery mascot, although he thinks of himself as one who, though small of stature, must be tall in integrity—and that he is. He does not hold his tongue or his fists when a standard is in jeopardy—a trait that frequently causes him pain. He sees his drummer friend die in battle, and before he can get over that, he and 19 other soldiers are captured by the enemy. They suffer many indignities, as they are robbed, starved, and deprived of clothing and human needs at the hand of prison keepers and guards at Andersonville prison camp in Georgia. Although he will not sign the parole offered him to drum for Southern troops, he is afforded some opportunities by a Southern lieutenant, who sometimes takes him hunting. Ransom is always mindful of the other 19 in his group and brings back meat and vegetables to them as long as any of them live. Later, because he can read and write, he keeps books for the cruel captain of the camp, who is later tried and hanged for atrocities there. Ransom is able to smuggle maps to the prisoners as well as food. His activities are discovered, and he is forced back into the prison camp where many of his comrades are dying. Eventually, he is the last surviving member of the group of 20. Because Sherman has taken Atlanta, the Confederate Army begins sending some of the prisoners north; Ransom is able to be among one group. He ends up in a hospital and is finally released to the Union Army. They give him a furlough for 30 days, but because of an intermittent fever, he never returns to duty. He later marries, has five children, and dies at the age of 50 of complications from the war.

Integrated Language Arts Experiences
- As students begin this theme study, have them keep a separate writing log called their "courage chronicle." Have them make a beginning entry into the chronicle with their initial thoughts about "courage."
- Either of the first two books listed in this cluster could be used as a read-aloud to the class. If used in this manner, use a visual presenter to show the illustrations to the whole class on a large screen. Students may also read the book chorally from the screen for a second reading.
- Students quick-write responses to the story in their courage chronicles and share thoughts in small discussion groups. The quick-writes remain as drafts until students wish to revise or edit the writing.
- *Red Cap* may be read in chapters by the teacher to the students or independently by students if multiple copies are available. It is a story that needs discussion, so provide that time either in small or whole groups each day as the story continues.
- Have students select a character from one of the stories to profile in the chronicles. Begin the profile with a character description web, then add a character's values web, then make a relationship web showing how the character relates to others, and finally make a character activity web near the end of the story to depict the character's role throughout the story. These webs should be kept in the chronicles to be used in later writings.

Literature Approaches
- Show students three ways authors display conversations or dialogue in stories: (1) quotation marks; (2) dialogue following a colon; (3) dialogue in balloons or boxes. Ask them to select a segment of one of the books they have read or heard in this cluster and create dialogue for two characters. Have them write the dialogue in two of the ways authors use to show conversation. They may record their writings in the chronicle. (literary convention)
- As a culmination to the theme study on courage, students will examine the character they have been studying and write a paragraph or an essay

about their own definition of courage. They may use examples of courage from the character's role. (personal experiences)
- The last writing assignment may be used as an evaluation piece when the teacher will grade the piece for mechanical accuracy. Students should have ample opportunity to revise, edit, proofread, and feel satisfied that the accountable criteria have been met. (literacy processes)

Story Branches

Elfwyn's Saga
- Students cooperatively retell the story in their own words as the teacher writes their story on chart pages.
- Separate the retold story into sections, giving groups of three or four students each a section to edit and illustrate for a big book.
- Groups make paper cut-outs in layers, similar to those used to illustrate the book, to accompany the retold story.
- Investigate the origin of the word "saga" and find other related words.

Don Quixote
- Break the story into the following adventures and assign groups to retell or dramatize each part:
    becoming a knight;
    declaring Dulcinea the fairest lady in the world;
    battling windmill "giants";
    rescuing a "princess";
    rescuing Rocinante;
    battling the "armies" of sheep; and
    getting a "helmet."
- Students may write to Don Quixote and try to persuade him to put down his sword and shield and lead a simpler life; or students may write from him to other students, explaining why he must fulfill his dreams of knighthood.
- Students may make shoebox dioramas of the adventures of Don Quixote and Sancho Panza.

Red Cap
- Students discuss in literary circles the reality of Ransom Powell's experiences. Can they imagine the exposure to weather without proper clothing, the lack of food, and fear for their lives? What would they have done if offered a parole as happened to Ransom?
- They may research prisoner of war camps during the Civil War and find where Union and Confederate camps were located.

- Invite a guest drummer to class who will demonstrate the drum rolls from the book. If possible, students might learn to beat some of the rolls, such as reveille and taps.
- Additional reading:
  Crane, Stephen. 1953. *The Red Badge of Courage.* New York: Little & Ives.
  Forbes, Esther. 1943. *Johnny Tremain: A Novel for Old and Young.* Boston: Houghton Mifflin.
  Sound recording: 1994. *Johnny Tremain.* Prince Frederick, MD: Recorded Books (7 cassettes, 9 hrs., 30 minutes).

Family and Friends

Students are keenly aware of the tenuousness of some friendships and of the steadfastness of others. They also know that family support is one of their greatest treasures.

Singer, M. 1990. *Twenty Ways to Lose Your Best Friend.* Illustrated by Jeffrey Lindberg. New York: HarperCollins.

Summary. Emma and Sandy become best friends after a rocky beginning that includes Emma's ridicule and her killer voice. It is after Sandy makes a list of "why friends are useless" and another of "why friends are useful" that Emma realizes they are very much alike. Emma's mother makes an impression on her by noting, in disgust, that on election day, during the recent presidential election, she overheard a man talking about voting for his friend instead of the one who could do the best job. She urges Emma to vote for the one who could do the best job, even if voting at school, and that is exactly what Emma does—in doing so, she loses her best friend, Sandy. Each of the girls pick other best friends and shun the other while hurting inside. Finally, Emma tries to write a list of "20 ways to lose your best friend" but could only think of 19. It is Sandy who thinks of the twentieth, and as each tries to understand the series of mistakes they made, they become good friends again.

Fleischman, S. 1992. *Jim Ugly.* Illustrated by Joseph Smith. New York: Greenwillow.

Summary. In 1894 in Blowfly, Nevada, Jake Bannock inherits a yellow, wolf-eyed mongrel named Jim Ugly from his father, who is brought home in a pine box and buried after a horse threw him over in Smoketree Junction. Jake is orphaned, as his mother has died sometime ago. His Aunt Aurora and Uncle Axie brought the body home and are going to stay on the farm for a while. Jake's father had been accused of stealing some diamonds and a bounty hunter had been after him before his death. Jake is not happy to inherit the dog because he is often afraid of him. But the dog soon seems to be trying to track down Jake's dad's scent, which makes Jake think his father might still be alive. Taking one of his dad's shirts for a better scent, he and Jim Ugly catch a train to Smoketree Junction. Not finding his dad's scent there, but picking up some other clues, Jake and Jim Ugly catch the train to the next station. There, Jim Ugly catches a scent and tracks it to the bounty hunter, who is looking for Jake's dad. Jake's dad had been an actor, and some of the actors and actresses are in this town for a show. One actress has special claims on Jake's father and the diamonds. Jake has numerous adventures while unraveling the mystery of what happened to his father. He begins to like Wilhelmina, the actress, and the acting crew and joins their troupe for the production of *Mrs. William Tell*. He and Jim Ugly are taken by train with the troupe to Oakland, California, where he continues searching for a scent of his dad. Clues are forthcoming, and Jake and Jim Ugly take a ferry to San Francisco and spot Jake's dad but do not talk to him because the bounty hunter is following them. During one of the shows, Jake's father appears in costume, and eventually the mystery is solved of Jake's missing father and the missing diamonds—thanks in part to Jim Ugly, the dog that has become Jake's dog instead of his father's and receives a name change also.

Birdseye, T. 1993. *Just Call Me Stupid.* **New York: Holiday House.**

Summary. Patrick Lowe, a fifth grader, lives in Arizona with his mother whom he has called Paulette ever since his dad left them two years before. His life at school is miserable, with a reading resource teacher who forces worksheets on him and a kid named Andy who constantly calls him "stupid." Stupid is the word his father called him when, in drunken stupors, he would lose control of himself and shut the child in a dark closet. Patrick's answer to not being able to read and having to cope with Andy and Mrs. Nagle, a less-than-sensitive teacher, is to retreat to his dream world of the White Knight.

When Celina, a creative girl, who has just moved to the neighborhood from Spain, tries to make friends with him, he recoils and withdraws into his shell at first, only to find it intriguing that she is a good chess player. They begin playing chess over the back fence without seeing each other move the pieces. Finally they meet face to face and become good friends. He is happy to have her company in The Kingdom, a hiding spot beyond the oleanders with a plywood roof on it, where she reads to him from *The Sword and the Stone* and piques his interest in the story. They ride bikes to the dry river bed and find a chuckwalla (lizard) that they declare "The Questing Beast" and which promptly attaches itself to Celina's nose and will not turn loose. It takes many tries and everybody's help at the café where Paulette works to free Celina. In the end, it is Patrick's idea for Celina to put her nose under water and breathe through her mouth. That is the solution and the lizard turns loose. Celina and Patrick let him live in an aquarium and find books on chuckwallas to know what to feed him.

Celina also brings books to The Kingdom on medieval times. Patrick begins drawing more and more. He draws figures of all the characters in *The Sword and the Stone,* while Celina cuts them out and stands them by the castle they made. Patrick still does not think he can read, but he cooperates with Mrs. Nagle and her worksheets and nonsense words games because he is happy with his drawing and the world of make-believe he is creating. A series of events, including a chess tournament, a writing contest, the betrayal of his friend, Celina, and a boastful vow, nearly destroy him. Despite his problems, he pulls himself to heights that he did not realize he could reach as the story climaxes.

Integrated Language Arts Experiences
- All three of the books in this cluster are chapter books and will take several sessions of reading. One suggestion for using them is to obtain multiple copies of the first two books and allow one group to read one of them while another group reads the second book during readers' workshop (including group discussions). Giving students choices is always a good idea. The third book may be read by the teacher to the whole class, as it contains strong emotions and will need teacher-led discussion.
- After each reading session with one or more of the books, students should have some time for individual or paired response projects. Writing in literature logs, making dioramas, or hanging book reports are suggestions.
- Students may create questions for literature tic-tac-toe. The questions from a book will be placed in a shoebox for safe keeping until the game starts. The tic-tac-toe board may be drawn on the chalkboard or a plastic toy set may be used if available. During their turns, team members must answer a question before being permitted to mark an X or O.
- The book, *Just Call Me Stupid,* will be especially meaningful to students who have had problems in learning to read. Care must be taken that other students do not point out those who may identify with the character. But if an *esprit de corps* has been established among the students in the class, reading the book aloud and discussing it as a group should be successful.

Literature Approaches
- Students select a character from one of the stories and write about why that person was or was not a good friend or good family member. Students should use their own criteria for what makes a good friend or family member. (personal experiences)

- Examine text from one or more of the stories to determine how writing is punctuated in current texts. Look at the use of commas, semicolons, and colons as age appropriate or writing-level appropriate. Students look at a writing piece on friends and family and edit for correct punctuation. (literacy processes)
- Compare one or more of the stories with each other or with other juvenile novels to see techniques authors use to describe characters and events. Find examples of such techniques as:
    character thinks about own or other characteristics;
    characters' dialogues; and
    flashbacks of previous events.
- Encourage students to use these examples as models in their own writing. (literary conventions)

Story Branches

Twenty Ways to Lose Your Best Friend
- Students may make their own lists of how to keep or lose friends. These may be mounted and made into a bulletin board.
- Students may create individual projects by making a shoebox diorama of one of these scenes from the book:
    1. when Sandy was trying to become friends with Emma in the beginning;
    2. Marguerite's party;
    3. dinner at Emma's house when she insulted her mother; or
    4. in the hall where the teacher sent Emma and Sandy for laughing out loud.
- Have students review this book, determining the best audience for the book and why that audience will enjoy it. Submit the review to the school or class newsletter if the book is highly recommended.
- In chapter 3 the magnetism of the television is discussed: "You have lots of interesting stuff to talk about. But the TV is on. No matter how hard you try to pay attention to your friend, you end up looking at the TV instead. That's what Marguerite was like—a TV. She pulled your eyes right to her" (p. 19). Students may react to the chapter and to its implications either through disucssion or writing.

Jim Ugly
- After reading the story, have students decide on a better name for Jim Ugly and explain their choice. If they think Jim Ugly or Amigo is the very best name, ask them to explain their reasons.

Themes

- Students may write their own dog story and post it on a bulletin board called "Canine Concoctions."
- As a group, retell the story in this way: Assign these characters to different students and have them each talk about what that character did in the story: Jake Bannock, Sam Bannock, Jim Ugly, Wilhelmina, Mr. Cornelius, Aurora, Axie, D. D. Skeats, and Miss Jenny.
- Students may describe a character using as many adjectives as possible. They might also try describing a character by using metaphors (Jim Ugly was a bushy pile of brush).

Just Call Me Stupid
- Provide opportunities for small group discussions of how children learned to read and what they remember about the learning process, which will help them digest this story.
- Set up a chess board on an overhead transparency and read the excerpts of the chess game aloud. Move the chess pieces on the overlay as were moved in the story so all students may see the movements as well as hear them.
- Begin a unit on medieval times and include as many activities as possible that Patrick and Celina did while they were learning about medieval times. Above everything else, show the video of *The Sword and the Stone* or read the book aloud to the class at the same time this book is being read.

Comparisons

No creature lives in its own world without the influences of others. To look at those worlds and to consider how they are alike and different provides another glimpse into our own lives. The wild animals in these stories may be compared to each other and to ourselves.

Mason, C. 1993. *Wild Fox, A True Story*. Illustrated by Jo Ellen McAllister Stammen. Camden, ME: Down East Books.

Summary. The author tells her story of a red fox who lives on Deer Isle off the coast of Maine and who visits with her often. The first glimpse of the fox is on one summer day when, as a pup, he invades her strawberry patch. Six months later, she sees a red fox again, this time getting suet from her birdfeeder when there is snow on the ground. This time, the fox is wounded; his right front leg was nearly severed above his foot—the work of a steel-jawed trap. She grabs a chicken drumstick that is thawing for her dinner and runs outside to give it to the fox. Of course, he runs away, but as she watches from a window, he returns to devour it. The next day he returns, and she talks to him softly and leaves more chicken for him. Day after day, the routine becomes the same, as the fox seems to grow stronger. The dangling foot has also disappeared. She keeps feeding him and names him Vicky for Vixen, although he never seems to learn his name. Each day she tries to get a little closer to him, but he is still wary of her, although he lies in the driveway or puts on jumping shows for her as he practices pouncing. Another fox joins him near her house, and she makes a peanut path to show him a burrow that he might use for a den. He doesn't seem impressed. Summer comes and he still visits, often stretching out in the grass not far from where she weeds her flowerbeds. He is often around at night also—maybe to get his favorite blueberry muffins or Swiss cheese that she often feeds him. He will even come to the screen door and look in as he waits for his treats. For one moment that summer, she is also able to feed him a peanut from her hand and barely strokes his nose. As fall comes, he seems to turn to "fox" business, visiting less frequently and depending less on her for food. As it should be, he is still a wild fox.

George, J. C. 1992. *The Moon of the Wild Pigs.* **Illustrated by Paul Mirocha. New York: HarperCollins.**

Summary. In this nonfiction account of a peccary piglet, separated from his relatives during a thunderstorm in the Sonoran Desert in Arizona, the author creates a vividly descriptive story of how he tries to survive. It is morning in the desert but already more than 100 degrees when the peccary becomes lost. Peccaries are similar to pigs, but have three toes instead of four on each foot and have musk glands on their backs that pigs do not have. The clan has just taken precautions about becoming separated as a storm is on its way. A boar has rubbed his musk odor on the piglet and his mother, as it does on the other peccaries in the clan, so they can tell which pigs belong together if they are separated during the storm. The piglet can smell his clan off and on as well as the approaching thunderstorm, but he is not with them. He meets the spiny lizard, insects and birds, including a woodpecker and an owl, runs across a tarantula, and disturbs a rattlesnake. A bolt of lightning strikes a saguaro cactus, which lites up in the dark sky, and the piglet run in fear—right to his mother and the clan, waiting out the storm under a rocky ledge not 50 feet from where they had been separated.

Nelson, D. 1991. *Wild Voices.* **Illustrated by John Schoenherr. New York: Philomel.**

Summary. From the genre of animal fiction, this book carries the reader into the thoughts, emotions, and fears of six wild animals and a domestic dog. Reading like nonfiction with its environmental descriptions, the book begins with the misery felt by the red fox as she carefully and painstakingly ventures into the cold winter nights in search of food and in fear of predators. Pitted against Jim, the dog, she knows the tricks of survival and plays them all. Not so lucky is the young, healthy lynx who falls to the steel-jawed trap and cannot get his foot released, even after breaking a fang as he fights against this cold, steel enemy that can not be beaten. Ironically, the boy who sets the trap never profits from his pelt as a wolverine lies in wait for the lynx's demise. Other animals living in and on these mountains are the horse, who leads his harem and yearlings to safety against an army of wolves led by a wolf with one eye; the elderly puma who finds life hard as she tries to hunt prey that is much younger and much faster; the nanny goat who gives birth during a blinding snowstorm; and faithful Patch, the dog who has seen Jim come to live with them as a pup and whose days of watching the farmyard are over. Although these are fictionalized accounts of animals' struggles, insights into their way of life provide sensitivity to their voices.

Integrated Language Arts Experiences
- Comparison of these stories will require that the students read or hear all of the stories. It is suggested that the teacher read aloud the nonfiction, *Wild Fox*, and conduct a whole class discussion. Questions include:
  How much of the wild animal's natural life habits can be learned from this book?
  What other values, particularly about nature, are found in this nonfiction narrative?
  How does the story make you feel?
- The other books in the cluster may be read independently, in small groups, or shared through read-aloud. The questions listed above should guide the discussion for all books and a comparison chart may be posted to help keep a record of the results of the discussion.
- Have students take the perspective of one of the wild animals and imagine how the animal felt in one of the episodes. Tell them to list and discuss all the emotions the animal might have felt at given times in the story. Then they may write their conclusions in their literature log.
- Have them find other nonfiction sources for information on the wild animals. They may use Venn diagrams to compare information from one of the books with that from the other source.
- Have them select two wild animals from those read about and write a comparison-contrast paper on their habits, food, and habitat.

Literature Approaches
- As a class, list books about animals from personal knowledge that are factual and some that are fiction. Each student may make personal lists of the same. (personal experiences)

- As a class, use a Venn diagram to compare the differences in nonfiction and fiction stories about wild animals. Guide students as they think and talk about why it is important to know whether you are reading nonfiction or fiction when reading about wild animals. (Could you believe something was true when it was only an author's conjecture if you didn't know the difference?) (literary conventions)
- Provide opportunities for students to make papier mache masks of the faces of wild animals, using descriptions from the books. Encourage them to show emotions on the animals' faces as were expressed in the texts. Try to make the masks as accurate as an illustrator of one of the texts would have done in matching the author's words. (literary conventions)
- Take a field trip around the school or in a nature preserve and have students observe a wild creature's behavior. They will write about the behavior from a nonfiction perspective, describing exactly what they observe. Make sure that only observable information is written and avoid projecting emotions onto the creatures. Birds and squirrels as well as many insects can be watched without their knowing it. (literacy process)
- Have them prepare the final copies of their nonfiction piece and their fiction piece to be mounted on matching construction paper side by side for a display of nonfiction and fiction comparisons. (literacy processes)

Story Branches

Wild Fox, A True Story
- Students may read more about foxes and determine how likely it was for this story to have happened. Can they find other accounts of wild foxes becoming friendly with humans?
- They may write an essay on the life and habits of the New England red fox and share it or post it for others to read.
- They will draw pictures of the red fox to go with their essays.

The Moon of the Wild Pigs
- Using the lid of a box, such as a shoebox or envelope box, students may make a replica of the part of the Sonoran Desert where the piglet was lost during the thunderstorm. Include paper cacti and wildlife as described in the story.
- Although this is a nonfiction narrative, students may fictionalize the story of the piglet and write the piglet's thoughts as he was searching for his mother or write the dialogue for the piglet, telling his mother of his adventures.

- As a class project, locate other books in the series of "The Thirteen Moons." Find out the names of the moons and why there are 13 when there are only 12 months in the calendar.

Wild Voices
- Divide the class into seven groups and have one group research the type of animal found in each chapter. Computer-generated reports may be edited and published for a classroom library.
- On a large sheet of butcher paper, have students design a mountain range, placing each animal in its own place on the range. Draw dotted lines to show how the animals interacted with each other. There were definite interactions between Jim, the dog in the Foxtrot story, and Patch, the dog in the last story; Roan and Lone Wolf also interacted.
- Individually or in pairs, students may build a fictionalized prequel or sequel to this story for each animal: what had happened to him or her prior to this story; what happened in the future? Use all of the materials from these activities for a bulletin board.

CHAPTER 5

Evaluating a Literature-Based Language Arts Program

The assessment and evaluation of a literature-based language arts program must begin with a clear statement of the purposes and goals of such a program. Integration of language arts is a foundation stone for communication; various aspects of language arts must be woven together as they are used in real life. In daily living, we read, write, listen, and speak without separating the processes; we spell as we write; we use standard English as we speak and write; and we implement our penmanship not for show, but for the practical purpose of communicating. When the language arts are integrated in the classroom, they are fused into purposeful, real-life experiences for children.

A corresponding foundation stone is the use of literature as an instructional base. Because children learn language by day-to-day use and by interacting with other practitioners, it is logical to use models of excellence. Those models are good pieces of literature. By reading, hearing read, talking about, and imitating the writing in such works, children are exposed to many models of language use. These models provide exhaustive use of the language in ways that children will not experience if left to read basal texts and publisher worksheets. Even with ordinary conversation with people in a child's environment, the child will lack breadth and depth of language use as compared to experiences with literature. Through literature, children meet characters with interesting vocabularies; they encounter vivid descriptions and realize that words can almost equal pictures. Because literature may be revisited over and over, they can examine the language used, determine how the authors use language to make a point, or how they use punctuation to tell the reader when to take a breath, when to pause, when to get excited, and when to stop.

Nothing can surpass human interaction for learning to communicate; children must have people with whom they can talk, listen to, and learn to appreciate different opinions. On the other hand, for learning refined communication skills, for recognizing and using fine nuances of language, and for moving beyond the language of the neighborhood, literature is essential.

PROGRAM GOALS

1. Students will read, write, speak, and listen on a daily basis with a variety of purposes. Children use language for entertainment, information gathering and sharing, imitation of models for learning purposes, self-fulfillment, aesthetic purposes, and clarification of thinking.
2. Students will employ mechanical supports as needed on a daily basis for communication purposes. As children use oral and written language, they will need to practice correct usage of the English language, such as verb agreement, pronoun and noun use and agreement, and appropriate vocabulary choices. When writing, they also need to use appropriate punctuation and capitalization to insure better communication. Legibility in handwriting is a courtesy to the reader that children should recognize and follow.
3. Students will take risks to spell words not yet in their written vocabularies and will use developmentally appropriate strategies in the process of standard spelling acquisition. Spelling is a developmental process requiring time and experience with writing for standard production. It is more important for children to attempt to write their thoughts than to be bound by a correct spelling standard. Young children spell the way they think a word sounds if given the encouragement to do so. In accepting their transient spellings, adults are encouraging their risk taking and allowing for normal development to take place. On the other hand, when children are forced to spell correctly from the beginning of their writing, they learn to use only those words they can spell. Appropriate developmental strategies for correct spelling are implemented by many teachers as they:

   - encourage drafting of writing to be followed by editing of spelling if the piece is going to be completed for a purpose;
   - use mini-lessons to call attention to spelling generalizations as children's work indicates the need;
   - model appropriate spelling as children dictate labels and stories individually and in groups;

- require children to keep spelling journals or word banks of words they can spell; and
- begin formal spelling instruction when children have developed phonological awareness, can recognize many of the vowel sounds, and have an interest in "correct" spelling.

4. Students will know that literature has different forms and that their own writing, too, may be expressed in a variety of ways. Through hearing and comparing stories from early childhood through the school-age years, children will notice different structures among stories. They will learn that "genre" refers to specific types of literature based on how it was created, how it came to be told or written, whether it is in prose or poetry, and how it meets various criteria. They will begin writing in assorted genres as they gain confidence in their abilities.
5. Students will know that, in addition to genres, structures such as narrative, expository, and poetic forms reflect how and why selections are written. As with the recognition and imitation of genres in their own writing, children also write with these forms of literature. When taught the choices that an author has, students consider purpose and audience as they begin the communication process.
6. Students will find role models and solutions to problems that lead to strengthening values that promote human harmony. As students find other diverse characters whose problems are not so different from their own, they are able to explore ways of solving problems, developing attitudes, and taking stances that will enable them to meet their own conflicts through life.
7. Students see connections among all areas of the curriculum as they practice communication skills naturally as a function of interacting with the subject areas. When children find that they use language arts when they write math problems, that they read literature as part of their social studies unit, and that the science observation log they keep will provide data for an expository writing piece, they can celebrate the joy of learning without the artificial barriers of subjects.
8. Students find joy and excitement in their learning. When children know they are gaining knowledge, processing information, and developing skills needed for daily living, they become more confident and pleased with themselves. The result is a cycle, a wonderful growing cycle that cannot be stopped. When children are caught up in this cycle, they initiate their own homework by reading and writing for their own pleasure and needs, they perform well in school because they understand the rules of the "learning game" and have skills needed to

play it, and each day and each experience with content builds onto a base that will eventually grow into a productive, literate adult.

CONTINUOUS ASSESSMENT AND EVALUATION

As teachers plan for theme studies and focus units around which curriculum will be integrated, they also plan ways to assess the experiences and their effectiveness in terms of students' progress in pacing and application of content.

Overall goals are supplemented with specific objectives for definite periods of time. Some teachers develop goals by grading periods while others set weekly or monthly objectives. Traditionally, teachers have specified objectives, held students accountable for them, and kept records of students' achievement. Many teachers maintain profile charts on students' progress and may keep daily records such as this one.

Name	Read aloud	Read silently	Write in journal	Draft a description	Participate in a discussion	Edit: spelling punct. handwriting	Book report or book talk on animal fiction	Research on wild animal: collect data

By maintaining such a profile on a weekly basis, teachers are able to determine that students are making progress with the objectives. By carrying profiles on a clipboard during the class activities, teachers have a consistent reminder that they need to be continually assessing the students' experiences.

Especially when content is integrated, teachers are interested in assessing the processing of content. It is for this reason that many teachers are beginning to make their own checklists and square box charts to help them with ongoing record keeping. Checklists allow teachers to mark specific indicators of progress and to return to it at the end of the grading period to view it in a holistic manner. For example, with the following checklist, a teacher may determine a child's fluency in reading on a given day:

Name:	Date:
1. Selection: 2. Unbroken reading: a. sentence b. paragraph c. page d. more than a page	

Teachers also observe their students during literature discussion groups, as they are interested in how the students think and carry on a discussion without the teacher's contributions. Teachers often stand on the sidelines with a clipboard and a box chart to record processing:

Participates	Initiates	Responds	Relates to own life	Summarizes

As the teacher listens to the discussion, it is easy to record names and short remarks regarding the criteria stated in each column. Such anecdotal information is valuable at the end of a grading period or for sharing information at parent conferences.

Student Involvement in Assessment

Some teachers allow student involvement at the beginning of the assessment process. They plan for students to have a voice in the weekly activities that will produce grades. They may have already planned a group of possible activities and present them to the students, allowing students to select from the group. Sometimes teachers suggest possible projects, and students design a contract to be submitted to the teacher that details the number and types of projects to be attempted during a theme or unit study. If the teacher concurs, the contract then is stapled inside a working folder that is filed in the classroom, where the student and the teacher will have access to it during the working period. The contract becomes the guide for the teacher and the student in assessing the on-going progress. A contract might look like this:

Name:
Grading Period: November 20—December 10
I will accomplish these projects:

1. Read three nonfiction books on animals.
2. Read three fiction books on animals.
3. Write about all six books in my literature log.
4. Write to the author of one of the books.
5. Read a favorite section in a book to my reading partner twice a week.
6. Make questions from my reading for the class animal scrapbook.

7. Practice my handwriting by writing the questions and forming each letter correctly.
8. Review my lit log and find five new words I am not sure I can spell correctly and add them to my spelling list.
9. Meet with my reading group twice a week to talk about animal stories.
10. Complete two art projects on animals.

This type of assessment focuses on the quantity of experiences, while the evaluation of the quality must be viewed separately.

Teachers certainly know the criteria for acceptable performances, but unless they are willing to discuss them, their students are often not aware of how they are graded or what they need to be working toward. For this reason, many teachers not only give students a voice in the number and type of projects and activities but also include them in decisions on criteria for acceptable performance.

Each of the objectives in the sample contract may be viewed with definitive, yet very different criteria for performance. For example, to read three nonfiction books over a ten-day period might produce a simple check mark on a profile chart, indicating that the child did read three books. In this case, the objective is for the child to read. It is an easily met objective and one that the teacher can verify simply by having him or her read aloud from some of the books during conference time and by viewing the literature log to see what has been written about the books.

Another objective may have more stringent criteria, such as writing to an author. In this case, it would be expected that when the child wrote a letter to be mailed to an audience such as the author of a children's book, the letter must meet standard criteria for correctness: form, spelling, punctuation, sentence formation, and it must have purposeful content. Those criteria are expected by teachers who have taught letter writing standards. Children may have been exposed to such criteria for several years, but they may not have mastered them. When the student brings the letter to the teacher for approval, the teacher will assess the letter and either approve its mailing or provide additional instruction. A slash through the check on the profile chart might indicate that the first attempt was unsuccessful. Later, successful performance will also be noted on the chart, and the final grade will reflect both attempts. Daily and weekly records of performance allow teachers to continuously know the progress and the rate of progress of their students.

Writers' and readers' workshops are instructional techniques that include record keeping and assessment as an integral part. The workshop method has many forms, and teachers must determine which aspects of it work best for them. A basic structure for workshop time includes a short mini-lesson (sometimes preceded by a read-aloud related to the mini-lesson content) on literary conventions or literacy processes that are needed; silent sustained writing or reading to allow for those who need quiet time; working blocks when students may read or write in pairs, in groups, or individually, while the teacher conducts conferences; and sharing when students either discuss what they have read in literary discussion groups or read from their compositions in the writers'-share chair (author's chair).

Teachers often have a separate block of time for readers' and writers' workshops although some teachers rotate or give students choices on some days. The assessment aspect of these workshops is that students work independently much of the time. For accountability, they need a list of objectives or goals. Often teachers spend the first workshop of a grading period structuring experiences that lead to the individualized goals that will govern the ultimate outcome of the workshops. The teacher may require some goals and give choices for others. For example, if the grading period is nine weeks, the teacher might require that three writing pieces be completed and submitted for grading. There would probably be six to eight pieces begun, but the writer would decide which pieces to revise, edit, and submit to the teacher for grading and possible inclusion in a portfolio. All other pieces would be kept in a working folder, and at a future date, even during another grading period, the child might return to the piece for revision and completion.

Portfolio assessment has been widely acclaimed as a fair way to collect data and document progress over time. It is also a process that may involve students and allow them a voice in their own evaluation. Materials collected for a portfolio must be representative samples, however, rather than just a collection of paperwork. Students should have opportunities to include materials in the portfolio and to make considered judgments about what they will insert. They are often asked to look back through a working folder, holding materials in progress, and select one or two items that reflect the student's drafting, editing, thinking, problem-solving, or calculation efforts. They will probably be asked to attach notes to the materials indicating why those materials were selected. From folders holding completed works, students may also select for the portfolio and follow a similar procedure of determining what represents the work done during the grading period. Teachers may guide children in selection of materials for portfolio assessment by asking them to select one item that meets each of these needs:

1. Show that you have read regularly during the grading period. (The student will probably elect to submit the reading record on which daily readings, including title and pages read, have been recorded.)
2. Show that you have written a response to a book that caused someone else to think. (The student might search through literary letters [where a student writes to another student about a book and the one receiving

the letter must respond] written during the grading period and find one letter and its response that shows someone disagreeing with the writer or that shows new thinking on the part of the person receiving the letter.)
3. Look at your writing goals for the grading period and find examples of how you have met each of them. Label the examples by the goal number so the teacher can tell exactly what you are using as an example. (Students may use Post-it notes to show documentation of progress in specific areas, such as underlining titles, using a variety of words instead of "said," practicing penmanship, reading from three genres, and writing in expository form.)

The teacher will also include tests, quick-writes (when students are asked to quickly write a reaction or their opinion on a topic; these are assessed for content rather than mechanics as they are always in draft form), and other materials deemed pertinent to the student's status at the end of the grading period. All of these materials together become the basis for a letter grade, when required, and certainly a narrative report to parents even when not required.

Assessment of Literature

To maintain the use of quality literature, the evaluation of materials is ongoing. So many new books from all genres are published every year in huge quantities that few people can really keep up with all the new titles that are available. Here are some ways that teachers can stay abreast of good quality literature.

1. Read professional journals that review current literature. Either obtain a personal subscription or find access to the journals through school libraries, school professional libraries, and university or public libraries. Some journals that regularly review children's literature are *Childhood Education*, by the Association for Childhood Education International; *Language Arts*, published by the National Council of Teachers of English; *The Reading Teacher*, by the International Reading Association; and *The Horn Book*, published by Horn Book, Inc.
2. Read publications that review books such as *The Horn Book Guide* (Horn Book, Inc., 11 Beacon St., Suite 1000, Boston, MA 02108-3017).
3. Review serials in libraries that provide book summaries by subject matter. One excellent source for such information is *The Book Finder*, published by American Guidance Services, Circle Pines, MN.
4. Participate in an adult reading circle where books are read and shared by members, noting top quality selections. Teachers form these groups

as a way to increase their own literacy while they update their knowledge on recent children's publications.
5. Listen to the suggestions of students and ask them for favorite book titles. Many children visit libraries regularly and read avidly. These are the children who can advise teachers on the interest level of books, on the quality of the content, and on the book's readability. Use this most valuable resource.
6. Make friends with some media specialists and librarians who will also make recommendations regarding good and upcoming books. Teachers certainly will find a friend in their own media specialist in their school and should take advantage of this resource.

LOOKING AT THE TOTAL PROGRAM

Using the suggested strategies will allow teachers to determine how well each child is progressing with the integrated language arts and literature goals. Information will also be available in judging good books to use and in keeping the reading balanced between classic literature and more recent selections.

Another major area for consideration is to assess the total program and how it meets the program goals. The following questions in relation to goals can guide teachers in self-assessment, helping clarify daily activities in an integrated language arts literature based program.

Students will read, write, speak, and listen on a daily basis with a variety of purposes.

1. Is there excitement in the classroom that invites students to read and write, speak and listen?
2. Are there comfortable reading areas with at least five books per child on the reading shelves?
3. Are the books from all levels of reading?
4. Are all genres of books included?
5. Are there books related to the unit or theme being studied on the shelves?
6. Does the schedule provide for daily reading and writing?
7. Does the plan for the day include teacher read-alouds to the students?
8. Is there a silent sustained reading period when everyone in the classroom reads?
9. Is there a silent sustained writing period when everyone in the classroom writes?
10. Are there materials available for children to use for writing, such as unlined paper, lined paper (by second grade), colored paper, markers, pencils, and crayons?

11. Is there a daily talk and listen time when children have a chance to talk to a friend?
12. Is there evidence in the room of writing and reading for real purposes?

Students will employ mechanical supports as needed on a daily basis for communication purposes.
1. Are mechanical support skills directly and indirectly taught to children with developmentally appropriate strategies at the relevant time for each child?
2. Are students involved in developing their own literacy goals?
3. Do students have some choices in activities to meet their goals?
4. Do children draft first and then worry about mechanics?
5. Do they read for meaning first and then after a second reading, participate in activities to promote support skills?
6. Does the curriculum show real life reasons for learning the mechanics of literacy?

Students will take risks to spell words not yet in their written vocabularies and will use developmentally appropriate strategies in the developmental process of standard spelling acquisition.
1. Do children go beyond their spelling vocabularies and reach into listening and reading vocabularies for their writing?
2. Are young children encouraged to spell words as they sound?
3. Are older children encouraged to spell words as they sound while they draft, with a suggestion that there are places to find those words after the thoughts are on paper?
4. Are experience charts being written by teachers who take dictation from students in kindergarten through fifth grade?
5. Are experience charts hung on walls for frequent choral readings even days and weeks after they were written?
6. Are students encouraged to copycat a story with a few changes to give them confidence that they can use the standard language?
7. Does spelling instruction begin only after children start using short vowels and have phonemic awareness of basic sounds?
8. Are there games and activities for trying out stage appropriate spelling generalizations?
9. After spelling instruction has begun, do children have a chance to select at least five of their own spelling words?
10. Do all children who write keep a word bank or a spelling notebook of words they can spell?

Students will know that literature has different forms and that their own writing, too, may be expressed in a variety of ways.
1. Do children have opportunities to hear a variety of literary genres?
2. Do they have opportunities to respond personally to the literature they hear and read?
3. Are there many opportunities for books to be reread?
4. Do they write group copycat stories to imitate different genres?
5. Do they have genre studies and compare stories within a genre?
6. Are students aware of literary conventions that authors and illustrators use as they write and illustrate?
7. Do they have author and illustrator studies and focus on models of excellence in children's literature?
8. Are children aware of books that have won awards?
9. Do students keep reading records of how much and what they are reading?

Students will know that, in addition to genres, other structures such a narrative, expository, and poetic forms reflect how and why selections are written.
1. Do students write with a balance of all structures?
2. Have they been taught graphic organizers to help determine effective forms?
3. Are there opportunities for students to excel in writing with various structures?
4. Do students know the names of well known authors who write in expository text?
5. Are they familiar with more than two or three poets?

Students will find role models and solutions to problems that lead to strengthening values that promote human harmony.
1. Are theme studies conducted that lead to discussions of values that promote better human relationships?
2. Are the worth of humans, animal life, and the earth on which we live valued through literary discussions?
3. Are possibilities of conflict resolutions clearer to students because of literary discussions and experiences?
4. Through this program, are students able to think for themselves and accept the responsibility of making decisions?

Students see connections among all areas of the curriculum during their practice of communication skills as a natural function of interacting with the subject areas.
1. Are subjects related as much as possible without being artificially connected?
2. Are there always books and stories related to themes and units?
3. Does the planning show large blocks of time with several integrated objectives met through each activity?

Students find joy and excitement in their learning.
1. Do students enjoy reading during class and on their own?
2. Do they read at home?
3. Do they have library cards and visit the library often?
4. Do they sometimes spontaneously mention storybook characters?
5. When asked, "If you could select anyone in the world, who would you like for a friend," do they ever mention a character from a story?
6. Do students ever indicate that they would like to be authors or illustrators of books someday?

The answer to each question is "yes."

APPENDIX

• • • • • • • •

Selected Book Titles for Author Studies

Aardema, Verna

* *Anansi Finds a Fool*
* *A Bookworm Who Hatched*
  Bimwili and the Zimwi
* *Bringing the Rain to Kapiti Plain*
  Oh Kojo! How Could You!
  Pedro and the Padre
  Princess Gorilla and a New Kind of Water
  Rabbit Makes a Monkey of Lion
* *Sebgugugu the Glutton, A Bantu Tale from Rwanda*
  The Vinganenee and the Tree Toad
  What's So Funny, Ketu?
  Why Mosquitoes Buzz in People's Ears: A West African Tale
  Borrequita and the Coyote: A Tale from Ayutla, Mexico
  Misoso: Once Upon a Time Tales from Africa
  Traveling to Tondo: A Tale of the Nkundo of Zaire
  Who's In Rabbit's House?

Ackerman, Karen

Araminta's Paint Box
The Banshee
Broken Boy

---

*Books summarized in this volume

By the Dawn's Early Light
I Know a Place
Just Like Max
The Leaves in October
* Song and Dance Man
This Old House
The Tin Heart
Walking with ClaraBelle
When Mama Retires

Babbitt, Natalie

* Bub or The Very Best Thing
The Eyes of the Amaryllis
Goody Hall
Kneeknock Rise
Nellie, A Cat on Her Own
Phoebe's Revolution
The Search for Delicious
The Something
* Tuck Everlasting

Banks, Lynne R.

The Adventures of King Midas
The Fairy Rebel
* The Farthest Away Mountain
I, Houdini
The Indian in the Cupboard
The Magic Hare
The Return of the Indian
The Secret of the Indian

Baylor, Byrd

Amigo
The Best Town in the World
The Desert is Theirs
Desert Voices
Everybody Needs a Rock
* Guess Who My Favorite Person Is
Hawk, I'm Your Brother
If You Are a Hunter of Fossils

I'm in Charge of Celebrations
And It Is Still That Way
Moon Song
One Small Blue Bead
The Other Way to Listen
The Table Where Rich People Sit
The Way to Start a Day
When Clay Sings
Your Own Best Secret Place

Bunting, Eve

The Big Red Barn
Coffin on a Case
Day Before Christmas
A Day's Work
Demetrius and the Golden Goblet
Dream Dancer
Face at the Edge of the World
Fifteen Flower Garden
Fly Away Home
The Girl in the Painting
Happy Birthday, Dear Duck
* How Many Days to America?
Nasty Stinky Sneakers
Our Teacher's Having A Baby
Red Fox Running
* Smoky Night
Someday a Tree
The Wednesday Surprise
The Wall

Byars, Betsy

The Animal, the Vegetable and John D. Jones
Bingo Brown and the Language of Love
The Blossoms and the Green Phantom
The Cartoonist
* Coast to Coast
The Computer Nut
The Cybil War
Good-bye, Chicken Little
The Nightswimmers

Summer of the Swans
The TV Kid
* *McMummy*

Carle, Eric

All Around Us
Do You Want to Be My Friend?
* *The Grouchy Ladybug*
Have You Seen My Cat?
The Mixed-Up Chameleon
My Very First Book of Colors
La Oruga Muy Hambrienta
Pancakes, Pancakes!
Rooster's Off to See the World
The Very Busy Spider
The Very Hungry Caterpillar
The Very Quiet Cricket

Cherry, Lynne

A River Ran Wild
Follow Me
* *The Armadillo from Amarillo*
The Dragon and the Unicorn
Great Kapok Tree
Who's Sick Today?

Cooney, Barbara

Hattie and the Wild Waves
Island Boy
* *Miss Rumphius*
Snow White and Rose Red

de Beer, Hans

Ahoy There, Little Polar Bear
Little Polar Bear
* *Little Polar Bear and the Brave Little Hare*
Little Polar Bear Finds a Friend

Denslow, Sharon

At Taylor's Place
* *Bus Riders*

Hazel's Circle
Night Owls
Radio Boy
Riding with Aunt Lucy

de Paola, Tomie

The Art Lesson
Big Anthony and the Magic Ring
Bill and Pete
* *Bonjour, Mr. Satie*
Charlie Needs a Cloak
The Cloud Book
Helga's Dowry
The Legend of the Bluebonnet
The Legend of the Indian Paintbrush
Michael Bird-boy
Pancakes for Breakfast
Stega Nona
* *Tom*

Fleischman, Paul

The Birthday Tree
* *Bull Run*
I Am Phoenix
Joyful Noise: Poems for Two Voices
Rondo in C
Shadow Play
Time Train

Fleischman, Sid

Here Comes McBroom
* *Jim Ugly*
The Midnight Horse
The Scarebird
The Whipping Boy

Fox, Mem

Guess What?
Hattie and the Fox
Koala Lou
Night Noises

* Shoes from Grandpa
  Time for Bed
* Tough Boris

George, Jean Craighead

The Cry of the Crow
Dear Rebecca, Winter is Here
The Everglades
Julie of the Wolves
The Missing Gator of Gumbo Limbo
The Moon of the Alligators
The Moon of the Bears
The Moon of the Chickarees
The Moon of the Deer
The Moon of the Fox Pups
The Moon of the Gray Wolves
The Moon of the Moles
The Moon of the Monarch Butterflies
The Moon of the Mountain Lions
The Moon of the Owls
The Moon of the Salamanders
* The Moon of the Wild Pigs
  The Moon of the Winter Bird
  The Talking Earth

Houston, Gloria

But No Candy
Littlejim
Mountain Valor
My Great Aunt Arizona
* The Year of the Perfect Christmas Tree

Lowry, Lois

All About Sam
Anastasi
Autumn Street
The Giver
* Number the Stars
  Rabble Starkey
  A Summer to Die

MacLachlan, Patricia

Arthur, For the Very First Time
* Baby
Cassie Binegar
The Facts and Fictions of Minna Pratt
Journey
Mama One, Mama Two
Sarah, Plain and Tall
* Skylark
Through Grandpa's Eyes

Paterson, Katherine

Bridge to Terabithia
Come Sing, Jimmy Jo
Flip, Flop Girl
The Great Gilly Hopkins
Jacob Have I Loved
The King's Equal
Lyddie
The Tale of the Mandarin Ducks

Rylant, Cynthia

All I See
Appalachia: The Voices of Sleeping Birds
A Blue-Eyed Daisy
A Fine White Dust
Miss Maggie
Missing May
Mr. Putter & Tabby Pour the Tea
The Relatives Came
When I Was Young in the Mountains

Spinelli, Jerry

Do the Funky Pickle
Dump Days
Fourth Grade Rats
* Maniac Magee
Who Put That Hair in My Toothbrush?

Van Allsburg, Chris

Ben's Dream
The Garden of Abdul Gasazi
* *Jumanji*
Just a Dream
The Mysteries of Harris Burdick
Polar Express
The Stranger
The Sweetest Fig
Two Bad Ants
The Widow's Broom
The Wreck of the Zephyr
The Wretched Stone
The Z Was Zapped

INDEX

• • • • • • • • •

by Nancy Fulton

Aardema, V., 34, 181
   Anansi Finds a Fool, 32, 181
   A Bookworm Who Hatched,
     27–28, 181
   Bringing the Rain to Kapiti Plain, 77,
     181
   *Sebgugugu the Glutton, A Bantu
     Tale from Rwanda*, 85, 181
Aaseng, N.: *The Problem Solvers,
   People Who Turned Problems into
   Products*, 92
Accorsi, W.: *My Name is Pocahontas*,
   28–29
Ackerman, K.: *Song and Dance Man*,
   130, 182
Adams, John Quincy, 103
Adams, Lucy, 103
Adams, Sarah, 103
Alex Is My Friend (Russo), 127
   story branches for, 129
Alexander, L.: *The Fortune-Tellers*,
   145
Along the Santa Fe Trail (Russell), 87
   story branches for, 88
Altman, L. J.: *Amelia's Road*, 20

Amelia's Road (Altman), 20
   story branches for, 21
American Guidance Services, 175
American Way West, The (Franck),
   88
Anansi Finds a Fool (Aardema), 27,
   32, 181
   story branches for, 34–35
Anastasia (Lowry), 46, 186
*Animals Should Definitely Not Wear
   Clothing* (Barrett), 68, 90
   story branches for, 70
Annie's Promise, 45
Are You My Mother?, 53
Armadillo from Amarillo, The
   (Cherry), 80, 184
   story branches for, 81
Arnold, C.: *On the Brink of Extinction,
   The California Condor*, 89–90
Art Lessons (Schick), 120
   story branches for, 122
Asch, F.: *The Earth and I*, 56
Assessment program
   of literature, 175–176
   student involvement in, 172–75

Assessment program *(continued)*
  total, 176–79
Association for Childhood Education International, 175
Auch, M. J.: *Peeping Beauty*, 16
Aurora Means Dawn (Sanders), 120–21
  story branches for, 122
Autobiographies, 11

Babbitt, N.: *Bub or The Very Best Thing*, 116–17, 182
  Tuck Everlasting, 36, 182
Baby (MacLachlan), 40, 187
  story branches for, 42
Ballads, 11
Banks, L. R.: *The Farthest Away Mountain*, 37, 182
Banneker, Benjamin, 90
Banneker-Douglas Museum, 92
Barrett, J.: *Animals Should Definitely Not Wear Clothes*, 68, 90
Barrett, M. B.: *Sing to the Stars*, 82
Baylor, Byrd, 47
  Guess Who My Favorite Person Is, 46, 182
Beanpole (Park), 134
  story branches for, 136
Beginnings and endings (theme)
  intermediate resources, 140–42
  primary resources, 116–20
Bennett, J.: *A Cup of Sunshine*, 75
Berger, M. and Berger, G.: *The Whole World in Your Hands, Looking at Maps*, 70
Binch, Carolina, 59
  Hue Boy, 59, 105
Biographies, 11
Bird Watch: A Book of Poetry (Yolen), 46
  story branches for, 48
Birdseye, T.: *Just Call Me Stupid*, 160–61
  story branches for, 163

Birth-Order Blues, The (Drescher), 148
  story branches for, 150
Blackberry Ink (Merriam), 94
  story branches for, 96
Bonjour, Mr. Satie (de Paola), 133–34, 185
  story branches for, 136
Book Finder, The, 175
Bookworm Who Hatched, A (Aardema), 27–28, 181
  story branches for, 31
Booth, George, 96
Borrequita and the Coyote (Aardema), 28
Boulton, J.: *Only Opal, The Diary of a Young Girl*, 48
Boy Who Sailed with Columbus, The (Foreman and Seaver), 141–142
  story branches for, 144
Bridge, The (Neville), 113
  story branches for, 115
Brierly, Louise, 32
Bringing the Rain to Kapiti Plain (Aardema), 77, 181
  story branches for, 79
Brown, Kathryn, 54
Brown Honey in Broomwheat Tea (Thomas), 99
  story branches for, 100
Brownstone, David: *To the Ends of the Earth*, 88
Bryant, Michael, 55
Bub or The Very Best Thing (Babbitt), 116–17, 182
  story branches for, 119
Bull Run (Fleischman), 149, 185
  story branches for, 150
Bunting, E.: *How Many Days to America?*, 19, 183
  Smoky Night, 39–40, 183
Bus Riders (Denslow), 113–14, 184
  story branches for, 116
Byars, B.: *McMummy*, 145–46, 184
  Coast to Coast, 148–49, 183

Index

CBS. *See* Cooperative book sharing
Can't You Sleep, Little Bear? (Waddell, M.), 62
   story brances for, 64
Carle, E.: *The Grouchy Ladybug*, 56–57, 184
Carmi, Giora, 82
Carpenter, Nancy, 113
Carr, T.: *Spill! The Story of the Exxon Valdez*, 89
Carrick, C.: *Two Very Little Sisters*, 103
Carter, Gil G., 145
Cartons, Cans, and Orange Peels, Where Does Your Garbage Go? (Foster), 92
   story branches for 94
Casey Over There (Rabin), 43
   story branches for, 45–46
Cause and effect, 67–70, 89–92
Celia's Island Journal (Thaxter), 48, 50
   story branches for, 50–51
Cervantes, Miguel de: *Don Quixote*, 156
Changes (theme)
   intermediate resources, 137–40
   primary resources, 106–09
Cherry, L.: *Armadillo from Amarillo, The*, 80, 184
Childhood Education, 175
Clark, Emma Chichester, 84
Clay, Wil, 28
Clouse, Nancy, 85
Coast to Coast (Byars), 148–49, 183
   story branches for, 150
Cobb, V.: *Writing It Down*, 64
Cole, S.: *The Hen That Crowed*, 123
Comparisons (theme)
   intermediate resources, 163–67
   primary resources, 129–33
Conover, Chris, 61
Considering others (theme)
   intermediate resources, 151–55
   primary resources, 120–22

Contemporary fiction, 39–42
Cooney, Barbara, 21, 22, 48, 184
   illustrations by, 22, 48
   Miss Rumphius, 21, 184
Cooper, Floyd, 99
Cooper, Martha, 64
Cooperative book sharing, 5–6, 37–38
Couplets, 73
Courage. *See* How much courage did it take? (theme)
Crane, Stephen: *The Red Badge of Courage*, 159
Crespo, G.: *How the Sea Began*, 140
Cumulative texts, 76–79
Cuneo, M. L.: *How to Grow a Picket Fence*, 87
Cup of Sunshine, A (Bennett), 75
   story branches for, 76
Cyclical stories, 56–58, 70–82, 79–82

de Beer, H.: *Little Polar Bear and the Brave Little Hare*, 123, 184
de Paola, T.: *Bonjour, Mr. Satie*, 133, 185
   Tom, 117, 185
Daly, N.: *Papa Lucky's Shadow*, 129–30
Dear Benjamin Banneker (Pinkney), 90
   story branches for, 92
Denslow, S.: *Bus Riders*, 113–14, 184
Dialogue journals, 5
Diaries, 48–51
Diaz, David, 39
Dickinson, E.: *I'm Nobody! Who Are You?, Poems of Emily Dickinson for Children*, 95
Dicks, Jan T., 76
DiSalvo-Ryan, D.: *Uncle Willie and the Soup Kitchen*, 152
Dixon, A.: *How Raven Brought the Light to People*, 13
Doctor DeSoto Goes to Africa (Steig), 151
   story branches for, 154
Doherty, B.: *Willa and Old Miss Annie*, 62

Don Quixote (Cervantes), 156
   story branches for, 158
Dreamcatcher (Osofsky), 46
   story branches for, 47–48
Drescher, J.: *The Birth-Order Blues*, 148
Drummer Hoff (Emberley), 77

Earth and I, The (Asch), 56
   story branches for, 58
Egielski, R., 16
Ehlert, L.: *Moon Rope–Un lazo a la luna*, 13
Elfwyn's Saga (Wisniewski), 155–56
   story branches for, 158
Eliot, T. S.: *Mr. Mistoffelees with Mugojerrie and Rumpelteazer*, 97
Emberley, Ed: *Drummer Hoff*, 77
Epics, 11
Evans, D.: *Monster Soup and other Spooky Poems*, 97
Explanatory animal tales, 10
Expository texts, 67, 86–89
   cause and effect, 67–70, 89–92
   intermediate resources, 86–94
   primary resources, 64–73
   problem-solution, 70–73, 92–94
   sequence, 64–67, 86–89

Fables, 10
Fairy tales, 10, 11
Family and friends (theme)
   intermediate resources, 159–63
   primary resources, 126–29
Fantasy, 11, 16–17, 35–39
Farthest Away Mountain, The (Banks), 37, 182
   story branches for, 39
Fiction
   contemporary, 39–42
   folk literature, 10
   historical, 42–46
Field, R.: *If Once You Have Slept on an Island*, 73
Filipovic, Zlata, 45
   Zlata's Diary, 48–49, 51

Firth, Barbara, 62
Fleischman, P.: *Bull Run*, 149, 185
Fleischman, S.: *Jim Ugly*, 159–60, 185
"Fog" (Sandburg), 51
Folk literature, 32–35, 53
   primary resources, 13
   subgenres of, 10–11
Folktales, 10, 11
Forbes, Esther; *Johnny Tremain: A Novel for Old and Young*, 159
Foreman, Michael M.: *Boy Who Sailed with Columbus, The*, 141–42
Fortune-Tellers, The (Alexander), 145
   story branches for, 147
Foster, J.: *Cartons, Cans, and Orange Peels, Where Does Your Garbage Go?*, 92
Fox, M.: *Shoes from Grandpa*, 130, 186
   Tough Boris, 54–55, 186
Frampton, David, 149
Franck, I.: *The American Way West*, 88
   To the Ends of the Earth, 88
Franklin, K.: *The Old, Old Man and the Very Little Boy*, 110
   The Shepherd Boy, 57, 105
Fraser, M. A.: *On the Top of the World, The Conquest of Mount Everest*, 92–93
Free verse, 46–48, 98
Friends of Benjamin Banneker Historical Park, The, 92
From the Hills of Georgia, An Autobiography in Paintings (O'Kelley), 87
   story branches for, 89
Fuchshuber, A.: *Giant Story, A Half Picture Book*, 114
Fun poetry, 74–76

Gammell, S., 130
Garland, S.: *The Lotus Seed*, 98, 105
Genres
   fantasy, 11, 16–19
   fiction, 10

Index

folk literature, 13–16
  intermediate resources, 32–51
  nonfiction, 11
  poetry, 11
  primary resources, 13–32
  realistic fiction, 19–20
  types and traits of, 12
George, J. C.: *The Moon of the Wild Pigs*, 164, 186
Giant Story, A Half Picture Book (Fuchshuber), 114
  story branches for, 116
Gilgamesh the King (Zeman), 33
  story branches for, 35
Giraffe on the Moon, A (Nightingale), 25
  story branches for, 27
Godden, R.: *Great Grandfather's House*, 137
Gordon, G.: *My Two Worlds*, 64–65, 105
Gourbault, Martine, 127
G.P. Putnam, 118
Great Change, The (White Deer of Autumn), 137
  story branches for, 139
Great Grandfather's House (Godden), 137–38
  story branches for, 139
Great Potato Book, The (Hughes), 71
  story branches for, 72–73
Grigg, Carol, 137
Grouchy Ladybug, The (Carle), 56–57, 184
  story branches for, 58
Guess Who My Favorite Person Is (Baylor), 46, 182
  story branches for, 47

Hafner, Marylin, 64
HarperCollins Publishers, 118
Harry and Tuck (Keller), 103
  story branches for, 105
Hastings, S.: *The Singing Ringing Tree*, 32–33

Hen That Crowed, The (Cole), 123
  story branches for, 125–26
Hey, Al (Yorinks), 16–17
  story branches for, 18–19
Hilda Hen's Search (Wormell), 59
  story branches for, 61
Hillary, Edmund, 93
Himler, Ronald, 113
Historical fiction, 21–25
Hoban, Lillian, 73
Hodges, M.: *The Little Humpbacked Horse*, 61–62
Hogrogian, Nonny: *One Fine Day*, 77
House That Jack Built, The, 53, 77
Homer, 11
Hong, L. T.: *How the Ox Star Fell From Heaven*, 13
Hopkins, L. B.: *To the Zoo*, 25
Horn Book, The, 175
Horn Book Guide, The, 175
Horn Book, Inc., 175
House That Crack Built, The (Taylor), 76–77
  story branches for, 78–79
House That Jack Built, The (Hogrogian), 53, 76, 77, 133
Houston, G.: *The Year of the Perfect Christmas Tree*, 22, 186
Houston, Whitney: *One Moment in Time*, 45
How Many Days to America? (Bunting), 19, 183
  story branches for, 21
How much courage did it take? (theme)
  intermediate resources, 155–59
  primary sources, 122–26
How My Family Lives in America (Kuklin), 65, 105
How My Family Lives in America (cont.)
  story branches for, 67
How Raven Brought Light to People (Dixon), 13
  story branches for, 15–16

How the Ox Star Fell From Heaven
   (Hong), 13
   story branches for, 15
How the Sea Began (Crespo), 140–41
   story branches for, 144
How-to books, 11
How to Grow a Picket Fence (Cuneo), 87
   story branches for, 89
Howard, E. F.: *Mac and Marie and the Train Toss Surprise*, 145
Hue Boy (Binch), 59, 105
   story branches for, 61
Hughes, M. S. and Hughes, E. T.: *The Great Potato Book*, 71
Hutchins, Pat: *Rosie's Walk*, 80
Hyman, Trina Short, 145

"I Have a Problem" stories, 53, 58–61, 82
I Sailed with Columbus (Shlein), 142
   story branches for, 144
If Once You Have Slept on an Island (Field), 73
   story branches for, 74
If You Give a Mouse a Cookie, 53
I'm Gonna Tell Mama I Want an Iguana (Johnston), 73
   story branches for, 74
I'm Nobody! Who Are You?, Poems of Emily Dickinson for Children (Dickinson), 95
   story branches for, 96
Information books, 11
Integraged language arts approach viii–x, 1–6
Integrated language arts experiences, defined, ix
Intermediate (grade level) resources
   contemporary fiction, 39–42
   expository resources, 86–94
   fantasy, 35–39
   folk literature, 32–35
   historical fiction, 42–46

narrative resources, 76–86
nonfiction diaries, 48–51
poetry, 46–48, 94–101
themes, 133–167
International Reading Association, 175

Jafta, the Homecoming (Lewin), 106
   story branches for, 108–09
Jafta's Mother (Lewin), 126–27
   story branches for, 128
Jefferson, Thomas, 90
Jericho's Journey (Wister), 138
   story branches for, 140
Jim Ugly (Fleischman), 159–60, 185
   story branches for, 162–63
Johnny Tremain: A Novel for Old and Young (Forbes), 159
Johnson, A.: *The Leaving Morning*, 19
   Tell Me a Story, Mama, 105
Johnston, T.: *I'm Gonna Tell Mama I Want an Iguana*, 73
Journals, 4
Journey to America (Levitin), 43
   story branches for, 45
Jumanji (Van Allsburg), 79, 188
   story branches for, 81
Just Call Me Stupid (Birdseye), 160–61
   story branches for, 163
Just for Fun, 96–98

Kachenmeister, C.: *On Monday, When It Rained...Photographs by Tom Berthiaume*, 106
Kaleidoscope (theme)
   intermediate resources, 133–37
   primary resources, 103–06
Karas, G. Brian, 71
Kastner, Jill, 57, 120
Kate Shelley and the Midnight Express (Wetterer), 123–124
   story branches for, 126
Keller, H.: *Harry and Tuck*, 103

Index

Kherdian, D.: *A Song for Uncle Harry*, 152–53
Kiuchi, Tatsuro, 98, 99
Kopper, Lisa, 106, 126
Kroll, V.: *The Seasons and Someone*, 99
Krupinski, Loretta, 48
Kuklin, S.: *How My Family Lives in America*, 65, 105

Laan, N. V.: *Possum Come a-Knockin'*, 96–97
Language arts
 integrating literature with, 1–6
Language Arts, 175
Learning to Swim in Swaziland (Leigh), 67–68
 story branches for, 69
Leaving Morning, The (Johnson), 19
 story branches for, 20–21
LeCain, Errol, 97
Legends, 10
Leigh, Nila, 69
 Learning to Swim in Swaziland, 67–68
Letting Swift River Go (Yolen), 22
 story branches for, 24–25
Levitin, S.: *Journey to America*, 43
Lewin, H.: *Jafta, the Homecoming*, 106
 Jafta's Mother, 126
Lewin, Ted, 46
Lewis, Kim, 62
Lindberg, Jeffrey, 159
Literary circles, 45
Literary conventions, 5
Literary process, 5
Literary publications, 6
Literature
 approaches to, ix, 4–6
 assessment of, 175–76
 integrating language arts with, 1–6
Literature-based curriculum, 3
"Literature-based reading revolution," 4

Literature-based language arts program
 continuous assessment of, 171–76
 evaluation of, 168–79
 program goals for, 169–71
Literature logs, 4, 5
Little Humpbacked Horse, The (Hodges) 61–62
 story branches for, 63
Little Pigs Puppet Book, The (Watson), 67
 story branches for, 69
Little Polar Bear and the Brave Little Hare (de Beer), 123, 184
 story branches for, 126
Littlewood, Valerie, 137
Livingston, Myra Cohn, 25
Lobel, Anita, 74
Los Angeles Zoo, 90
Lotus Seed, The (Garland), 98, 105
 story branches for, 100
Lowry, L.: *Anastasia*, 46, 186
 Number the Stars, 42–43, 186

Mac and Marie and the Train Toss Surprise (Howard), 145
 story branches for, 147
MacLachlan, P.: *Baby*, 40, 187
 Sarah, Plain and Tall, 79, 187
 Skylark, 79, 187
Macaulay, David: *Why the Chicken Crossed the Road*, 78
Machotka, H.: *Outstanding Outsides*, 70
Maniac Magee (Spinelli), 134, 187
 story branches for, 136–37
Mason, C.: *Wild Fox, A True Story*, 163
Matisse, Henri, 136
McAllister, Jo Ellen, 163
McCoy, Elijah, 28
McDermott, G.: *Papagayo, the Mischief Maker*, 16

McMummy (Byars), 145–46, 184
　story branches for, 147
Medearis, A. S.: *Our People*, 55
Merriam, E.: *Blackberry Ink*, 94
　You Be Good, I'll be Night, 75
Minstrel and the Dragon Pup, The
　(Sutcliff), 84
　story branches for, 86
Miracle of the Potato Latkes, The, A
　Hanukkah Story (Penn), 82, 105
　story branches for, 84
Mirocha, Paul, 164
Miss Rumphius (Cooney), 21, 184
　story branches for, 23–24
Mitten, The (Brett), 133
Mojave (Siebert), 95
　story branches, 96
Monster Soup and other Spooky Poems
　(Evans), 97
　story branches for, 98
Moon of the Wild Pigs, The (George),
　164, 186
　story branches for, 166
Moon Rope–Un lazo a la luna
　(Ehlert), 13
　story branches for, 15
Mr. Mistoffelees with Mungojerrie and
　Rumpelteazer (Eliot), 97
　story branches, 98
Mrs. Katz and Tush (Polacco), 103–04
　story branches for, 105–06
Mullins P., 130
My Name is Pocahontas (Accorsi),
　28–29
　story branches for, 31–32
"My Shadow" (Stevenson), 132
My Two Worlds (Gordon), 64–65,
　105
　story branches for, 66
Myths, 10

Napping House, The (Wood), 76, 133
　story branches for, 78

Narrative forms
　Cumulative form, 53
　Cyclical Patterns, 53
　Repetitive patterns, 53
　Story grammar, 53
Narrative texts
　intermediate resources, 76–86
　primary resources, 54–76
National Council of Teachers of
　English, 175
Naylor, P. R.: *Shiloh*, 40
Nelson, D.: *Wild Voices*, 164–65
Neville, E. C.: *The Bridge*, 113
Newsom, Tom, 142
Nichols, B. P.: *Once a Lullabye*, 74–75
Nightingale, S.: *A Giraffe on the Moon*, 25
Nonconforming poetry, 98–101
Nonfiction, 11
　Biographies and autobiographies,
　27–32
　diaries, 48–51
Norgay, Tenzing, 93
"Note to Carl Sandburg" (Yolen), 51
Number the Stars (Lowry), 42–43, 186
　story branches for, 45
Nursery rhymes, 10, 11

O'Brien, A. S.: *Princess and the*
　Beggar, 84
O'Kelley, M. L.: *From the Hills of*
　Georgia, An Autobiography in
　Paintings, 87
Oh, Kojo! How Could You!
　(Aardema), 27
Ol' Possum's Book of Cats (Eliot), 97
Old, Old Man and the Very Little
　Boy, The (Franklin), 109
　story branches for, 112
On Monday, When It Rained . . .
　Photographs by Tom Berthiaume
　(Kachenmeister), 106
　story branches for, 108

Index

On the Brink of Extinction, the California Condor (Arnold), 89
   story branches for, 91–92
On Top of the World, the Conquest of Mount Everest (Fraser), 92
   story branches for, 94
One Fine Day (Hogrogian), 77, 133
One Moment in Time (Houston), 45
Once a Lullabye (Nichols), 74–75
   story branches for, 76
Only Opal, The Diary of a Young Girl (Whitely and Boulton), 48
   story branches for, 51
Orchard Books, 118
Osofsky, A.: *Dreamcatcher*, 46
Our People (Medearis), 55
   story branches for, 56
Outstanding Outsides (Machotka), 70
   story branches for, 72

Papa Lucky's Shadow (Daly), 129–30
   story branches for, 132
Papagayo, the Mischief Maker (McDermott), 16
   story branches for, 18
Park, B.: *Beanpole*, 134
Parker, Robert, 46
Paterson, Katherine, 187
Peck, Beth, 19
Peeping Beauty (Auch), 16
   story branches for, 18
Penn, M.: *The Miracle of Potato Latkes, A Hanukkah Story*, 82, 105
Percy, Graham, 75
Personal response journals, 5
Perspectives (theme)
   intermediate resources, 148–51
   primary resources, 116–20
Peter and the Pigeons (Zolotow), 127
   story branches for, 129
Peter Rabbit (Potter), 147
Picasso, Pablo, 136
Pinkney, A. D.: *Dear Benjamin Banneker*, 90

Pinkney, Brian, 90
Pip's Magic (Walsh), 58–59
   story branches for, 61
Pocahontas, 28, 29
Poetic narratives, 98
Poetry, 11, 25–27
   free verse, 46–48
   intermediate resources, 94–101
   just for fun, 74–76, 96–98
   nonconforming, 98–101
   primary resources, 73–76
   rhyming, 73–74, 94–96
Polacco, P.: *Mrs. Katz and Tush*, 103
Portfolio assessment, 174
Possum Come a-Knockin' (Laan), 96–97
   story branches for, 98
Power Point (Microsoft), 51
Powhatan, Chief, 28
Primary (grade level) resources
   expository texts, 64–73
   fantasy, 16–19
   folk literature, 13–16
   historical fiction, 21–25
   just for fun, 74
   narrative texts, 54–64
   nonfiction: biographies and autobiographies, 27–32
   poetry, 25–27, 73–76
   realistic fiction, 19–21
   rhyming, 73–74
   themes, 103–133
Princess and the Beggar (O'Brien), 84
   story branches for, 86
Problem-solution text form, 70–73, 82–84, 92–94
Problem Solvers, People Who Turned Problems into Products, The (Aaseng), 92
   story branches for, 94

Quackenbush, Robert, 70
Quatrains, 73

Rabin, S.: *Casey Over There*, 43

Raining Cats and Dogs (Yolen), 25
  story branches for, 27
Ransom, C. F.: *We're Growing Together*, 106
Raschka, C.: *Yo! Yes?*, 116
Reading, 5
Reading Teacher, The, 175
Real McCoy, The (Towle), 28
  story branches for, 31
Realistic fiction, 11, 19–20
Red Badge of Courage, The (Crane), 159
Red Cap (Wisler), 156–57
  story branches, 158
Response journals, 4, 5
Rhyming, 94–96
Ritz, Karen, 123
Robinson, Charles, 43
Rogers, Jacqueline, 97
Rogoff, Barbara, 123
Rolfe, John, 29
Rose, a Bridge, and a Wild Black Horse, A (Zolotow), 120
  story branches for, 122
Rosenblatt, L., 4, 52
Rosie's Walk (Hutchins), 80
Russo, M.: *Alex Is My Friend*, 127
Rylant, Cynthia, 187
Rynbach, Iris Van, 73

San Diego Wild Animal Park, 90
San Diego Zoo Animals (CD ROM), 27
Sanchez, Enrique O., 20
Sandburg, Carl: "Fog," 51
Sanders, S. R.: *Aurora Means Dawn*, 120
Sarah, Plain and Tall (MacLachlan), 79, 187
Schick, E.: *Art Lessons*, 120
Schlein, M.: *I Sailed with Columbus*, 142
Schmidt, Karen, 75
Schneider, Rex, 95

Schoenherr, John, 164
Seasons and Someone, The (Kroll), 99
  story branches for, 100
Seaver, R.: *The Boy Who Sailed with Columbus*, 141–42
Sebgugugu the Glutton, A Bantu Tale from Rwanda (Aardema), 85, 181
  story branches for, 86
Sequence, 64–67, 86–89
Seven Blind Mice (Young), 82
  story branches for, 83
Shaffer, T., 110
Sharing groups, 6
Shed, Greg, 43
Shepherd Boy, The (Franklin), 57, 105
  story branches for, 58
Shiloh (Naylor), 40
  story branches for, 42
Shoes from Grandpa (Fox), 130, 186
  story branches for, 133
Siebert, D.: *Mojave*, 95
Silent sustained reading, 44, 174
Silent sustained writing, 50
Silly Sally (Wood), 55
  story branches for, 56
Silver Days, 45
Sing to the Stars (Barrett), 82
  story branches for, 84
Singer, M.: *Twenty Ways to Lose Your Best Friend*, 159
Singing Ringing Tree (Hastings), 32–33
  story branches for, 35
Skylark (MacLachlan), 79–80, 187
  story branches for, 81
Smith, John, 28
Smith, Joseph, 159
Smoky Night (Bunting), 39–40, 183
  story branches for, 42
Soman, David, 19
Song and Dance Man (Ackerman), 130, 182
  story branches for, 132–33

Index

Song for Uncle Harry, A (Kherdian), 152–53
   story branches for, 155
Speidel, Sandra, 82
Spill! The Story of the Exxon Valdez (Carr), 89
   story branches for, 91
Spinelli, J.: *Maniac Magee*, 134, 187
Spowart, Robin, 120
SSR. *See* Silent sustained reading
Steig, W.: *Doctor DeSoto Goes to Africa*, 151–52
   Sylvester and the Magic Pebble, 35–36
Stevenson, Robert Louis: "My Shadow," 132
Story branches, defined, ix
Story grammar, 61–64, 84–86
Structures
   cause and effect form, 67–70
   cyclical stories, 56–58, 79–82
   expository forms, 54
   intermediate resources: expository texts, 86–94
   intermediate resources: narrative texts, 76–86
   intermediate resources: poetry, 94–101
   narrative forms, 53
   poetic forms, 54
   primary resources: expository texts, 64–73
   primary resources: narrative texts, 54–64
   primary resources: poetry, 73–76
   problem-solution, 70–73, 92–94
   repetitive stories, 54–56
Subject-specific books, 11
Surprises (theme)
   intermediate resources, 145–48
   primary resources, 113–16
Sutcliff, R.: *Minstrel and the Dragon Pup, The*, 84–85
Sword and the Stone, The, 161, 163

Sylvester and the Magic Pebble (Steig), 35–36
   story branches for, 38

Tall tales, 10
Taylor, C.: *The House that Crack Built*, 76–77
Tell Me a Story, Mama (Johnson), 105
Text
   expository, 52–54, 86, 89, 92
   narrative, 53
   poetic, 53
   reader's response to, 4
Thaxter, Celia, 51
   Celia's Island Journal, 48
Themes, 102–103
   beginnings and endings, 109–13, 140
   changes, 106–09, 137–40
   comparisons, 129–33, 163–67
   considering others, 120–22, 151–55
   family and friends, 126–29, 159, 163
   how much courage does it take?, 122–26, 155–59
   intermediate resources, 133–167
   kaleidoscope, 103–06, 133–37
   perspectives, 116–20, 148–51
   primary resources, 103–133
   surprises, 113–16, 145–48
"Thirteen Moons, The," 167
This Is the House That Jack Built, 76, 77, 133
Thomas, A.: *Wake Up, Wilson Street*, 109
Thomas, J. C.: *Brown Honey in Broomwheat Tea*, 99
Three Days on a River in a Red Canoe (Williams), 110
   story branches for, 112–13
To the Ends of the Earth (Franck and Brownstone), 88

To the Zoo (Hopkins), 25
　story branches for, 27
Tom (de Paola), 117, 185
　story branches for, 119–20
Tough Boris (Fox), 54–55, 186
　story branches for, 56
Towle, W.: *The Real McCoy*, 28
Travel books, 11
Trickster tales, 10
Triplets, 73
Tuck Everlasting (Babbitt), 36, 182
　story branches for, 39
Twenty Ways to Lose Your Best Friend (Singer), 159
　story branches for, 162
Two Very Little Sisters (Carrick), 103
　story branches for, 105

Uncle Willie and the Soup Kitchen (DiSalvo-Ryan), 152
　story branches for, 155

Van Allsburg, C.: *Jumanji*, 79, 188
Vidal, Beatriz, 77

Waddell, M.: *Can't You Sleep, Little Bear?*, 62
Wadsworth, M.: *Along the Santa Fe Trail*, 87
Wake Up, Wilson Street (Thomas), 109
　story branches for, 111–112
Wallace, Michael, 89
Wallner, John, 25
Walsh, E. S.: *Pip's Magic*, 58–59
Watling, James, 87
Watson, N. C.: *The Little Pigs Puppet Book*, 67
Watts, James, 13
Weather Reports (Yolen), 51
Weihs, Erika, 103
We're Growing Together (Ransom), 106–07
　story branches for, 109

Westcott, Nadine B., 87
Wetterer, M.: *Kate Shelley and the Midnight Express*, 123
White Deer of Autumn: Great Change, The, 137
Whitely, O.: *Only Opal, The Diary of a Young Girl*, 48
Whole World in Your Hands, The, Looking at Maps (Berger and Berger), 70
　story branches for, 72
Why Mosquitoes Buzz in People's Ears (Aardema), 27
Why the Chicken Crossed the Road (Macaulay), 78
Wild Fox, A True Story (Mason), 163–64
　story branches for, 166
Wild Voices (Nelson), 164–65
　story branches for, 167
Wilhelm, Hans, 94
Willa and Old Miss Annie (Doherty), 62
　story branches for, 64
Williams, V. B.: *Three Days in a River in a Red Canoe*, 110
Wisler, C: *Jericho's Journey*, 138
　Red Cap, 156–157
Wisniewski, D.: *Elfwyn's Saga*, 155–56
Wood, A.: *The Napping House*, 76
　Silly Sally, 55
Wood, Don, 76
Workshops, writers' and readers', 173–74
Wormell, M.: *Hilda Hen's Search*, 59
Wright-Frierson, Virginia, 106
Writing It Down (Cobb), 64
　story branches for, 66

Year of the Perfect Christmas Tree, The (Houston), 22, 186
　story branches for, 24

Index

Yo! Yes? (Raschka), 116
  story branches for, 119
Yolen, Jane: *Bird Watch: A Book of Poetry*, 46
Letting Swift River Go, 22
"Note to Carl Sandburg," 51
Raining Cats and Dogs, 25
Weather Reports, 51
Yorinks, A.: *Iley*, Al, 16–17
You Be Good, I'll Be Night (Merriam), 75
  story branches for, 76

Young, Ed, 46
  Seven Blind Mice, 82
Zeman, L.: *Gilgamesh the King*, 33
Zlata's Diary (Filipovic), 48–49, 50, 51
  story branches for, 51
Zolotow, C.: *A Rose, a Bridge, and a Wild Black Horse*, 120
Peter and the Pigeons, 127